Merry Xmas 1984!
with our love.
Mom and Dad

Kongur

Kongur
China's Elusive Summit
Chris Bonington

FOREWORD BY H R H THE DUKE OF EDINBURGH

INTRODUCTION BY MICHAEL WARD

HODDER AND STOUGHTON

London Sydney Auckland Toronto

British Library Cataloguing in Publication Data

Bonington, Chris
KONGUR, CHINA'S ELUSIVE SUMMIT
1. Mountaineering – China – Mount Kongur
2. Mount Kongur (China) – Description and travel
I. Title
915.1'6   DS793.S62

ISBN 0 340 26514 0

Printed in Great Britain for Hodder and Stoughton Limited,
Mill Road, Dunton Green, Sevenoaks, Kent by
Hazell, Watson and Viney Ltd., Aylesbury, Bucks
and bound by Dorstel Press Limited, Harlow.
Typeset by Rowland Phototypesetting Limited,
Bury St Edmunds, Suffolk.

Hodder and Stoughton Editorial Office:
47 Bedford Square, London WCB 3DP.
Designed by Trevor Vincent.

FRONTISPIECE] *The knife-edged ridge below the summit pyramid.*

To David and Carolyn

Even the simplest mountaineering expedition requires planning, preparation, climbing skill, team-work and the expectation of the unexpected. In order to mount the first foreign climbing expedition of one of China's major mountains, the difficulty of all these factors was very much greater than usual. The Mount Everest Foundation spent 10 years trying to organise a climbing expedition in China and it is due to the persistence and diplomatic skills of its China Committee that the Kongur expedition finally took place.

In the event, there were plenty of problems in all departments but the expedition was a great success, thanks largely to the vision and determination of Michael Ward, the generosity and support of Jardine, Matheson Limited, the mountain leadership and skill of Chris Bonington and the individual contributions of each member of the expedition.

It was not just a mountaineering success. After many years a new, if specialist, avenue of communication was opened with Chinese people and there can be little doubt that ripples of the friendly atmosphere in which the whole expedition took place will spread widely both in China and in Britain.

Philip

1982

Contents

Appendices

Note

by Sir Douglas Busk
Chairman of the Mount Everest Foundation 1980–2

The Mount Everest Foundation was established as a Charity by the Alpine Club and the Royal Geographical Society as a result of the successful first ascent of Mount Everest in 1953 by the British and New Zealand expedition led by Brigadier (now Lord) Hunt. Under its constitution, it gives financial support to carefully selected British expeditions with both scientific and climbing objectives in the mountain regions of the world. Since it was set up the Foundation has made grants totalling over £280,000 to some 550 projects. The Foundation twice organised and ran expeditions itself – the first ascent of Kangchenjunga, the third highest mountain in the world, in 1954 and the Annapurna South Face expedition in 1970. In both cases the Foundation ultimately made profits, which enabled it to give more generous grants to other expeditions.

For over a decade the Foundation worked to obtain permission to mount a mixed scientific/mountaineering project in the vast area of Chinese Central Asia. Contacts were maintained with Peking and success came when Chairman Hua and his entourage visited London in 1979. The Prime Minister and Lord Carrington invited the Chairman and Vice Chairman of the MEF to meet Chairman Hua and it was agreed in principle that one of the many projects suggested by the MEF could be favourably considered. In the result, as set out in the introduction to this book, Mount Kongur was chosen. It has now been climbed and the scientific results will, when evaluated, be of great importance, not only to mountaineers, but in wider fields.

The MEF wishes to express its thanks to all who have helped during many years to achieve such a happy outcome and also to Jardine, Matheson & Co., Ltd. who not only made a massive financial contribution to the project and underwrote the costs, but who also placed at the disposal of the expedition their vast experience of the Far East and an assiduous organisational capacity that was beyond all praise.

D.L.B.
April 1982

Author's note

The expedition book is very similar to the expedition itself and without the help not only of my fellow expeditioners, but many others as well, I could not possibly have written this book. I should like to give my special thanks to Michael Ward, the expedition leader, for his advice, support and the many invaluable contributions he has made to the text of the book, and the team members who provided their diaries and letters home, as well as contributing to the text.

I should also like to thank Sir Douglas Busk, chairman of the Committee of Management, who provided a delightful note on the origins of the game, *buzkashi*. To Martin Henderson, financial director of Mathesons in London, go my grateful thanks for the notes on the fauna of the area and to Christopher Grey-Wilson of the Royal Botanic Gardens, Kew, for identifying the flora.

My own home front has as always provided tremendous support, my wife Wendy sorting and helping select the pictures and my secretary, Louise Wilson, doing a first line edit and keying in all the corrections in the magical Wang word processor that I used for writing the book. Anders Bolinder of the Himalayan Club very kindly provided us with a wealth of detail on the climbing history and topography of the area, which was invaluable both in the main text and the historical appendix.

Finally I should like to thank Margaret Body, my editor, and Trevor Vincent, who has designed the book, for all the help they have given me.

CHRIS BONINGTON

Introduction:
Fragments of history

by Michael Ward

The mountains that form earth's bones jut starkly out of the high deserts of Central Asia. This antique land has always stimulated the curiosity and imagination of travellers with a strong sense of history. Better known to older civilisations than our own and described for thousands of years as the roof of the world, this is the home of gold-digging ants, of men who know the arts of levitation and self-warming without fire and of peaks on whose slopes grow herbs that cause heads to ache.

The ancient worlds of Greece, China and India joined in this vast upland waste of wind, stones and ice and the Silk Roads were the tenuous link between alien cultures. In 1951 when I was exploring the Nepalese side of Everest with Eric Shipton he often talked of his years as Consul General in Kashgar. Every journey that he made on horseback outside this oasis town could bring him within minutes to the borders of the known world. This laid a train of hope that smouldered for thirty years. Expeditions are created by individuals and our venture in Southern Xinjiang* bore the imprint of my desires, wishes and interests. In 1972 I started my extended search for a 'passport' to the uplands of Central Asia. Not surprisingly this failed, despite a request being taken to Peking by a mission led by Sir Alec Douglas-Home.

From occasional articles in *Scientia Sinica* and other sources, I knew that the Chinese had been carrying out a series of projects in Central Asia, concerned mainly with geology and glaciology. In the course of these a number of peaks, including Everest in 1960, were climbed by them and medical research on the effects of altitude was completed. It seemed to me that a project with a similar pattern containing both scientific investigation and mountaineering would have the best chance of success. Also research and exploration have dominated my attitude and interest towards mountains. Over the next few years I wrote innumerable letters to the British Embassy in Peking and the Academia Sinica, and persuaded some of the relatively few people, politicians, scientists or businessmen, who were able to visit China to plead the cause of such a project.

In 1977 as acting chairman and in 1978–80 as chairman of the Mount Everest Foundation, my main task was to bring this to fruition. My requests to the Chinese were always for areas that I thought would be politically insensitive and I therefore chose regions as far away from frontiers as possible. One of the main ranges of the world and one of the least known is the Kun-lun, 'the Mountains of Darkness', that separate the northern edge of the Tibetan plateau from the Taklamakan desert. This range stretches from the Pamirs on the Russian border with China eastwards for a thousand miles or more. In the centre is a peak called Ulugh Mustagh (7,724 m) which was discovered by Sven Hedin during his travels in North Tibet over eighty years ago. This was my prime target, though I mentioned a number of other areas as alternatives.

*Xinjiang is the modern Romanised spelling of Sinkiang. See Appendix X, 'On Names'.

Everest was one obvious choice, but this had been extensively explored and mapped on both the Tibetan and Nepalese sides by many expeditions of all nationalities from 1921 onwards. It is almost as well known as Mont Blanc. We wished to break entirely new ground and for this reason a number of other regions in China where peaks had been climbed were also ruled out. Central Asia is so vast that to return again and again to well-known areas would show a lack of imagination and enterprise and, more practically, could threaten the charitable status of the MEF, which was set up specifically for the purpose of exploration. In this respect it is like other research councils and bodies such as the Royal Society and the Medical Research Council, that provide money for pushing forward the frontiers of knowledge, not for repeating the same routines.

In the course of much correspondence with China, one letter I received does stand out. This described a meeting between Shi Zhanchun of the Chinese Mountaineering Association, Wang Fuzhou, who made the first ascent of Everest from the Tibetan side in 1960, and Sir George Bishop, (former chairman of Booker-McConnell). Also present was Phundob, the first Chinese (Tibetan) woman to climb Everest in 1975 within six months of giving birth to her third baby. She breathed oxygen on the summit, but climbed it without. Shi told Sir George Bishop that at 8,200 m he had found the rope, crampons and ice axe that could possibly have belonged to Mallory and Irvine.

As far as the MEF was concerned perhaps the most important next event was a visit to Peking by the late Malcolm MacDonald, Sir Harold Thompson and Sir John Keswick on behalf of the Great Britain–China Centre. Sir John Keswick was a former chairman of Jardine Matheson, the well-known Hong Kong trading company. In the 'thirties in Shanghai, he had lent a rook gun to Peter Fleming for his epic journey to Kashgar with Ella Maillart. He had also been very friendly with Chou En-lai and present members of the Chinese Government whom he visits every year. Edward Heath, also well liked by the Chinese, pleaded our case when he visited Peking and Lhasa in September, 1979.

At about this time Sir Douglas Busk, a former Ambassador and vice-chairman of the MEF, and I learnt that Chairman Hua Guofeng would be coming to the United Kingdom at the end of the year. Naturally we had already been in touch with the Chinese Embassy in London about our plans and the relevant departments of the Foreign and Commonwealth Office. One way and another a great number and diversity of people were now involved in helping us and, thanks to Lord Carrington and the Prime Minister, some members of the MEF were able to meet Chairman Hua at a reception at the Banqueting Hall in Whitehall. We were also able to spend some time with Huang Hua, the Chinese Foreign Secretary who spoke English well. He was very interested in the whole project, particularly as we wished to include Chinese members. The Cultural Revolution had blocked knowledge in so many fields that they were anxious to enquire about the latest advances in science. A direct result of this meeting was that we talked to Denis Thatcher, who became most enthusiastic about the project.

At the end of November, I received a letter from Professor Weng Qingzhang of the Institute of Sports Science Research in Peking who mentioned that he had read my textbook, *Mountain Medicine*, published in 1975. This was the first direct contact that we had had with China. Shortly afterwards Sir Edward Peck, formerly of the Foreign and Commonwealth Office and on the Management Committee of the MEF, sent me a cutting from a Chinese newspaper, *Ta Kung Po*, published in Hong Kong. This had been

sent to him by David Wilson, the Political Adviser to the Governor of Hong Kong, Sir Murray (now Lord) MacLehose. It said that eight mountains would be opened to foreign climbers. All these peaks had been climbed by British, American or Chinese parties except for one – Mount Kongur. It was amazing to me that five of the peaks were near a border and three, including Kongur, in Southern Xinjiang, one of the least known regions, were within a few miles of the Russian border. The Chinese must have felt very secure in Xinjiang.

The MEF were unanimous that Mount Kongur, possibly the highest unclimbed peak wholly in China and situated in the west Kun-lun, should be our choice. The Chinese Mountaineering Association was informed immediately. Their reply was that negotiations should take place in Peking at the end of February, 1980. We all felt it would be better if I could be accompanied by one other person in these negotiations. As Chris Bonington was a member of the MEF Management Committee and a likely member of any team in China it was an excellent idea that he should accompany me.

The main and most recent information about Kongur was from an article in the *Geographical Journal* by Sir Clarmont Skrine, Consul-General in Kashgar 1922–24. Not only was he the first to identify Kongur as a separate peak but he had explored the surrounding Shiwakte and Tigarman groups. His photographs and maps gave some flesh to our project.

Although I had not yet been confirmed as leader, the vital factor was to decide the exact scope and form of our project. I had already decided that it should include scientific investigation and mountain exploration. In the back of my mind, too, was the hope that a diplomat could be taken as interpreter and the project be sponsored by a trading firm, thus extending its scope well beyond most expeditions. Money was, as ever, a problem, especially in the United Kingdom. Alan Tritton, a director of Barclays Bank Ltd. and member of the MEF Management Committee, suggested Hong Kong might be a better source of funds. In contrast to Britain Hong Kong seemed to be fizzing financially, and there they were much more aware of the long term potential for trade in China, and its place in world affairs. They understood too that things take a long time in the Far East and hurry is counter-productive.

Of the firms in Hong Kong, Jardine Matheson, whose 150th anniversary was to fall in 1982, seemed to be one to approach, especially as Sir John Keswick was able to give us an introduction to David Newbigging, the chairman and managing director of this celebrated trading house.

Xinjiang with its oil deposits has been compared to the Yukon. A far better comparison would be with California, as it is a hot desert country. Water is as precious as platinum; when it is available the desert blooms and rice, fruit and vegetables grow in abundance. Turfan grapes and Hami melons are famous throughout Asia. Jade and gold are also found, whilst wool from yaks and sheep is exported and Urumchi, the capital, is a manufacturing centre. Jardines already had some contacts in this developing region.

Mountaineering and research have often run together. In the life sciences the emphasis has been on the effects of chronic oxygen lack which affects mountaineers at altitude, and sea-level sufferers with chronic bronchitis and heart disease. However since 1977, Jim Milledge from Northwick Park Hospital, Edward Williams from the Middlesex Hospital School, and I had been involved in a field programme investigating the effects of prolonged exercise taken by hill walkers and mountaineers on the fluid content of the body. This caused oedema or excess fluid to appear in certain places. Named 'Exercise Oedema' by a *Lancet* editorial, its significance was that, as the oxygen lack of altitude also caused oedema, the two combined could, we thought, cause lethal complications. Work carried out by the others and led by Jim Milledge at the Gornergrat (3,130 m) in Switzerland, when I was on the Kongur Reconnaissance in 1980, produced some most interesting results and we could continue this in China in 1981. Also I hoped that this research could be communicated to Chinese scientists.

Another doctor, Charlie Clarke, by the use of photography had recorded both oedema of the optic nerve, which is a projection of the brain, and haemorrhages at the back of the eye, due to a change in permeability of the blood vessels, the result of the oxygen lack of altitude. This would extend our oedema studies.

Another project that was simple yet rewarding would be to collect, photograph and record any flowers and grass we found for the Herbarium at the Royal Botanic Gardens, Kew. The director, Professor Patrick Brenan, provided us with the necessary presses and collecting books for some very amateur work, for they had no data of any sort from this part of Central Asia.

Having both a scientific and mountaineering aim could pose very great problems, as I knew from previous Himalayan expeditions. Both were demanding and jealous masters. I thought that I had an understanding of the way both groups thought and worked and success would depend on whom I chose and how the whole was structured. Right from the start I determined to have a group of four climbers whose main task was to climb Kongur and four scientists whose main task was to do the research work. Both groups would act as subjects, whilst the scientists would be good enough mountaineers to support the summit attempt if necessary.

By the time the negotiations with Shi Zhanchun and the Chinese Mountaineering Association were ended, I had committed the MEF to a large investment, the cost of a reconnaissance in June and July 1980, as well as the attempt on Kongur in 1981. It was therefore an enormous relief when a meeting with David Newbigging, the chairman of Jardines, resulted in his board's agreement not only to make a massive financial contribution, but also to underwrite the whole of the Kongur venture. I was elated and we were soon to discover how splendidly equipped this famous trading company was to give us maximum assistance. For Jardines had just opened an office in Peking which was managed by David Mathew, who proved really invaluable. Conveniently for me, the head office of their British subsidiary, Mathesons, was situated in the City of London, near to the hospital where I work, so I asked that our home based administrative support should be run from there. Martin Henderson, the financial director of Mathesons, and his assistant, Pippa Stead, ran this side of things with all the professional skill and enormous facilities available to one of the world's richest trading companies. There are not many expeditions that have had this advantage. They worked in conjunction with a sub-committee set up by the MEF under the chairmanship of Sir Douglas Busk.

The scientific programme was financed from traditional sources – substantial grants from the Medical Research Council and St. Bartholomew's Hospital. Some very sophisticated equipment was provided for us out of those funds.

During our climbing negotiations with Shi Zhanchun in Peking in February 1980, I was also able to give a medical lecture after which I was approached by Professor Liu Dengsheng of the Academia Sinica and asked if I would like to take part in a meeting organised by the Academia in Peking in June. The subject was work carried out by Chinese scientists in both the earth and life sciences on the Tibetan plateau; the guest delegates talked about their work in the Himalaya and other mountain regions.

So before I joined the reconnaissance of Kongur in June 1980, I attended this meeting, read a paper and met Professor Hu Xuchu of the Shanghai Institute of Physiology. His department, together with that to which Professor Weng Qingzhang of Peking belonged, had been working on the effects of high altitude in man on the many ascents undertaken by the Chinese. (The proceedings of the Peking symposium were published at the end of 1981, run to 2,000 pages and are a monument to Chinese scholarship in Central Asia.) In 1981 before the start of the successful expedition to Kongur, Jim Milledge and I visited Shanghai where we lectured in his department and had a meal with his wife, a dietitian at the main hospital, and their family. We visited the theatre and also the Botanical Gardens, as well as contacting Michael Jardine, who had just opened Jardines' office there. Whilst we were in Shanghai the others flew to Urumchi, where Charlie Clarke and Edward Williams lectured at the Xinjiang Medical College and then went on to Kashgar. In 1981 both Professor Hu, Professor Weng and Liu Dayi, our liaison officer, visited the United Kingdom as guests of the MEF who were given great assistance by the Great Britain-China Centre. They visited the Royal Geographical Society and the Alpine Club and were also entertained by Jardine, Matheson and Sir John Keswick. The professors lectured at the Clinical Research Centre, Northwick Park Hospital, while Liu Dayi and Professor Weng also visited the Mountain Training Centre at Aviemore, where they climbed Cairngorm in suitably atrocious weather.

The foundation of our project was now laid. The Chinese had surrounded Kongur with elements of a legend. When asked why they had not climbed it, they admitted that it had posed unusual problems. They described it as enigmatic, and weather conditions were notoriously fickle. They were not able to give us any real information about the best approach. This was why reconnaissance was essential. Unlike Everest in 1951, when six of us explored one aspect of a mountain and discovered the route by which we made the ascent in 1953, on Kongur in 1980 there were only three of us to look at all sides of this elusive peak. Within a week this was dramatically reduced to a party of two and thereby hangs a tale.

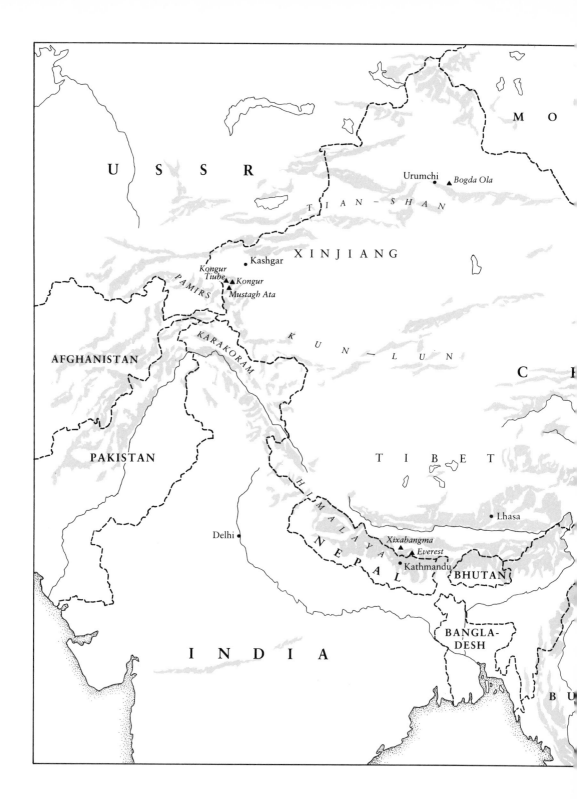

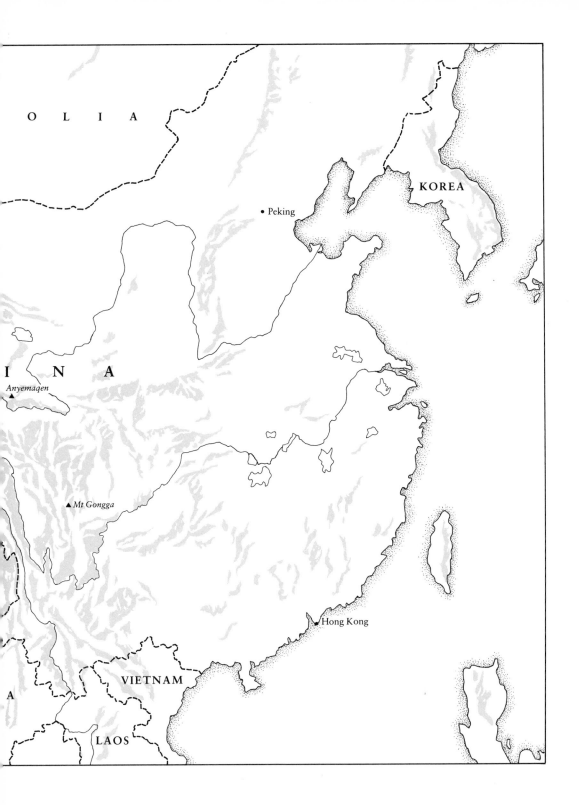

1

A wealth of mountains

19TH FEBRUARY–3RD MARCH 1980

How does an expedition begin? For me it was at the Charles de Gaulle Airport on the 19th February 1980, waiting to catch the Air France 707 to Peking, though for Michael Ward, who was sitting on the bench seat beside me, it had started some years earlier. For it was he who had not just dreamt of going climbing in China, as many of us mountaineers had done over the years, he had actually worked at it, firing off applications like space probes to a distant star system, hoping that some day there would be a return. And now there was; the two of us were on our way to China, emissaries of the Mount Everest Foundation, to negotiate permission to climb a mountain and carry out medical research.

It had happened very quickly, all part of the opening of China to the western world. Already, a Japanese expedition had permission to attempt the north side of Everest that spring, while the West Germans were going for the only 8,000-metre peak entirely within China, nowadays spelt Xixabangma but perhaps more familiar to old 8,000-metre watchers as Shisha Pangma. Michael had received a copy of the Chinese regulations only a couple of days before we set out, with lists of rules and an even longer list of prices. They had opened up just eight mountains: Everest and Xixabangma in Tibet; Kongur, Kongur Tiube and Mustagh Ata in South-West Xinjiang; Bogda Ola near Urumchi, capital of Xinjiang, and finally Mount Gongga and Anyemaqen in China proper. With the exception of Mount Kongur, (7,719 m) which, as far as we knew was unclimbed, this represented the majority of main peaks already climbed within China. A look at the map emphasised just how much more there was still to do in the vast area that lay to the north of the serrated barrier of the Himalayan chain.

It was like a mountain reserve, preserved for some future generation, for in the last thirty years the main Himalayan chain in Nepal and the Karakoram mountains in Pakistan have been thoroughly explored. Before 1950 a bare handful of mountains had been climbed in the Himalaya, the highest being Nanda Devi (7,816 m) in the Garhwal range in India, but since then, all the peaks of over 8,000 metres and almost every mountain of over 7,000 metres has been climbed; many have more than one route up them. Almost every valley has been explored, every pass crossed.

But the mountains of China, guarded by political turmoil before the second world war, and then by the isolationist policies of her government after the success of the Communist revolution, have remained almost untouched, with only a handful of her thousands of mountains climbed. There were complete ranges on the north side of Tibet with mountains of over 7,000 metres that had not even been explored. It was these that we were most interested in. The Kun-lun range stretches for approximately 1,000 miles to

LEFT] *The summit of Kongur emerges through distant cloud, seen from Pik Kommunizma, 160 miles away.*

the north of the Tibetan plateau, forming a high wall between the cold, arid sweeps of upland Tibet and the vast expanse of the Taklamakan desert. Probably the highest mountain of the Kun-lun is Ulugh Mustagh (7,724 m) and this one particularly interested Michael. We resolved to apply for this even though it was not on the list.

The original approach by the Mount Everest Foundation had been for a joint Chinese/British expedition which would have both a scientific and mountaineering programme. This had seemed a sound approach politically, since the suggestion of co-operation seemed essential and we knew that the Chinese had had a strong scientific content in all their expeditions. Later Michael learnt to his surprise that his work was well known to those scientists in China who were concerned with high-altitude research on the Tibetan plateau. Over the past twenty years he has established himself as a leading authority on the diseases of cold and altitude and had written the first definitive textbook on mountain medicine.

We had a couple of hours' wait for our connection. I must confess if I had been alone, I should almost certainly have read a book, but Michael Ward, who is a hard worker, opened his brief case and suggested we start costing out the expedition. Only now that we had the regulations could we do any detailed planning. It had been decided in principle that there would be a team of four climbers and four mountain scientists, but that was all. At this stage not even the leader of the expedition had been formally nominated by the Mount Everest Foundation. Michael at that time was chairman of the foundation and had provided all the initial drive. This concept of a combined mountaineering and scientific project was quite different from the type of Himalayan expedition with which I am normally associated. Only a medical scientist with an extensive knowledge of both field research and mountaineering could plan and co-ordinate this type of party.

Michael Ward was fifty-five, nine years older than myself, and had made his first climb at the age of fourteen, just before the start of the second world war. At Cambridge in 1943 he joined the University Mountaineering Club and it was during this period that he met Menlove Edwards, probably one of the finest rock climbers of the pre-war and war-time era, and led a variation finish to Longland's Climb on Clogwyn Du'r Arddu which was certainly as difficult as anything that had been done at that time.

Once the war was over he was eager to get out to the Alps and expand his horizons still further. He was talented and very ambitious but essentially an amateur climber in the traditional mould of British alpinism. There was no thought of throwing everything up and making a living around climbing. In those days there was very little chance of doing this anyway, but it probably would never have occurred to him. The son of a colonial civil servant, he learnt about independence and self-reliance the hard way at Marlborough. From there he went on to Cambridge and a medical career. But his imagination went much wider and farther than that of most young climbers or, for that matter, doctors. Even though he had never been to the Himalaya and had only experienced one Alpine season, he began planning a reconnaissance expedition to Mount Everest in 1951. Eric Shipton, who had just returned to England from a post as British Consul in Kunming in China, was the obvious choice as leader, since he was not only one of Britain's best known mountaineers but had been a member of some of the pre-war Everest expeditions.

The expedition found the way up into the mouth of the Western Cwm of Everest and showed that there was undoubtedly a route from there to the summit. Eric Shipton, an inveterate mountain explorer, also took off with Michael to enjoy some exploration, wandering inadvertently into Tibet. The Sherpas accompanying them had to bribe their way out of a brush with Tibetan militia before they got back over the Nepalese frontier. Michael felt a close affinity to Eric Shipton and it could have easily altered his entire life if he had decided to concentrate on expeditioning rather than medicine. But in his book, *In This Short Span*, he commented:

Although I was very happy on this expedition and found immense satisfaction and delight in mountain exploration, I was still not satisfied. Opportunities were being missed. Observation of the reactions of the expedition members to high altitudes was very rudimentary, and in any case, even as a doctor I did not know what to look for.

This was the start of his interest in high-altitude medicine and it was also during this expedition that he resolved to become a surgeon. The discipline of research and learning appealed to him. He therefore stood down from the Everest training expedition to Cho Oyu in 1952, a sign of how seriously he took his own medical career, but went on the successful 1953 Everest expedition as medical officer, taking a full and active part in the climb itself and carrying out research with Dr. Griffith Pugh of the Medical Research Council.

After Everest he concentrated on his career but also took part in a series of expeditions that combined mountain exploration and medical research, spending the winter of 1960–1 in the Himalaya at an altitude of between 5,000 and 6,000 metres carrying out research into the long-term effects of oxygen lack which is relevant to chronic heart and lung disease. He and his team ensconced themselves at the Silver Hut just below Ama Dablam, a beautiful and technically difficult unclimbed peak of 6,856 metres in the Sola Khumba region. At the end of the winter four of them, led by Michael Ward, climbed it. It was one of the most technically difficult ascents to have been made at that time.

Michael was one of the very few Europeans who have been allowed to explore and do medical research on the fascinating and remote border of Tibet and Bhutan when he and a cardiologist and climber, Fred Jackson, were invited there to treat the King of Bhutan.

I had first met Michael in 1963 when I was invited by him to join a projected expedition to Xixabangma, the last peak of over 8,000 metres then still unclimbed. It was on the northern side of the Nepal Himalaya and at that time it was not quite certain whether it was in Nepal or Tibet. The Chinese settled the question by climbing it in 1964, and it is now agreed to be entirely in China. I next came across Michael in 1966, when Dougal Haston and I got frostbite on the final stages of the Eiger Direct climb and were treated at the London Hospital, where Michael had gained the reputation of being an expert on cold injury.

But, apart from these few encounters, I could hardly claim to know Michael. I had sat on committees with him, had talked to him over the phone, but for the next week, and probably for a lot longer we were going to work closely together. Although there was only a difference of nine years in our ages, I somehow felt that he was of a different generation. How much this was the shock of white hair and the half-frame granny glasses he used for paper work, and how far his manner, I am not at all sure. Michael has an analytical and enquiring mind. He is impatient and does not suffer the slow or lazy gladly. He has an instinctive sympathy for academic training.

Seated on the airport bench, we started the chore of detailed budgeting that took us through the stop-over in Paris and then high across Europe, the Middle East, the Indian subcontinent and finally China. The regulations were certainly very explicit and the price list comprehensive. It quickly became evident that climbing in China was going to be an expensive business. The mountain itself would cost around £1,000, only slightly more than the peak fees in Nepal or Pakistan, but it was in the cost of services that everything was so much more expensive. The liaison officer and obviously essential interpreter would cost £8 a day in salary and another £7 a day for their rations. In addition we had to insure them through the Chinese Mountaineering Association and this would cost £300 each. Then there was transport. A truck cost a pound a kilometre. A yak was £10 a day and you also had to pay for the yak driver. By the time we were close to Peking we had worked out that an eight-man expedition was going to cost around £140,000, about five times the cost of a similar expedition in Nepal. In the event our financial projections were surprisingly accurate.

We had seen little of the ground below us since leaving the Middle East, just a carpet of cloud, but now, as we lost height on the final run into Peking, we had our first glimpse of China – a patchwork of dusty brown fields, neatly squared off, veined with the grey of old snow. And then the runway was before us and with it the uniformity of all air travel; the great tarmac highway, the terminal buildings, characterless and new, much bigger and more extensive than the scatter of planes, all bearing the ubiquitous star of Communist China, justified.

We taxied up to the waiting tentacle of the outlying terminal pod and were disgorged into the building. There was even one of those long horizontal escalators to carry us to the main building down a great empty corridor. Immigration was quick and easy. We handed our passports to a trim, pretty girl with an unsmiling face, in a drab olive uniform with a pistol at her side, and we waited little longer than in Heathrow for our baggage to come chuntering out on the conveyor belt. Customs were no worse than anywhere else in the world, though we had to list every camera, wrist watch, and tape recorder we had, to ensure we didn't sell them during our stay.

And then, feeling very lost, not knowing whether we were going to be met, or where we were going to stay, we walked out of the customs hall into the reception area. The first impression was to be repeated over and over again; the drab uniformity of dress, the ubiquitous blue or grey Mao suit, the little peaked cap, and now, in February, the huge shapeless padded greatcoat. As we came uncertainly out of the door, a smiling little group bore down on us and the next few moments were taken up with introductions by the interpreter.

After these formalities, we piled into the limousine that was going to take us into Peking. It was an hour's drive along straight roads bordered by poplar trees. Everything was grey; every stretch of water, stream or river was iced over. The frozen ground was lightly dusted with snow, with little more than patches of old snow clinging to the sides of roads, the remnants of drifts. Cyclists, bundled in greatcoats, on clumpy, upright push-bikes, pedalled at the side of the road. In the country there were almost as many horse-drawn carts as there were motor vehicles. The houses were windowless, single-storied mud huts surrounded by a compound wall. There was a feeling of grey drabness that continued into the city itself, as we bowled down the huge wide road which seemed too big for the scanty traffic using it.

Now there were blocks of flats on either side, characterless and rather ugly, though probably better to live in than the hovels they replaced. The traffic increased; flocks of bicycles, all travelling at a sedate uniform speed, packed buses, laden lorries, but still comparatively few cars. There are no privately owned cars in China; they are all a perk of the job, or state-owned taxies. Status is indicated, as all the world over, by the size of the car, but in China, in memory perhaps of the mandarin's curtained palanquin, the big black cars of senior officials have curtains over their back windows – the Communist equivalent of the darkened windows favoured by western pop stars.

We were now near the centre of Peking, driving past Tian-an-men Square. Six times the size of Trafalgar Square, it gave an impression of the vast space of China. On one side the outer wall of the old Forbidden City, home of the emperors, was part concealed by the review stand which stretched out on either side of its great gateway. This in turn was dominated by the huge portrait of Mao Tse-tung, set over the gate. On the other side was the great expanse of the square, out of which, like islands, rose the square columned bulk of the Mao Tse-tung Memorial Hall in its centre, the obelisk to the People's Heroes, and, to its right, the mass of the Great Hall of the Peoples. On either side of the square, almost incongruous, still hung huge portraits of Marx and Engels, Lenin and Stalin. Abutting the walls of the Forbidden City is the gatehouse to the modern-day forbidden city, where the present party leadership live. Sentries with fixed bayonets stood at either side of the gateway and it reminded me of how the present régime in China is simply part of the great evolutionary process of the oldest civilisation of the world. Former imperial dynasties had arisen through a revolutionary process, had been progressive to a degree unimaginable in the western world of the time. Can the present socialist dynasty be viewed in the same light? It has certainly brought peace and a fairer system and a much greater level of prosperity to the vast majority of the people than has ever been known in the history of China. Driving through Peking or any other Chinese city there are none of the signs of abject poverty that can be seen throughout so much of Asia.

We drove on for another mile down the great avenue to reach our hotel, a massive block built in the 1950s Russian style, and called the Minorities Hotel. Michael and I had been given a double room which was pleasantly furnished and had its own bathroom, with a big old fashioned bath and limitless quantities of very hot water. The universal feature of all Chinese hotels was the big, gaudily decorated thermos of hot water and little tin of green tea leaves, infinitely preferable to the electric kettle, cluster of tea bags and UHT milk that you get in most British hotels.

We quickly discovered that our stay had been minutely programmed, not only with meetings with the Chinese Mountaineering Association, but also with scientific lectures that Michael was going to give, and a climbing lecture to be presented by myself. In addition we had brought out copies of both the 1953 and the 1975 Everest films. When we were not taking part in meetings we even had some tourist trips laid on for us. It was certainly going to be a full few days. The following afternoon we had our first meeting. It followed the pattern of all subsequent ones. On each floor of the hotel were meeting rooms, furnished with heavy settees and small coffee tables on which were set large tea cups for the inevitable green tea. Mr. Shi Zhanchun, vice chairman and effective executive head of the Chinese Mountaineering Association was waiting for us.

Stockily built and dressed in an immaculate grey high-collared suit, of a cloth much finer than any of his subordinates, Mr. Shi had an air of genial authority, a smile coming very readily to his face. He was the party official who had been put in charge of mountaineering in 1956 when it was decided that the Chinese should climb their own mountains. He had started as a bureaucrat but had come to enjoy and love the mountains and consequently had taken an active part in the expeditions, co-leading the first Russian/Chinese expedition to Mustagh Ata in 1956 and then leading the Chinese Everest expeditions of 1960 and 1975. He spoke practically no English which meant we were entirely dependent on an interpreter. The introductions were made. Mr. Shi made a short speech welcoming us and Michael replied. It was some time before we got through the exchange of compliments and down to the detailed negotiation. Michael did all the talking which enabled me to think out the next step and occasionally suggest either an additional point or perhaps a change in tactics. In this respect the process of interpretation was very useful, since it gave both sides more time to consider each other's points.

That afternoon Michael did no more than describe our own proposal for a joint scientific and mountaineering expedition and our request for Ulugh Mustagh, with Kongur, the only unclimbed peak on the list, as an alternative should this not be possible. Mr. Shi told us that they would consider our suggestions and let us know in two days' time. I spent the following morning sight-seeing, while Michael had a session with the mountain scientists at the Institute of Sports Medicine where he met Professor Weng Qingzhang and other members of the Institute.

The next day was to be the crucial meeting. After the usual courtesies, Mr. Shi came to the point. First, we could not climb any other mountain outside the list already laid down, but we could have Kongur.

'When do you want to climb it?' he asked.

This was almost too fast for us. We had been planning on an expedition for 1981 and said so. Mr. Shi smiled, and said, 'Well in that case someone else might climb it this year. Surely though, you will need to make a reconnaissance?'

This was something we hadn't even thought of. A recce would take up both time and money. From my own point of view I was struggling to complete a book against a tight deadline and Michael, of course, had his job as surgeon. We hurriedly conferred. They obviously expected a recce and very little was known about Kongur anyway. Even though the Chinese had climbed its sister peak, Kongur Tiube, they had been unable to give us a single photograph of the mountain or even an accurate map. However the immediate objective was to stake a claim which would block any other expedition from getting there before us and, since there was no way we could have mounted a full scale scientific and mountaineering expedition in the 1980 season, we agreed to mount a reconnaissance expedition that summer.

Then the question of a joint expedition arose. It emerged that the Chinese definitely did not want a joint mountaineering venture, though they were considering the possibility of sending some scientists with us. With this decided we got down to the specifics of detailed planning, costs, how many yaks we should need from the road head, how far it was by road from Kashgar to the Karakol Lakes, what the terrain was going to be like and so on. The meeting lasted through the day and at the end of it there were still several points to clear up and we still hadn't signed the protocol.

But the following day was once again to be devoted to sight-seeing. In sub-zero temperatures we were taken first to the Summer Palace, which is just outside Peking. There were practically no other tourists, being out of season, but the palace grounds were crowded with Chinese visitors, avidly gazing at their heritage. The Kunming Lake was frozen over and people were skating over its wide expanse. Even though the trees were bare and the ground frozen, one could appreciate the beauty of the place – the long wooden painted gallery along the north shore of the lake and the exquisite folly of the marble barge lying marooned in ice by the bank, a token of the corruption of the old imperial régime, for this picturesque but useless boat was built from funds diverted from the creation of a modern navy to withstand the rapacious demands of the foreign powers in the late nineteenth century.

We drove on to the Ming tombs, with their guard of more-than-life-size animals lining each side of the road – lions, camels, horses and mythical beasts in enigmatic grey stone. In the days of the empire only members of the imperial retinue were allowed up this long avenue to the site of the imperial mausoleums.

And then on northward to the Great Wall itself, where a section of a mile or so has been fully restored. The wall clings to the top of a ridge line, winding serpentine along the crest of steep rock hills as far as the eye can see. It is difficult, indeed impossible, to grasp the concept of a wall that stretches over 3,000 miles across Northern China, that was built 2,000 years ago. When one compares it to Hadrian's Wall, which was built at about the same time and is a mere eighty miles long, with today little more than a few foundations nudging above the turf, it is all the more remarkable. Staring through one of the turret windows of the square watch tower at the broken ice-veined hills barring the view to the north, I could imagine the dark threat of nomad hordes in the cold reaches of Manchuria and Mongolia, poised to strike against the soft wealth and sophistication of the Chinese Empire.

We made the long drive back to Peking with Michael talking of hospital politics and some of the more bizarre crises confronting a surgeon in his work. We had been brought close together those last few days, often working jet-lagged and tired till midnight, getting ready for the meetings or lectures we were giving each day. Michael was very much the surgeon, used to absolute command of his operating theatre. I, of course, had already led several expeditions and was used to taking my own decisions. It was certainly a situation that could have led to conflict, but, in fact, we worked together extraordinarily well, complementing each other in many ways. Michael undoubtedly had a stronger work drive than I did, believing in meticulous preparation for each meeting. But I probably had greater experience of the basic problems of expedition organisation, having been closely involved in the last few years. There is no doubt that Michael's age and presence, as well as his status as a surgeon and scientist, impressed the Chinese.

We had now come near the end of our visit and were due to fly to Canton on our way to Hong Kong the next day. These were to be the crucial meetings when we hoped to sign the protocol or contract which guaranteed us the first attempt on Kongur. The meeting went on interminably through the day as we went over each separate point. We still had not signed the protocol at 6.00 p.m. when we were due to attend a banquet given by the Chinese Mountaineering Association. Mr. Shi smiled amicably and said we could carry on with the meeting after dinner.

The Chinese Mountaineering Association entertain us to a banquet as our negotiations come to an end.

This was our first Chinese banquet. It was held in a private room in one of the Peking restaurants, at a large round table at which about twelve of us sat. They were officials of the Chinese Mountaineering Association and of the Institute of Sports Medicine, with Michael and I the only Europeans. We had already become adept at using our chopsticks and as a result could enjoy the superb meal to the full. It started with an hors d'oeuvre of cold meats, nuts and pickled vegetables, followed by course after course of fat juicy crayfish, Peking duck, beautifully cooked vegetables, fungi and button mushrooms – the ultimate in chopstick manipulation. This was all accompanied by a mixture of beer and toasts of *mao tai*, the fiery spirit, which is a little like schnapps, and accompanies all Chinese banquets.

Toasts are drunk through the meal. Someone stands, proposes a toast to Anglo–Chinese friendship, the Chinese Mountaineering Association, the Mount Everest Foundation or anything else he can think of, and then everyone else stands up, clinks each others' glasses, and drains the contents in one, ending by turning the glass over to show it's empty. The only variation is when the person making the toast favours the glass of sweet red plum wine which is also kept constantly topped up.

At the end of the banquet we were all happily mellow, certainly not in the mood for a further session of negotiation. But back we went to the hotel. It was ten o'clock before we were ready to sign the protocol but then we had to go through the appendix to the protocol, specifying just how many Chinese personnel, how many yaks and how many trucks we were going to need. I found myself typing this out at two in the morning on my little portable typewriter. Then it was down to the deserted hotel dining room for another meal and more beer before finally signing the appendix at three o'clock in the morning.

There was no respite the next day for we had to be up early for an appointment with Sir Percy Cradock, the British Ambassador. We were both very pleased with ourselves. Not only had we buttoned up the protocol but we now had the chance of being the first expedition to make a major ascent of an unclimbed peak in China. Sir Percy quickly brought us back to earth, pointing out that there was no guarantee in the protocol that they would not allow another expedition on to Kongur at the same time as ourselves or even in front of us. We composed yet another letter to Mr. Shi and then rushed off to catch our plane.

Our mission was by no means over. True, we had got permission, but the reconnaissance and main expedition were going to cost around £180,000, which was close to the entire capital of the Mount Everest Foundation. There was no way that the foundation could embark on the expedition without sponsorship from somewhere to underwrite the costs. We had already been warned that it was most unlikely this kind of money would be available in England. We should have to look farther afield and Hong Kong, less affected

Michael Ward and Shi Zhanchun sign the protocol for our reconnaissance expedition.

than Europe by the recession, with its strong links with China, seemed the best bet. I already had one good contact in Hong Kong, in the shape of Adrian Gordon, who had been with me on the South-West Face of Everest in 1975. He had served with the Ghurkas and, although he had only done a little climbing, had been invaluable in an administrative rôle supervising our Sherpa high-altitude porters and organising some of the lower camps. He was now working in Hong Kong as the secretary of the Hong Kong Jockey Club and had managed to get us a concessionary rate in the Hong Kong Hilton, which seemed a very pleasant base for a couple of mountaineering fund raisers. He had also organised a press conference and various television interviews.

After a week in China the impact of Hong Kong was extraordinary, from the moment our plane dived through the clouds over Hong Kong harbour, seeming to fly direct at the jutting high-rise buildings of Kowloon, skimming the top of the ridge then dropping down into the packed airport crammed with planes bearing the insignia of the world's major airlines. The first person we saw as we came out of the plane had been an airport policeman toting a sub-machine gun. In China there had been no security check of our hand baggage and hardly a weapon in sight. We were back in the affluent free west, but we were also back into the world of violence and potential hijackers.

Adrian was there to meet us in an unfamiliar dark suit and striped shirt. He had soon plunged us into our round of press conferences and interviews, but the key meeting was to be at lunch the following day. This was when we were to meet David Newbigging, chairman of Jardine, Matheson, the 'taipan' of one of the oldest and most prestigious of all the Hong Kong traders. Their head office was the Connaught Centre, an elegant tower that dominated the Hong Kong water front. Express lifts swept us up to the 48th floor. The reception hall was panelled in light oak, with a dark-suited Chinese porter standing guard in front of an impressive coat of arms. We were shown up to the penthouse where we were to have lunch in a private room that must have one of the finest city views in the world, looking out across the crowded Hong Kong harbour over to the mainland shore of Kowloon, with the bustling streets far below.

Over lunch, Michael and I described the objects of the expedition and our experience in Peking. David Newbigging listened, occasionally posing a question. I had a feeling it was going well, particularly when he told Michael that he would have to talk it over with some of his colleagues but that he would let us know their decision in half an hour's time. In less than half an hour the phone went in our hotel room and Michael heard that Jardines were prepared, in principle, to underwrite the expedition.

It was amazing how easy it had seemed; but this often appears to be the case. You either stumble immediately upon the executive, ideally the man at the top, who is inspired by your particular adventure, or you just never seem to find him. The chemistry of sponsorship is not entirely one of cool business analysis, I suspect. I think the first essential is to gain an emotional response or sympathy for the project.

In this respect we were lucky, for David Newbigging was a keen walker and had explored most of the paths and back country of Hong Kong Island and the New Territories, which, for one of the most densely populated regions of the world, are very wild and unspoilt. He had also gone on several treks to Nepal. This at least ensured a sympathetic hearing but he was too sound a business man to make purely emotional decisions. Fortunately, not only was there the magic of our being the first British

The business centre of Hong Kong, dominated by the Connaught Centre in which Jardine, Matheson have their headquarters.

Jardine, Matheson agreed to make a massive financial contribution and underwrite the expedition. l to r, William Courtauld, Michael Ward, Chris Bonington, Tom Harley, and chairman David Newbigging.

expedition into China, tackling an exciting unclimbed peak, but Jardines, with their long tradition of Chinese trade, were busy strengthening their trading links and other contacts there, and our venture could undoubtedly help in this respect.

Our expedition seemed to be off to a good start, but time was now short, for we were due to set out on our reconnaissance to Kongur in May, just three months hence. Michael and I agreed that a team of three would be adequate, Michael, myself and one other. We had to decide on this as soon as possible, but I was not going straight back home, since I had a week's lecturing in Singapore.

We tossed some names around. The number of top British climbers with good Himalayan experience, even today, is limited to about half a dozen. We had decided on four climbers for the team, of whom I would be one. It wasn't so much a matter of fielding the four best climbers, as of selecting four who were obviously very competent but who could also get on with each other. Equally important, they would have to fulfil the role as ambassadors of British climbing in China and at the same time co-operate and take part in the scientific studies, acting as guinea pigs.

Quite a few potential members of the team I knew were already involved in other expeditions, but one climber, who represented the younger generation, was Alan Rouse and, as far as I knew, he was free that summer. Michael agreed that I should phone him from Hong Kong to invite him to join our recce. He took some tracking down, for he was running a climbing course on Ben Nevis, but Louise, my secretary, finally found out where he was likely to be and I called him from Singapore to ask if he was interested in joining us. Our expedition was under way.

RIGHT] *Kongur glimpsed from the Karakol Lakes.*

2

To the Karakol Lakes

28TH MAY–12TH JUNE 1980

The time between our return to England and setting out for the reconnaissance went all too quickly. Al Rouse and I got together the equipment and food we were going to need, assembling and packing it at my home in Cumbria. At the same time we got to know each other. The age difference between Al and myself was eighteen years; I was the same age as his mother, and yet there seemed very little generation gap between us. Part of the reason might well have been a lack of maturity on my part. I don't think I've every really grown up. I love playing games, of which climbing is one. I still enjoy my climbing as much as ever I have done and thoroughly enjoyed snatching the odd rock climb with Al while we were getting the gear together. His climbing is much better, I suspect, than mine had ever been, but that didn't matter. In the early 'seventies, particularly, Al was one of the most outstanding rock climbers in the country. He also has an excellent, very quick mind. He went to Birkenhead Grammar School, played chess for Cheshire and went on to Cambridge to study Mathematics. He had stumbled across climbing whilst still at school, starting on a little sandstone outcrop near his home in Wallasey, then graduating to North Wales, hard climbing and everything else the anarchic Welsh climbing scene had to offer. He had moved quickly through the evolution of British rock, hard winter climbing in Scotland, alpinism and then two seasons in South America. He and five others spent a year working their way from Patagonia up to Yosemite, completing a series of very bold climbs. They then turned to the Himalaya, and as a foursome in 1978 Al, Rab Carrington, Brian Hall and Roger Baxter-Jones climbed Jannu (7,710 m) in five days using alpine-style tactics. It was a remarkable tour de force, for the mountain had only been climbed once before by a large French expedition. The following year Al and Brian joined Doug Scott in a very bold ascent of the North Face of Nuptse from the Western Cwm of Everest.

Al has an essentially buoyant nature with a bubbling enthusiasm and self-confidence. He loves talking and is happy to voice an opinion on almost any topic. We set out on our reconnaissance on the 28th May. Michael was already in Peking, taking part in a scientific seminar, but Al and I were going out through Hong Kong, both to discuss plans for the main expedition and also to talk to the Hong Kong press. We had with us the inevitable pile of last-minute gear which was both costly in terms of excess baggage and awkward for the two of us to shift around. And yet the fact that there were only two of us, and just one more member of the team to catch up with in Peking, gave our trip a light-hearted flavour. This was enhanced by the fact that we did not have a single, over-awing objective, but, being a reconnaissance, we could wander at will, climbing as

LEFT] *Al Rouse gives a demonstration of rock climbing on the Great Wall of China, but our hosts remained unimpressed.*

33

many minor peaks as possible. We talked over plans, and I was as relaxed as I have ever felt at the start of an expedition.

We were met in Peking by David Mathew, Jardines' manager there. In his mid-twenties, he has the languid air of the old Etonian, but we quickly found that this was little more than a protective front. Sensitive to the feelings of others, he got on very well with the Chinese and had already put in a great deal of work on our behalf. He was also determined to accompany us as far as Kashgar, partly to smooth our path, partly to investigate commercial potential, but most of all to visit some of the ancient cities on the old Silk Road.

We met up with Michael Ward, whose scientific seminar had finished, the following morning. Our three days in Peking went by all too quickly. It was a very different place to what it had been in February. With the warmth of early summer there was no longer the same drab uniformity of dress. David Mathew commented on how rapidly the Chinese were adopting greater individuality. Most women still wore trousers, but there were blouses of many different colours and there was even a variety of hair styles.

Leaving my hotel just after dawn, I found the streets filled with people carrying out their own form of exercise, some in big groups, others by themselves. One group would be practising *tai-ji-quan,* which is a form of ritual shadow boxing, with slow, graceful movements, each member of the group acting as part of it and yet maintaining his own individual self-expression. Another group would be practising *wu-shu,* the traditional martial arts, wielding their wooden swords in the gentle light of the morning sun. In the grounds of the Forbidden City there were people singing, each individual having his own little territory in the vast space of the great outer courtyard. Vendors, with fresh vegetables, soft drinks or even ice cream, were pushing their wheeled carts along the broad streets. Droves of cyclists were already on their way to work, pedalling beneath the great billboards, which today not only carry socialist tracts but also big consumer advertisements for Japanese television sets, radios and even cars.

I had come to Peking this time with an almost evangelical aim. Although the Chinese government had adopted mountaineering as a worthy sport and felt a need, perhaps for national pride as much as anything else, to climb their highest mountains, there had been no interest shown in the sport of rock climbing, in spite of the fact that China is an extremely rocky country, with outcrops or even major cliffs close to many of the population centres. I felt that rock climbing was, in many ways, more accessible to the Chinese than more ambitious mountaineering which was both remote to the average city dweller and, of course, extremely expensive. Rock climbing was something that the individual could do at weekends with comparatively little equipment. With this in mind I had written a short paper extolling the virtues of the sport and had suggested that Al and I gave a demonstration of rock climbing on the crags that could be seen from the road leading to the Great Wall of China.

We started off with a traverse on the Great Wall itself, and then found a spot for our picnic lunch by a large boulder lying at the bottom of the valley. Out with the chalk bags and light climbing shoes and we were soon finding various routes up the boulder, when an old peasant came rushing up to us, shouting and gesticulating. At first we thought he was the local farmer, angry at our trespass, but then he beckoned us round to the back of the boulder and pointed out some steps that had been cut into the rock. He was merely being helpful, quite unable to understand how anyone could take a difficult route by choice. We found another small crag just high enough to justify a rope, but the Chinese Mountaineering Association remained unimpressed.

It was a question perhaps of priorities, for China is stretched to the limit in every sphere, whether it be in industry, commerce or sport. At the moment the Chinese Mountaineering Association is concentrating its entire resources and personnel, not on its own climbing development, but in the servicing of foreign expeditions. Rock climbing is perhaps an indulgence which only the affluent west, with its greater leisure and wealth, can really afford.

We set out on the next stage of our journey on the 4th June. There were the four of us, and Liu Dayi, our liaison officer. Tall by Chinese standards, broad-chested and big-boned, he was one of their most outstanding mountaineers. He was the same age as me, with a son and a daughter almost exactly the same ages as my own two sons. His introduction to climbing was similar to that of most of the Chinese mountaineers. He came from Shandong province in eastern China, son of a cook in a leatherwork factory. He went to technical school and then became a factory electrician. He was a keen sportsman and excelled at basketball. One day in 1956 he saw a notice asking for volunteers for a climbing camp in the Tai-bai mountains in Shansi province. The climbing course was run by Russian instructors. Sixty started the course but this was soon whittled down to thirty, and then the best twelve joined nineteen Russians in an expedition to climb Mustagh Ata. Shi Zhanchun was the deputy leader. Liu Dayi was able to use his experience as an electrician to wire their Base Camp for electric light and he also went to the summit of Mustagh Ata with thirty others. The Russians went on to climb Kongur Tiube in a very bold, fast push, taking with them two Chinese.

Liu took part in most of the subsequent Chinese expeditions, climbing Mount Gongga in 1957 and Mustagh Ata again in 1959, when eight women reached the top. He took part in the Chinese Everest expedition of 1960 and also a Chinese women's expedition to Kongur Tiube in 1961. He became a member of the Communist party in 1965, and during the cultural revolution, when climbing was out of favour as an activity, he coached a volleyball team. With the return to more normal times, he was able to resume his mountaineering activities, leading a successful expedition to Mount Tumor in the Tian-shan range and as Chinese leader of the proposed joint Iranian/Chinese expedition to Everest in 1978. He had also made a reconnaissance of the north side of K2. It took some time to get to know Mr. Liu, since he spoke no English, and he reminded me of a slightly worried sheepdog trying to control a particularly unruly flock. The Chinese are always very punctual and I am afraid we were anything but that.

But we were at last on our way, accompanied by an array of rucksacks, boxes and kitbags. Liu quickly showed himself adept at cutting through red tape and certainly had our interests very much at heart. We flew out to Urumchi in a four-engined Russian jet. It was a four-hour flight, most of it over featureless desert which reminded us again of the vast scale of China. As we came down into Urumchi, capital of Xinjiang, we saw, to the north, Mount Bogda Ola, which was one of the mountains open to foreigners. Although only 5,445 metres in height, it was a fine looking peak, steep and rocky, dominating everything around it. As we lost height we could see the intriguing patterns of different mineral deposits in the barren foothills, great streaks of rusty red, presumably from iron ore, and black fields of coal deposits. Urumchi was an industrial centre with factories sprawling all around it and the airport was a big modern building, characterless as all airports are.

We had a sizable delegation from the Xinjiang Sports Federation to greet us and once we had got through the hand-shaking were whisked away to a guest house on the outskirts of the city. Our first impression of Urumchi was not particularly favourable. Broad streets, drab blocks of flats and offices, and factories ever intrusive. The dress was uniformly Chinese – blue trousers and jackets – but the features of the people were different. The majority of the population of Xinjiang are of varied Turki-based stock, people of Central Asia, descendants of the nomad tribes who wander the empty grasslands and desert. The majority belong to the Uighur race, but there are also Mongols, Tadzhiks and Kirghiz. Imperial sway over this region varied with the strength of the central government and the fortunes of the nomad tribes. With the rise of the Russian Empire in the nineteenth century and its spread eastward into Siberia, Russian influence was brought to bear on Xinjiang with the presence of Russian merchants and advisers. It was this that made Chinese Central Asia the playing board for the Great Game between two great colonial empires, Russia and Britain, throughout the latter part of the nineteenth century and for the beginning of the twentieth, as Russia manoeuvred to gain increasing influence, if not total control of Xinjiang, while Britain endeavoured to preserve Turkestan, either as an independent nation or as a province of China, to act as a buffer between the dark threat of Russia and her own Indian Raj. The Chinese still feel the looming threat of Russia, whose divisions are deployed adjacent to their long, ill-defined frontier. The fact that the same tribes live on both sides of the border only increases the potential threat.

But we were hardly aware of this as we drove out of the city towards a low line of broken hills. The guest house was a pleasant airy building with two storeys. We were met by the manager and a friendly pigtailed Uighur lass, carrying hot towels for us to wipe our hands and faces. That night I went running across land that seemed to have been churned up by gigantic earth-moving machinery. It was wide and empty and somehow the smoke-belching factories that were scattered across its surface, did not seem intrusive. The land was so bleak and barren that even these eruptions of chimneys, pipes and pylons, seemed welcome. The old and the new were in strange juxtaposition. I came to a tattered yurt, a round-domed tent of felt over a wooden frame, the traditional mobile home of all Central Asian nomads. A flock of goats grazed near by and then suddenly round the corner of the yurt came one of the biggest dogs I think I have ever seen, all yellow teeth and growling. I was uncomfortably aware of my bare legs, picked up a rock, dropped to a walk and tried not to look too frightened. The dog stood and growled whilst I walked on, trying not to look back. I jogged over to the rampart of hills about two miles from the rest house. They were only 150 or 200 metres above the wide stretching plain with slopes of shaley stones and stunted scrub. On the top were old entrenchments and I wondered whether these had been used to defend Urumchi in the civil war or one of the many other struggles that had riven Xinjiang throughout the nineteenth and twentieth centuries. Behind the hills climbed in serried ranks and in the distance were the snow peaks of the Tian-shan. I was immensely happy to be there, to be at that moment on my own, yet knowing that Michael and Al were in the rest house a few miles away and that we were on our way to a delightful, light-hearted adventure.

That night we were invited to attend an opera in the city. It was a local production in the Uighur language, though the music had an almost European feel to it. It was a delightful piece of fairytale escapism, of the shepherd boy who falls in love with the princess, is framed by a wicked uncle, but who eventually wins through, marries his beloved and becomes king of the country. The theatre was packed but customs were very different from that of the West End of London. People got up and wandered around the theatre during the action. There was a constant undercurrent of conversation, and at the end, everyone simply got up and walked out. There was no tradition of applauding the actors.

We had three days in Urumchi. Michael visited the hospital and gave a lecture on mountain medicine, while Al and I went sight-seeing, though there was very little to see. We were also taken on a day trip towards Bogda Ola to view the Heavenly Lakes. It took several hours' drive along dust roads through desert country, relieved by small farming settlements irrigated from the melt waters of the nearby mountains, before we started climbing into the foothills. Suddenly from being very obviously in the heart of Central Asia we could have been somewhere in the Austrian Alps. Conifers grew on either side of the road, there were little grassy alps, tumbling streams and then the lake itself filling the bottom of a glacial valley, with craggy pine forests on either side. The small settlement of wooden chalets at the road head could easily have been in Europe. An old fashioned steam-driven gun boat lay drawn out of the water, particularly incongruous since we were as far from the sea as anywhere else in the world. There was a leaden grey sky and rain threatened, but there was a feeling almost of coming home in the moist fresh air, the dark woods and emerald green of the grass.

As we set out to walk up the lakeside, Liu Dayi enjoined us to be back in two hours for lunch. We dashed off like a group of schoolboys escaping the teacher. A path of rocks had been built round the side of the lake to its end beneath a high rocky bluff. We paddled to the other side of the inlet stream and crossed a flat-bottomed valley filled with tall old pine trees. On the other side the hill rose steeply above a little group of farm buildings. The farmers gazed at us with quiet curiosity as we trooped along. A path led up through the trees and back along the farther side of the lake. We had already used up an hour of our free time but resolved to go a little farther. I stepped off the path to take a photograph, using a small flowering bush as foreground and glanced down only just in time to see that I was about to stand on a small viper-like snake. I was wearing shorts and didn't have any socks on, so would almost certainly have been bitten if I had stood on it. We should have realised that this was an omen, but ignored it.

The path soon faded out in the broken scrub and woodland. We were about half way round the lake, with less than an hour to our deadline. I suggested we should go back the way we had come to be sure of getting back in time, but the others were feeling adventurous. Out in the hills at last, Michael had dropped the dignity of the surgeon and scientist, was thoroughly enjoying himself, and readily responded to Al's suggestion that we try to circumnavigate the lake. After all it didn't look that far. David Mathew, clad in sports jacket, flannels and city shoes, was nevertheless game for anything, so we started walking round the lake, keeping close to the edge, where we could scramble along its rocky shore. But appearances were deceptive; there were little inlets and rocky promontories. Inland, the ground was covered in dense undergrowth or bristled with rocky outcrops. It was like an obstacle course and time was galloping by. We were only ten minutes away from lunch-time and seemed to be as far as ever from the end of the lake.

David Mathew in his leather-soled shoes was finding it particularly hard going. I therefore suggested that Al should run on ahead to warn Liu that we were going to be late. He set off alongside the lake but soon a steep rocky buff barred his way. The only way up it was by a flying buttress of piled blocks. It was horrifyingly loose and the top turned out to be both steeper and very much more difficult than it had looked from the bottom. By this time Al had passed the point of no return, and we were out of sight, having chosen a different and much easier route. He was about twenty-four metres above the ground and pulling up over some big overhanging flakes. He would have certainly been injured, probably killed, if he had fallen off. It was undoubtedly the most serious moment of the entire expedition yet Al, a very talented solo rock climber, was in his element, and handling the loose blocks with delicate care, eased his way out over the top. He was back at the little tea house three-quarters of an hour later.

Meanwhile, our progress was very much slower. I had chosen an easier route that took us about 150 metres above the lake shore, through dense prickly undergrowth, across loose scree and small rocky outcrops. David, who was worried about the drop and inadequately clad, was inevitably slow. And then came the rain in a steady torrent. We had nearly reached the end of the lake and had dropped once more to the shore, but

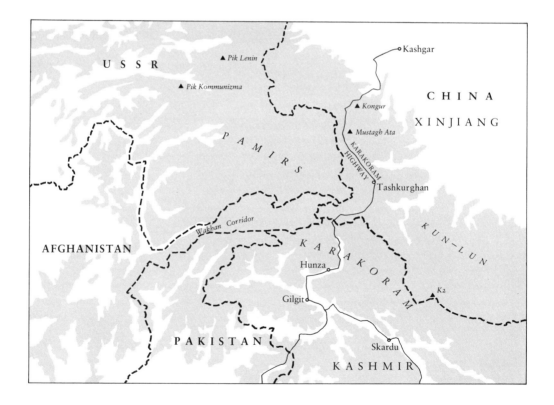

another bluff barred our way. I started making some desperate moves on the wet and slippery rocks, even using holds below the surface of the ice cold water. I certainly did not fancy a swim. A small boat set out from the little harbour half a mile away on the other side of the lake. For a delightful moment we thought it might be a rescue force led by Liu Dayi, who surely must be getting worried about his charges. But the boat put back to the pier. We were going to have to work out our own salvation. I returned to the other two and suggested that we climb up round the bluff. More struggles ensued over near vertical dripping vegetation. David was now showing all the signs of acute hypothermia, shivering, constantly stopping for a rest and seeming to have very little idea of what was going on. I did my best to encourage him, assuring him, with very little conviction, that the end was just round the next rise.

In some ways it reminded me of my days as an Outward Bound instructor back in North Wales. We took three hours to get back to the end of the lake, were soaked to the skin and yet, as we trudged along, I felt absurdly happy. It had been an enjoyable little adventure and had helped to bring us together as a team. Michael also had obviously thoroughly enjoyed it and had shown in the way he moved across the broken ground that he had lost none of his feel for rock over the years. David was not quite so sure about his enjoyment of the misadventure we had landed him in, but it certainly gave him a good after dinner story to recount on his return to Peking.

We were three hours late for lunch, but they had kept it back for us; a traditional Uighur meal of spicy shish kebabs grilled over an open fire. We swilled down Xinjiang beer and gobbled the shish kebabs, before piling into the car. We were now running late for our next function, a banquet given in our honour by the Xinjiang branch of the Chinese Mountaineering Association. Liu was obviously getting worried, the anxious shepherd with a particularly wayward flock of mountain goats. We got back just in time for the banquet, which was the best meal any of us so far had had in China. It was a mixture of Chinese and Uighur cooking. Dishes of boiled mutton and yet more shish kebabs alternating with delicious vegetables and local fish, all washed down by innumerable toasts in *mao tai*.

The following morning, nursing hangovers, we set out for Kashgar in a Russian built turbo-prop aircraft that seemed to be a copy of the Fokker Friendship. The plane was crammed with soldiers in their olive green, badgeless uniforms, giving no hint of rank except by the cut and quality of the material, others who were obviously cadre and a few who perhaps were ordinary workers. The plane flew over the end of Tian-shan range, over snow peaks and stunted glaciers to the featureless Taklamakan desert that stretches all the way to Kashgar, relieved only by the occasional oasis of cultivation. Half way to Kashgar we dropped down into Aksu, with its single runway and shack of a terminal building.

I couldn't help regretting the ease and speed of our progress. Only seventy years earlier this same journey would have taken a month by camel and, even with the introduction of lorries, the journey still took several days by road. I envied Peter Fleming and Ella Maillart who in 1935 took over six months to complete the journey from Peking to Kashgar, slipping into Xinjiang by the back door of the southern side of the Taklamakan desert, travelling on horseback and camel, living amongst the nomads. This is the only way one can really get the feel of a country and its people. Even a vehicle has an insulating effect and is travelling too fast, and a journey by plane is like travelling in a vacuum.

We were wonderfully looked after by Liu Dayi. Indeed it was like travelling on a magic carpet, for he carried out all the money transactions, ordered vehicles, checked our bookings, chased up any gear that might have gone missing, but all this insulated us once again from the people and country we were travelling through. I couldn't help pining for the shopping sessions I had had in the busy Rawalpindi bazaar, buying rice, dhal and flour for ourselves and our porters, or even the ferocious bargaining and arguments we had with our porters on the approach march.

Our party had now increased to five, for in Urumchi we had picked up our interpreter Peter Chen. He had an intriguing background. Aged fifty-five, he was half-Burmese and had even owned a British passport. His father, who was Burmese had married a Hopei girl and in 1933 moved to Tianjin to work as a pharmacist. They had been overtaken, first by the Sino/Japanese war and then by the liberation. Chen had gone to Peking University after the liberation to study art, but he was suspect because of his bourgeois background and Burmese nationality, and was exiled to Urumchi in 1955. At first life was quite bearable and he had a job teaching the making of model aeroplanes in a military school. This lasted for four years, but he was then purged and sent into the country for nine years to work as a labourer.

From 1959 to 1964 he was allowed back to Urumchi and worked as a pianist accompanying gymnasts in their training routines. However, with the coming of the cultural revolution, it was back to hard labour for another nine years, building houses, mining coal and helping to build a dam near Aksu. Life then came full circle, for in 1978 he returned to the military school where he started to teach model making once again. Looking at him it was impossible to guess the life he had led. He seemed to hold no bitterness but accepted, as I suppose he had to, everything that had been handed out to him. He had got married only two years before and at last his life seemed to have some degree of stability with the prospect of his being able to utilise his talents, which in our case included his command of English. A mild, bespectacled, gentle man, with a diffident, courteous manner, we were worried whether he would survive the rigours of the walk to Base Camp and life at around 4,500 metres. This was before we learnt of his background.

As we approached Kashgar the desert beneath us changed to the green of cultivated land and a chequerboard of fields demarked by irrigation canals and lines of trees. The flat-roofed, mud-walled houses grouped round courtyards were very similar from this height to those of Skardu or Gilgit on the southern side of the Himalayan divide.

The airfield once again was a tarmac strip with an adobe single-storied house for a terminal building. We were met by a delegation of the local Sports Federation and given green tea in the waiting room while our baggage was unloaded. The journey into Kashgar was exciting. It was as if we had been transported suddenly into a different country;

ABOVE RIGHT] *A corner of Kashgar market.*
BELOW RIGHT] *The letter writer plies his trade.*

OVERLEAF ABOVE LEFT] *Youth band, Kashgar.*
BELOW LEFT] *Kashgar schoolroom.*
RIGHT] *Formal monuments and makeshift transport, Kashgar.*

donkey carts jostled with lorries and jeeps. Although there were still the drab blue and green suits of standard Chinese wear, there were also the black coats of the nomads, sheepskin cossack-style hats over faces tanned brown by the sun and the wind, with hooked noses and features more Middle Eastern than Chinese. The women wore brightly coloured skirts, blouses and head scarves. A few of the older ones were veiled. The shops, little more than alcoves open to the street, with their bolts of coloured material, bags of spices, flour and rice, could easily have been in a hill town of Pakistan or Nepal. There were market stalls everywhere, selling cooked meats, soft drinks of an improbable pink colour in big bottles, sweetmeats and yoghurt. There were big umbrellas shading the stalls and everywhere there were flies. It was a rich, exciting, colourful scene which we were whisked through in our mini-bus, horn blaring, to a big compound surrounded by a high wall on the far side of town. Inside were gardens and various official guest houses, presumably for different grades of visitor. We were some of the very few westerners who had been allowed into Kashgar since 1949. Our guest house was clean and airy, its spacious bedrooms had their own bathrooms. Although some concern was expressed about the effect of our presence on curious crowds, there was no attempt to stop us going out and we wandered at will throughout our stay.

Kashgar has a long and turbulent history, for it is both the focal point of the great overland trade routes, the Silk Road between Europe and China, and the southern arm through the Karakoram to the Indian sub-continent. It is also a rich agricultural region in its own right. As a result it has been a coveted prize which has frequently changed hands through the millennia. Its importance as a trade centre is because of its position at the very root of the great mountain branches that stretch across the Central Asian plateau. These great ranges all reach towards the Pamirs, to the west of Kashgar. The range of the Tian-shan stretches to the north, that of the Kun-lun to the south of the city. In between is the arid waste of the Taklamakan desert. The high mountains that guard the Kashgar valley on three sides provide the melt water that turns this desert, with a rainfall of only a few centimetres a year, into a garden paradise, for the talus dust once watered provides an immensely rich soil, and almost every grain, fruit and vegetable can be grown in profusion around Kashgar.

Trade between the civilisations of east and west started many centuries before Christ, when the first caravans bearing silk set out on their long journey to sell it in the rich markets of the fast expanding Roman Empire. Even before the start of the silk traffic, jade had been exchanged from the west for lapis lazuli from the east more than 5,000 years ago.

The history of China has seen a constant struggle with the nomadic hordes sweeping across the empty steppes of Central Asia. The Great Wall of China represented an effort to deter incursion by means of an artificial barrier, whilst the great mountain wall of the Tian-shan and the Pamirs represented a natural barrier that gave the cities around the Taklamakan desert some degree of protection.

Kashgar was never a magnificent city. The building materials of all these desert cities made this almost impossible, for they are built of bricks composed of mud and straw,

ABOVE LEFT] *The Russian frontier is only thirty miles to the north beyond these foothills.*
BELOW LEFT] *The North-East Face of Kongur towers beyond the dust of the Karakoram Highway.*

which must inevitably crumble in the course of time. The buildings seem to blend into the dusty brown of the landscape in a discreet camouflage. Even so the old city of Kashgar has a charm and beauty of its own, with its winding lanes between high blank walls, broken only by doorways, which open on to the privacy of shady courtyards around which the houses are arranged. It is sad that the massive fifteen-metre defensive city wall, admired by every pre-war traveller, has recently been demolished. Modern Kashgar is less attractive with its wide streets and characterless buildings.

We visited the old British consulate, established by Younghusband in 1891 as part of the buffer zone between the British Raj to the south of the Himalaya and an expanding Russian presence in Chinese Turkestan. It was probably the most remote and at the same time most attractive British consulate in the world until it was finally withdrawn in 1947 with the success of the Communist forces in China. It provided not only the opportunity for British diplomats to play out the Great Game but, for those inclined, to explore and venture in this fascinating region. It was equally inevitable that it was the adventurously inclined who should be attracted to such a remote post. It was this that brought C. P. Skrine to Kashgar in 1922 and Eric Shipton there in the 1940s. Their description of the Kongur massif provided us with much of the background material of the mountain we were about to reconnoitre.

The building had fallen on hard times. It was being used as a lodging house with rooms let out to transient lorry drivers. The windows were dirty; scaffolding was lying abandoned on the once elegant verandah which overlooked what had been the carefully tended gardens. At its height the consulate had a community of around seventy, with its Indian born clerks, servants, a small force of locally recruited cavalry and all their families. It was difficult to imagine even the gracious and fairly leisured life style of just a few years before, so derelict was the house today.

You could not blame the Chinese for having no desire to preserve in style what was, after all, a relic of foreign influence if not imperialism. Much better cared for was the mausoleum of Apak Hodja, which is undoubtedly the most attractive and architecturally the most interesting building in Kashgar. Built in the seventeenth century, its design is similar to that of the Taj Mahal near Agra, but on a much smaller scale, and in a rougher, almost earthy vein that has a special charm of its own. The building is square cut with minarets at each corner and a fine dome of green glazed tiles rising from the centre. It is set amongst groves of poplars and is surrounded by a burial ground of sun-baked mud graves for those wanting to rest within sight of the mausoleum of the holy prophet and his family. It has become known as the Concubine's Tomb because the Hodja family sent one of their daughters, Mamrisim, to the court of the Emperor Qian Long, as a token of their loyalty to the Manchu dynasty. It took three and a half years to carry her in a sedan chair from Kashgar to Peking. At the imperial court she was called Xiang Fei, the Fragrant Concubine, and became one of the many lesser wives of the emperor. She only lived for a year after reaching Peking and it is said that she hanged herself, though it is not known why. Her body was allegedly brought back to Kashgar and she is buried next to her maternal grandfather, Apak Hodja, in a small plain tomb.

Outside the tomb, by the brown waters of a cistern, peasants were sitting talking under the shade of the poplar trees. Another was crouched behind little baskets of mulberries that he was offering for sale. They had a delightful, fresh flavour. In the town itself, there was evidence of thriving private enterprise wherever you looked. The day we arrived in Kashgar was that of the open market, when peasants from miles around came into the town with their own private produce and livestock to sell or barter. With the ending of the cultural revolution the collective system has been relaxed still further and each family is allowed a small tract of land to tend for themselves. It is difficult to tell from a superficial visit to an area just how well a system is working, but certainly in Kashgar there was no sign of any poverty or malnutrition. The streets are crowded and busy. The department stores, which are state run, have a surprising number of consumer goods which include a variety of transistor radios and watches, children's toys, clothes and kitchen goods, whilst the bazaar, which is privately run, is full of more traditional goods.

To give some idea of costs, one of the jeep drivers who took us to the Karakol Lakes told us that it took him a year to save up for a little battery cassette player. Compared with what can be seen in similar towns on the other side of the Himalaya in Pakistan, there certainly seemed many more goods for sale and a much higher standard of living for the majority than is apparent in Gilgit or Skardu. A jeep driver in Kashgar has more possessions and is probably living better than his opposite number south of the border. Looking at the average villager, the difference seems even greater. There also appeared to be more services. In Kashgar there was both a Chinese hospital, practising modern medicine and also a Uighur hospital practising the traditional herbal medicine. Certainly almost everyone we saw in the streets looked very healthy. Every child in Kashgar went to school and we were assured that the vast majority, even in the outlying villages, did as well.

We spent only three days in the city before setting out for the Kongur massif. When Skrine and Shipton went exploring in the mountains only sixty miles away they rode there on horseback, but today the Karakoram Highway skirts the mountain range on its way to Pakistan. We were to drive practically all the way by bus. It arrived at six in the morning, just before dawn. In the back was piled all the baggage that had been brought out from England and the food and cooking gear that Liu Dayi had been collecting in the last few days in Kashgar. We seemed to be accompanied by half the Sports Federation of Kashgar, though whether this was from solicitude for our comfort or just for the ride, I'm not at all sure.

Surprisingly, it was still dark at the height of summer at six in the morning, but the reason for this is a manifestation that I feel is revealing. Although China stretches 2,500 miles from east to west, which in every other large country in the world would necessitate three different time zones, the entire country is on Peking time.

But we were on our way at last, rolling through the empty streets of Kashgar, past yet another statue of Chairman Mao, towering over the entire town, through the central shopping area, past the mud-walled compounds of the new factories and the tree-lined irrigation ditches that mark out the fields of tossing wheat, still an unripe green. Little clusters of mud-walled houses are scattered amongst the broad stretch of the fields. It was a scene of immense, reassuring peace. The road was a smooth tarmacadam, and I wondered whether this great Karakoram Highway could be like this all the way. If it were, what an anticlimax! But this wasn't to be and before we had reached the start of the desert, the road became a dusty rutted track and our way was marked by a great banner of dust thrown high behind us.

43

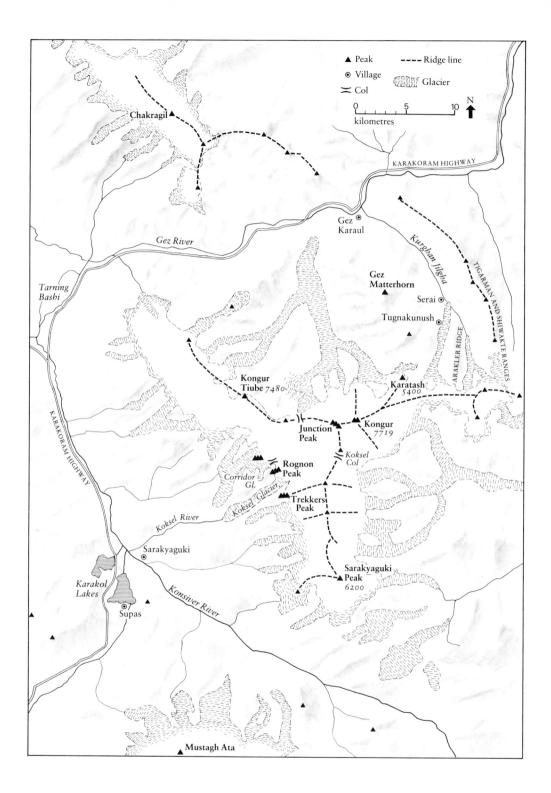

Peak
Village
Col
Ridge line
Glacier

0   5   10
kilometres

N

Chakragil

KARAKORAM HIGHWAY

Gez
Karaul

Gez River

Kurghan Jilgha

Tarning
Bashi

Gez
Matterhorn

Serai

TIGARMAN AND SHIWAKTE RANGES

Tugnakunush

ARAKLER RIDGE

Kongur
Tiube 7480

Karatash
5400

Junction
Peak

Kongur
7719

Koksel
Col

KARAKORAM HIGHWAY

Rognon
Peak

Corridor
Gl.

Koksel Glacier

Trekkers
Peak

Koksel River

Sarakyaguki

Karakol
Lakes

Konsiver River

Sarakyaguki
Peak
6200

Supas

Mustagh Ata

It was a perfect morning, the first we had experienced since arriving in Kashgar, for up to this moment the town had been shrouded in the dust cloud that covers it for most of the summer. I am not sure what meteorological trick had cleared the cloud, but it was a brilliant, clear dawn and for the first time we saw the wall of snow peaks, only sixty miles away, that guarded the southern horizon. We stopped the bus, climbed on to the roof and gazed at the peaks, trying to work out which was our objective. I thought I could recognise Kongur from a fine panorama in Skrine's book, *Chinese Central Asia*, which must have been taken from much the same position, but Liu Dayi, who had been here on two previous occasions, assured us we were wrong and that these were the outlying peaks of Chakragil. I was not convinced. The biggest peak, a great hump of a mountain with steep sides that dominated everything around it, surely must be our objective.

We drove on and, as the sun came up, the haze descended over the main peaks. We rolled across an empty stone desert to the next oasis, a haven of waving poplars and mud-built houses and compounds. There were even a few shops, and then on into the foothills up the wide valley containing the Gez river. Barren, sculptured hills of grey and brown and rich red ochre thrust up on either side. We passed a little hydro-electric power station in the course of construction and then a small coal mine, its huts, drab and grim like mining villages the world over; a lonely basketball net sagged against one wall and men in overalls, faces blackened by coal dust, moved to and fro. It was a desolate spot in which to work.

After a further hour we had another tantalising view of our mountain, now only ten miles or so away. This was the north-eastern aspect. In some ways it reminded me of the first view of Mont Blanc as you drive towards it from the west, not elegant and soaring, but rather squat and massive, threatening in its very bulk. Mount McKinley in Alaska gives the same impression as it rises abruptly from the flat forests that guard it from the east. The route from this side looked long and steep. Another problem was also becoming evident. There was no obvious pointed summit on Kongur. It looked from below as if it could be a huge plateau on top with several small summits, and it was difficult to ascertain which was the highest.

The valley now narrowed and Kongur was hidden by the steep rocky hillsides. The Gez river, which had flowed, untrammelled in a number of channels across the flat open valley bed of shingle and boulders was now squeezed into a single thundering turmoil of creamy brown waters that tore and battered the abutments of the road. Groups of labourers, some of them women, worked at the roadside in the ceaseless battle against the encroachment of the river. The gorge was ugly in its starkness with sun-baked mud and shattered rock unrelieved by vegetation. We reached Gez, a little group of buildings that resembled a frontier customs post. There was a hinged pole across the road and a scruffy policeman lolling in the shade of the verandah of a single-storied structure. Building materials were scattered around and the whole place looked only half finished. This was a police post on the Karakoram Highway and it looked like the sort of place one might be sent to when out of favour. And yet if you allowed your eyes to escape the starkness of the valley bottom, beyond and above soared a snow peak unlike any we had seen from a distance. This was a fairytale peak, a veritable Matterhorn, slender, shapely and pointed, with far-flung ridges reaching up into the skies. It was a mountain I longed to climb, one that I still dream of. It had no name, was probably only around 5,750 metres in height, but higher peaks behind it were hidden and it dominated the valley. Al and I enthused about the peak and speculated on our chances of climbing it when we returned to this side of the mountain for the second part of our reconnaissance.

But we were driving on for we had decided to look at the southern aspect of Kongur first of all. The road wound improbably up the gorge between steep slopes of shattered rock and mud that were obviously in constant movement. There was barely room for two vehicles to pass each other and every time we met a lorry coming the other way there was a frightening edging and creeping as the vehicle on the outside went to the very brink of the precipice that overhung the tumbling torrent of the Gez.

On the left of the road, we caught glimpses of the jumbled debris of the glaciers flowing down from the north side of Kongur with an occasional glimpse of high mountain walls and distant snow ridges beyond. Each bend in the road brought new and exciting vistas as we crawled in bottom gear up through the Gez gorge. On the other side of the river we could see the remains of the old track climbing across sheer rock walls. This was the old trade route that eventually led through Tashkurghan to the Himalayan passes and the wealth of India.

Then, suddenly, we escaped from the gorge. Everything opened out into high rolling hills and sweeping valleys. We had reached the Pamir plateau. Tarning Bashi, a huge empty lake bed, filled with silt and the occasional patch of water, stretched before us. On the other side, dunes of almost white sand rose tumescent, miniature mountain ranges to blend with the ochre coloured rocky hillside behind them. One branch of the road followed the northern side of that great empty lake to the closed Russian border just thirty miles away, though it was difficult to visualise man's artificial borders in this vast expanse of desert steppe. Our road wound round the eastern shore of the lake. It was now three o'clock in the afternoon and we were hungry, but Liu Dayi had everything in hand. We stopped by the ruins of a little fort that guarded the lake shore. All that was left was the eroded outer mud wall. He produced bread rolls, tins of Chinese Spam, butter and jams, tins of fruit, and even a crate of beer. It seemed incongruous but then so much of this trip was. The pace and ease of our progress made it very difficult to believe that we were in the heart of Central Asia, that the mountains we had just passed were comparatively unknown and had hardly been explored.

After having done full justice to the meal, we set out on the final leg of our journey, making a diversion to the headquarters of the local collective. It was rather like an army camp, with single-storied huts scattered over the gravelled desert floor, a basketball pitch of dried mud and most of the people wearing Chinese-style blue jackets and trousers, though from their features they were obviously Kirghiz or Uighur. The collective covered a huge area and owned all the herds of sheep, goats and yak in this part of the Pamir plateau. The buildings provided the essential services for the community, with a small hospital and school as well as the offices to co-ordinate and control this gigantic operation. The nomads were becoming more settled. In pre-revolutionary days, they lived in their tents throughout the year, moving from one grazing area to another, but now, they tend to spend the winter months settled in mud brick huts, resuming their nomadic way of life in the spring.

We paused at the collective just long enough for Liu Dayi to confirm arrangements for the yaks which were to carry our gear up to Base Camp, before driving on round the back

Looking across the desert plinth to the Kongur massif.

of Kongur to the Karakol Lakes where we planned to camp. There was no hint of their existence until we pulled over a slight shoulder and found ourselves beside a wide expanse of water, with a sward of close cropped grass on either side of the little exit stream; a perfect site for a camp. Once the bus had been unloaded and driven away with our retinue of helpers from the Sports Federation, we realised just how small an expedition we were. There were five tents, a makeshift cooking shelter and a little pile of baggage. Our team now numbered seven for we had been joined by a cook from Kashgar. He was a slightly sullen-faced Uighur, who complained of having a headache because of our fast gain of altitude. The bus had taken us from about 1,200 metres to over 3,000 in a matter of hours.

It was dark by the time we had pitched the tents and had something to eat, but that night we all had a sense of excited anticipation as we crawled into our sleeping bags. I woke with the dawn the next morning and, taking an assortment of cameras, climbed the steep little hillock immediately behind the camp. From its crest, about sixty metres up, there was a magnificent expansive view, so very different from those in the main range of the Himalaya or Karakoram, where the mountains, perhaps more magnificent and

47

dramatically sculptured, are often high retaining walls restricting distant views. But here on the high Pamir plateau the view seemed almost boundless and for the first time, just through the small effort of scrambling up the loose rocks of the broken ridge leading to this little top, I at last felt part of this limitless landscape.

Below me stretched the Karakol Lakes; the one by which we were camped and then, on the other side of a low rocky isthmus, an even greater stretch of water, dark and still in the subdued light of the dawn. Sprawling like a huge volcano beyond the lake, was the great cone of Mustagh Ata. Easy-angled snow slopes and ridges stretched invitingly up towards its top. It is not surprising that Sven Hedin, the famous Swedish explorer who came there in 1894, was attracted to such a magnificent yet easy-seeming prize. He spent a year living with the Kirghiz in the Karakol region and made several attempts to climb the mountain while surveying its many glaciers. He had little mountaineering experience, no crampons and tried to make the ascent by yak. It is remarkable that he reached a height of around 6.700 metres. Aurel Stein, the great archaeologist, also made an attempt with some Hunza guides, but he too failed at around the same height.

It was perhaps Mustagh Ata's accessibility, combined with its dramatic situation that also attracted Eric Shipton when his climbing partner, Bill Tilman, visited him in 1947, while Shipton was on his second tour of duty as Consul General in Kashgar. They made the most determined effort to date, getting within sixty-one metres of the summit before being turned back by the bad weather that is so characteristic of the region.

Sitting on the little hillock, I could see why Mustagh Ata had attracted all the attention, even though it is lower than the Kongur massif, for gazing eastward towards Kongur, the very extent of the range somehow diminishes its actual size. It fills the entire eastern horizon, but at a distance of about fifteen miles the snow-clad range seems little more than a band of rounded white mounds between the dusty grey brown of the desert plinth from which it rises, and the towering mountains of cloud that part conceal and dwarf the snows to which they cling.

And as for Kongur itself, it is hidden by those very clouds and even Kongur Tiube, the second highest peak of the range, with its great whaleback bulk, hardly draws the eye or challenges the imagination. It is not surprising that the Chinese/Soviet expedition first attempted and finally climbed Mustagh Ata before turning to Kongur Tiube almost as an afterthought.

We spent three days on the edge of the Karakol Lakes before setting out for our mountain. Michael Ward visited Supas, the nearby Kirghiz village, police and army post on the other side of the lakes. One of the possible subjects for scientific study the following year was the surprising fact that there was practically no incidence of goitre on the Pamir plateau, while on the southern watershed of the Karakoram and the Himalaya, the incidence was very high. When he visited Supas he found that there was no history of goitre ever having occurred in the Kirghiz. It was a condition well recognised by the nomads. The Chinese had some years previously started adding iodine to the food in areas with goitre but he was told that the condition had been extremely rare even before this. Meanwhile, Al and I explored the country immediately around our campsite,

ABOVE RIGHT] *A Kirghiz yurt.*
BELOW RIGHT] *In Urumchi, capital of Xinjiang, the dress was still Chinese, but the features of the people revealed their Turki-based Central Asian stock.*

stumbling across a small encampment of yurts only a mile or so away.

The yurt forms a squat dome of heavy felt laid over a wooden framework. It is about four metres across and around two metres high at its apex. A circular hole is left at the centre of the dome to enable smoke to escape and the entrance is usually covered by a rug, decorated here with a strong symbolic pattern. Inside they were delightfully clean and airy, the mud floor swept, and the folded, brightly coloured quilts and rugs used at night for sleeping stacked against a wall. In the middle was a stove made from an oil drum, with a chimney reaching up to the hole in the roof. A big cooking pot fits into the top of the stove and yak or sheep dung provide the fuel. To one side of the stove was the larder with an array of cooking vessels, goatskins full of milk or cream, and ladles and knives.

The Kirghiz have the easy, natural courtesy of almost all nomad peoples and whenever we visited one of their encampments we were always invited into the yurt and offered their traditional hospitality. A patchwork felt rug was laid in front of the piled quilts for us to sit on and bowls of yoghurt and a plateful of yellow cake-like bread would be set in front of us. If we finished the bowl, another would immediately be pressed upon us, while the entire family would squat around us, watching the intriguing spectacle. We had brought with us an instant camera and this was an immediate success. Everyone wanted their picture taken, both as a family group and then individually. They were certainly used to the idea of photography, freezing into the formal pose of those sepia-toned Victorian portraits that can be found in most family archives.

Most of the Kirghiz still wore something akin to their traditional costume, the men sporting the black sheepskin cossack-style hat, black corduroy high-necked jacket, and trousers tucked into leather boots, while the women wore colourful patterned skirts or dresses, with a short jacket, often of the standard blue cotton to be bought throughout China, and a white headscarf concealing their hair. In appearance the Kirghiz are much more Mongol than the Uighurs who have fine Aryan features. The Kirghiz, particularly the women, have much broader, flatter faces, with slanting almond eyes. To our European tastes the girls tended to be homely rather than pretty. Traditionally the women did almost all the work around the camp, collecting water, cooking, milking the sheep and watching the flocks in the immediate vicinity, whilst the menfolk planned, talked, supervised the moves from grazing area to grazing area and went off fighting in the frequent conflicts that took place either between different tribes or against whichever power happened to claim control over their territory. It certainly didn't seem to have changed very much, though conflict, at least for the time being, seemed to be over.

As in Kashgar, there were certainly more signs of material possessions here than among the hill people south of the border. Most yurts possessed a transistor radio and several even had portable sewing machines. Schooling was difficult because of their round of migration from one pasture to the next, but with their settled winter base and the small villages that have been built round this, there is regular schooling for all for at least part of the year. I saw several older youngsters who were home on holiday from secondary school from farther afield. They were the cadre of the future.

Michael had a constant stream of would-be patients, for the nearest qualified doctor

LEFT] *The traditional hospitality of bread and yoghurt.*

was at the collective headquarters fifteen miles away; but medical attention, albeit much of it the barefoot doctor variety, was available and everyone certainly looked extremely healthy. Their day-to-day life probably had not changed very much. In the old days the tribal chief would have owned most of the sheep, goats, yak, camels and horses that represented the wealth and living of the community. Today it is the collective, which in theory, if not in practice, is the entire body of the people. They are also allowed to own animals of their own – sheep, yak, camels and horses in the proportion of five large animals and ten small to each family. With improved wintering, sheds for the animals and the cultivation of more animal feed for the winter months, they have certainly increased the size of their flocks, which in turn must have increased the prosperity of both the collective and the individual. The very courtesy of our reception in their yurts and the generosity of their hospitality gave the impression of a stable and contented society.

I enjoyed our few days by the Karakol Lakes. On our last afternoon there Al announced that he was going to run across to the spectacular black rock peak we could see rising above the valley beyond the lake. It seemed a long way, but I immediately rose to the bait. I had been feeling lazy, content to lounge around the camp, but this challenge at once roused a spark of competition, enhanced perhaps by the fact that Al was so much younger and presumably fitter than myself. I also resolved to go for a run.

Al was away first. Clad in singlet and running shorts, he set out from our little group of tents and disappeared round the corner of the lake a few hundred metres away at a steady, powerful run. I set off about ten minutes later, jogging along the other shore of the lake. I had been running daily back at home, but nevertheless was pleasantly surprised at how well I was going even though the altitude here was around 3,650 metres. The ground underfoot was a firm gravel or sun-baked mud and a small flock of ducks took off from the lake shore as I ran past. A bird of prey hovered high above me, emphasising the immensity of the sky. I have come to enjoy the sensation of running and in the process am fully aware of the country around me. If anything, my perception is heightened from the rhythmic movement combined with the element of concentration that running demands. I had set my eyes on the top of a hill slightly nearer than the one of Al's choice, but nevertheless on what seemed the watershed of the great open plateau that held the Karakol Lakes.

The slope was now steepening and I began to feel the altitude, dropping into a fast walk, but still determined to push myself as fast as possible as I climbed an outlying hill that buttressed the skyline for which I was heading. At first glance the hillside seemed an empty desert, but on closer inspection it was covered with tiny sage bushes, while in every hollow slender shoots of grass, nurtured by the moisture left from winter snow drifts, formed an almost invisible cover that gave the gravelled ground underneath an imperceptible light sheen of green. A flock of sheep, followed by a Kirghiz, were slowly working their way across the slope above me. They seemed very close but the altitude was now having an effect. I had to pause for breath every few paces, and by the time I reached their level, they had already drifted away and had vanished into a fold in the mountainside. The rise now seemed interminable, but at last I reached the top. It was probably around 4,575 metres, but I still hadn't reached the far skyline. There was another higher ridge beyond and, looking back to the east, the entire Kongur range seemed to fill the horizon. Kongur Tiube's great bulk led to another ridge line and behind that, part covered in cloud, I could just see what must be the summit of Kongur itself, a black cap of snow-veined rock, protruding above the outer ramparts that guarded it. To the right of this was a low col from which appeared to flow a broad sweeping glacier reaching down into the very desert, and then, to the right of this, a whole range of peaks, all of which I knew were unclimbed.

It was now late afternoon and the sun was getting low in the west. I was only wearing shorts and a T shirt. Shivering with cold, I started running down the long flanks back towards the Karakol Lakes. I decided to go back by the opposite shore and as I came on to the level floor of the valley, noticed a Kirghiz encampment over to my left. A dog barked as I approached, but a youngster came running across to me, shooed the dog away, and made signs for me to accompany him to the yurts. The sheep and goats had just been herded in from their daytime pastures and women were crouched by the ewes, milking them. Smoke was rising from the little chimneys jutting out of the tops of the yurts. The timelessness of the scene enhanced its peacefulness. I could feel the tranquillity of it stealing over me, made all the stronger by the fact that I was on my own.

I was ushered into the yurt, invited to sit down and was offered the inevitable yoghurt and bread. They then demonstrated a picture being taken by clicking their fingers to their eye. Their hospitality was not entirely motiveless! The fame of our instant pictures had spread throughout the community. Alas I had no camera with me, but tried to tell them with sign language that we would photograph them if they came to our camp by the lake.

I walked back beside the lake in the gathering dusk. Dark clouds had driven in from the west and as I reached camp a snow squall swept across the lake, lashing the tents with hard, hail-like snow. Al had got back some hours before. He had assessed my own competitive instinct all too well, had only run for the hundred metres that took him out of sight, had then had a rest behind a boulder and continued his expedition at a more leisured stroll. His objective, the dark peak on the skyline, had been even farther than it looked and in the end he had turned back just short of it, traversing some frighteningly steep slopes of baked mud, on which it would have been impossible to stop had he slipped.

That night, wielding our chopsticks on a series of delicious vegetable dishes, we were well content with the day and excited by the prospect of moving up to the foot of the Kongur massif the following morning. Our very lack of knowledge of the area was a stimulus. It was as if we were stepping back in time, to the days of mountain exploration, of crossing uncharted passes, of penetrating valleys that had never been seen before. Even though the dust plumes of the occasional lorry or bus, the presence of the line of telegraph poles stretching across the desert, was a reminder of the modern world, the gigantic vault of the sky, the subtle pattern of colours presented by the desert, the huge snow upthrust of these mountains of Central Asia, had a scale that made man's technical progress and political change seem very puny.

3

Mountain explorers

13TH–19TH JUNE 1980

Twelve yaks with four Kirghiz to drive them arrived on the morning of 12th June. They made quick work of our little pile of gear, seeming unconcerned about the exact weights they were loading on to the backs of the yaks. I have a feeling that the total weight of our baggage was well within the statutory seventy kilos which represented the official loading and no doubt this is well within what a yak is capable of carrying. They were shaggy, likeable beasts that seemed amazingly docile, standing quietly while the Kirghiz, working in pairs on either side of them, strapped boxes and kitbags to their saddles. In less than an hour we were ready to set out on the next stage of our journey.

It was a dull, threatening day, with big cloud banners flying over the Kongur massif. Our route took us across a short stretch of desert to the gorge of the Konsiver river fed by the Koksel Glacier and the melt water from the entire Kongur range and the back of Mustagh Ata. Liu Dayi had warned us that it would turn into a raging torrent later on in the season but there was little evidence of this at the moment. The water barely came over our knees as we waded across it. Our party was now augmented by three sheep who were going to be our meat on the hoof at Base Camp. Unwilling to plunge into the water, their tethers were attached to the saddle of one of the yaks and they were hauled across the

Our yak transport were docile and likeable beasts, but we quickly outpaced them.

river. On the other side the hard-packed banks stretched easily in a series of low ridges and hillocks towards the mountains beyond. It was delightfully easy walking, but the Kirghiz obviously thought us mad, both to walk when there was a chance of a ride on a yak and even madder, not to say plebeian, to carry a rucksack. For the Kirghiz it was demeaning to walk and unthinkable to carry a load. They rode anything on four legs; horses, yaks, camels and even their diminutive donkeys.

We quickly outpaced the yaks who grazed as they ambled through the shrub-scattered desert. Liu Dayi was carrying an ancient service rifle. There were plenty of hares on the lower slopes that would break cover from almost beneath one's feet. The crack of his rifle showed he had managed to bag one.

We walked through the day, halting every now and then to wait for the yaks. Peter Chen, our interpreter, and our Uighur cook had accepted the invitation of rides on the yaks. Impatient to get on, Michael, Al and I slowly drew farther ahead, reaching the moraine wall of the Koksel Glacier debris at around three in the afternoon. It was obvious by this time that we might have a serious problem in finding running water in this mountain desert, so we pressed on through a barren jumble of old moraines until suddenly a little valley opened before us at about 4,500 metres. It was sheltered, with grass on its flanks and a stream bed, albeit with only a trickle of water, but it was the first we had seen for some hours. We were now so far ahead of the yaks that we resolved to wait for them there and while we waited we started to build dry stone walls for a cook shelter. Liu Dayi caught us up shortly, reassuring us that we must have stopped in a reasonable place and he was soon helping us, shifting boulders twice as big as any that we would attempt to lift for fear of straining our backs. I had the feeling that he was a man who had known real toil; we had only played at it.

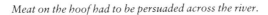

Meat on the hoof had to be persuaded across the river.

I was woken next morning by the sound of a birdlike chirping, peered out of the tent into the bright sunlight and saw a delightful little golden brown creature with a great bushy tail staring at me from the opposite bank of the moraine. It watched me for a second and then turned tail and dived down a hole. I quickly got dressed and set out to explore the surroundings of our Base Camp. Above our little valley it flattened out into an expanse of old moraine debris, part-covered by sparse grass and scattered with little primulas and other alpine flowers. It was a brilliant day with light streamers of very high cloud accentuating the deep clear blue of the sky. Behind me, the great wall of Kongur Tiube was piled high and steep, while across the great open divide of the Pamir plateau was Mustagh Ata, proud in its solitary splendour. But of Kongur there was no sight. A small subsidiary peak, shapely and pointed, rose from the end of the moraine ridge at whose foot our camp was set. It concealed both Kongur and even the approach to it. All I could get was a glimpse of a tumbled icefall leading down from what I imagined must be a glacier basin at the foot of our objective. Walking across the broken moraine to the alarm piping of the marmots who went scurrying off into their holes, I came to the edge of the glacier. We were very slightly above the petrified waves of tossing ice that stretched down in a great tongue into the desert.

By the time I returned the rest of the camp was coming to life. Al was feeling slightly

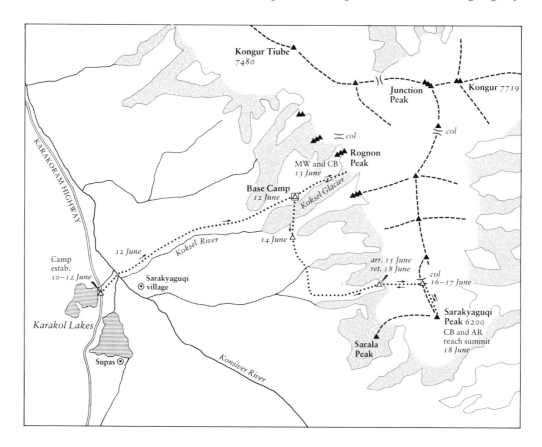

queasy from a combination of sun and altitude, but Michael and I were longing to see more of the glacier leading up to Kongur. We decided, therefore, to have a brief reconnaissance that morning and to spend the rest of the day preparing for our first serious foray, in which we planned to take a week's food and try to get up one of the valleys leading down from the range of mountains to the south of Kongur and then get over the col at the head of the valley into the glacier to the south side of the mountain.

The way now led up the narrow valley above the camp. Clumps of primula mingled with the scattered rocks and fine grass. A short distance above the shallow valley widened into a pasture and the concentration of sheep dung showed that this was a regular grazing area. Circles of beaten down mud marked out the sites where the yurts had stood and a low stone wall formed a fold. We continued up the valley which wound in and out of old moraines until it opened out once again into a perfect flat meadow of thick coarse grass with a stream bed meandering through it. On one side were some large boulders. It was the perfect site for a Base Camp if we ended up trying to climb the mountain from this side. A long grassy slope led up towards the crest of the moraine rib and we followed this, noticing on the way the magnificent horns and skull of a Marco Polo sheep. This large wild sheep still wanders the foothills of the Pamirs, though sadly its numbers have been seriously reduced by indiscriminate killing. We had already noticed that the local people shot almost anything that moved and as a result have decimated much of the wild life in the Pamir, and, I suspect, other mountain regions in China.

We were now above the glacier on the crest of the moraine ridge. It was clear of snow but very broken, a jumble of ice fins, towers and sérac walls, stretching about a mile across to the other side and up into an icefall, above which we presumed there was a glacier basin. It wasn't as big as the Khumbu Icefall on Everest, but, nonetheless, it was a formidable barrier. Once down on the ice, we found that it was slow going, an obstacle course of icy runnels and ravines that meandered, maze-like, into dead ends. We picked our way, slowly, tentatively, as always when first venturing on to a strange glacier. I wanted to see round the corner, to start building up a picture in my own mind of the structure of the mountain. After a couple of hours wandering we had reached an ice hummock from whose top we could see round the back of the small peak above our Base Camp. It appeared to be a rock island, or rognon, jutting out of the glacier. Could this mean that the glacier flowed more easily down the other side of it, or was there perhaps a col linking the peak with the main body of the mountain? As for the summit of Kongur, we were now too close beneath its retaining wall to see anything of that. We returned well satisfied to find that Al had spent the morning organising our provisions for the next ten days. They felt unpleasantly heavy when we tried our rucksacks for weight.

That night, tired from our excursion, I fell into a deep sleep, started dreaming of being engulfed in a flood and then, slowly coming into wakefulness, realised that it wasn't a dream. There was the roar and rush of running water from out of the dark. It seemed all around us, and suddenly I felt desperately vulnerable in this narrow bottleneck of a valley. The others were shouting from their tents; a light went on, and peering from the entrance I could see in the torch light that the stream bed was now brimming full with brown swirling waters. A snow dam had perhaps broken farther up the valley, but I think all of us started remembering stories of gigantic floods in the Himalaya caused by the collapse of glaciers containing large lakes. This was hardly in that class, but on a dark night it is amazing how freely the imagination can flow. We debated whether to move the tents but quickly abandoned the idea. It was too much effort and we were able to rationalise that the worst of the flood was probably over. Even so it took me a long time to drop off to sleep again as I listened to the urgent rush and gurgle of the water pouring down just a few feet away.

By morning it had settled into a steady flow of clear water which was to last for the rest of our stay. It was a dull, overcast day and we managed to fill most of it with our preparations for departure, almost as if we dreaded the moment of shouldering the heavy rucksacks for the first time. We were taking with us enough food for a week, the bare minimum of climbing equipment, consisting of a 7mm rope and a few ice pitons and karabiners, a three-man tent and our own personal gear. When packed it came to about eighteen kilos each and felt a lot heavier. We were a bizarre sight as we set off, for we were wearing bright red long-sleeved vests and long underpants with a pair of running shorts over them. This is the dress favoured by many fell runners and is really light and comfortable. Instead of boots we were using training shoes, which are a lot lighter than boots and ideal for walking below the snow line. The only thing out of keeping with this image of a quick run over the fells was the huge rucksacks we were going to hump.

Our first obstacle was the Koksel Glacier. It would have meant losing a lot of height to have gone round it and so we decided to strike out straight across. After all it was comparatively flat in its lower part, almost a gigantic basin, spread out over the desert surrounding it. However, this initial impression changed by the time we were half way across. It was a maze as confusing as the one that Michael and I had penetrated the previous day, with ice valleys winding back on themselves, sudden drops appearing or complete ranges of miniature ice mountains that limited our vision to a few metres around us. Our footwear was hardly ideal, but we couldn't bring ourselves to put on boots and crampons. Eventually we reached the other side, but it had taken us three hours to cover little more than a mile of ice. It was now into early evening and it was obvious that we were not going to reach the valley we were planning to follow the next day. In addition the country, which from a distance had appeared to be no more than open rolling desert, was very much more complex, seamed with little ravines and hidden valleys. Once again water presented a problem. Most of the stream beds were dry, but after an hour's walking we came across a Kirghiz campsite alongside the stream running down from the valley beyond the Koksel Glacier.

It was deeply satisfying to be on our own, just the three of us, on the brink of a journey of discovery, knowing that very soon we would stand where no one had been before. That night I slept outside a roughly built sheep fold amongst the rocks. Lying on my back, looking up at the black night sky in which glittered a myriad of stars, I felt a simple contentment, just happy to be there, to be wandering over this wild, empty unspoilt land.

We set out early next morning, skirting the line of mountains running south from the Kongur massif. There were two peaks which, according to the map and our own observation, were 6,700 metres in height. There then seemed to be a hump of around 5,800 metres on the right of which was a col which looked passable. To the south (or once again to the right) of this was another peak of 6,200 metres which Al and I were already thinking of as a possible objective. But first we had to get to the col and hopefully drop down into the valley on the other side.

It was easy walking but our packs were heavy and Michael, that little bit older, was finding both the pace and his load excessive. The previous day Al and I had reduced his load as much as possible, increasing our own to about twenty-five kilos each, but even so we still found ourselves pulling ahead and having to wait for long periods. This was quite useful since it gave us time to talk over plans, both for the immediate reconnaissance and for the climb the following year. With his climbing background Michael, not unnaturally, had ambitions for the summit of Kongur himself and in my own initial thinking I had imagined the scientists, all of whom would be climbers, would also like to get to the top.

This did, however, present problems, since it would inevitably affect both the choice of route and the style in which we tackled the mountain. There has been a lot written about the evolution of climbing techniques in the Himalaya, of the merits of alpine-style as opposed to siege-style tactics as a means of climbing Himalayan peaks. In essence, siege-style is what it implies. An expedition arrives at the foot of a mountain and lays siege to it, pushing up a series of camps, linking them with a line of fixed rope, should the angle be steep, ferrying supplies up to each camp and eventually making a bid for the summit from the top camp. Of necessity it is a slow process, involving the repetition of the lower stages many times over whilst ferrying supplies.

Alpine-style, on the other hand, means that the climber treats the mountain as he would a climb in the Alps, loading his rucksack in the valley and then tackling the climb in a single push, bivouacking on the way as necessary. It is therefore a much faster process, a more challenging one and infinitely more enjoyable, since new ground is being covered the whole time. There should be none of the drudgery of repetition.

The concept of alpine-style ascents in the Himalaya is nothing new. The great British Alpinist, Albert Mummery attempted Nanga Parbat (8,125 m) in 1895 with just two Ghurkas. He attempted it alpine-style since nothing was then known about the effects of altitude and he simply treated this huge mountain as he would have done Mont Blanc. But he and his two Ghurka companions vanished, probably swept away by an avalanche. Subsequent expeditions evolved the siege-style tactics which became standard practice on the higher peaks.

The attempts on Everest provide a good example of the development of the siege approach. Right from the first major expedition in 1922 it was obvious to the climbers that they would need a systematic approach, using a series of camps and Sherpa high-altitude porters to help carry all the gear. They were also already trying out a primitive oxygen system and when Mallory and Irvine vanished on their summit bid in 1924, they were using oxygen. The pre-war expeditions reached a height of at least 8,500 metres – and of course it is just possible that Mallory and Irvine did reach the summit of Everest. But the pre-war climbers didn't have either the equipment or the experience of altitude problems to finish off the climb. It was not until after the second world war that the peaks of over that magic height of 8,000 metres began to be attained.

Most of the ascents of the major peaks were made by large expeditions using siege tactics, but, at the same time, there were still climbers to whom the concept of the small, lightweight expedition was immensely appealing. One such was Eric Shipton, who, with a fellow tea planter, Bill Tilman, had done a series of bold climbs on Mount Kenya and then went on to the Himalaya. He became involved in the Everest expeditions of the

1930s, but his real love was for lightweight mountain exploration in which the ascent of peaks was almost coincidental. Even so he and Tilman achieved a great deal in the realms of Himalayan climbing. While Shipton was taking part in the 1936 Everest expedition, Bill Tilman and Noel Odell reached the summit of Nanda Devi (7,816 m) as part of a small expedition with only a few Sherpas, but they were still using siege tactics.

Shipton and Tilman had made a bold two-man attempt on Mustagh Ata in 1947, being just beaten by bad weather. In the 'fifties, while the 8,000-metre peaks were being climbed in what amounted to an international race, the move towards lighter expeditions continued. In 1957 Hermann Buhl, Kurt Diemberger, Markus Schmuck and Fritz Wintersteller from Austria climbed Broad Peak (8,047 m) without the help of high-altitude porters, though their ascent was not, strictly speaking, in true alpine-style since they first stocked some camps before making their bid for the summit. Schmuck and Wintersteller went on to climb Skilbrum (7,420 m) using pure alpine-style tactics, while Buhl and Diemberger tried to emulate them on Chogolisa (7,654 m), but were forced to turn back because of bad weather. On the way down, Buhl walked through a cornice and fell to his death. It was only in 1975 that an 8,000-metre peak capitulated to alpine-style tactics, when Reinhold Messner and Peter Habeler climbed Hidden Peak (8,068 m) in the Karakoram, by its North-West Face. They only took a lightweight tent with them, even leaving behind their rope, and made the ascent in a lightning two days. Messner went on to climb the Diamir Face of Nanga Parbat solo, using the same tactics and he was due in that summer of 1980 to go for the north side of Everest, once again solo.

The concept, you could almost describe it as a creed, of the alpine-style push had come into fashion. There was a strong feeling in the climbing media, and also amongst a lot of young climbers, which was beginning to filter through to the general media, that siege-style climbing was obsolete and that the only adventurous, challenging way of climbing a mountain was alpine-style. Al Rouse certainly felt this way and we had quite a few discussions on this subject that at times approached argument.

My own successful expedition to the South Face of Annapurna and then on the South-West Face of Everest had used siege tactics; indeed Everest had been almost like a military operation, with a small army of porters, the best available oxygen system and special box tents that were more like small fortresses and weighed as much – 150 pounds for a two-man tent. But I was unrepentant, feeling that we had needed everything we had to climb the mountain at that particular time, that this was part of the evolution of Himalayan climbing and that, although at some time in the future climbers might well climb the great Himalayan walls using alpine-style tactics, we had not been ready for it in 1970 on Annapurna nor in 1975 on Everest. Al, on the other hand, who had taken part in two highly successful alpine-style expeditions on Jannu and the North Face of Nuptse, felt that the entire siege phase of climbing in the Himalaya was an irrelevance and that in the course of time this would be seen to be the case.

Not unnaturally I was not prepared to dismiss my efforts in quite such a peremptory manner. My philosophy had always been to tackle a mountaineering problem with the minimum numbers and technical aids to give a reasonable chance of success. Certainly, at the moment the big Himalayan walls, such as the South Face of Lhotse, the Kangshung Face of Everest and West Face of Makalu, still need a siege approach to give any real chance of success.

As far as our ascent of Kongur went, however, Al and I were in complete agreement. For a mountain of 7,719 metres which did not seem desperately steep and which was awaiting a first ascent, alpine-style seemed the ideal approach, but the problem here was the possible imbalance of the team between the climbing scientists and the climbers. I had thought out a whole series of possible compromises – one was to make a siege-style ascent of the peak by its easiest possible route, which would enable the scientists both to climb the mountain and carry out their research. The climbing team could then go to the steep north side of the mountain and attempt a fast, alpine-style ascent of this huge north face. But, like most compromises, this idea was riddled with problems. We would have climbed the mountain in the first place by a method that had an element of overkill and a subsequent ascent of the same mountain, admittedly by a more challenging method and route, would still have an element of anticlimax. It was even possible that we might not have the energy or enthusiasm for such a second attempt.

Al and I talked around the problem, while we waited for Michael to catch up with us that day. For the time being the process and experience of mountain exploration, even though it was little more than glorified fell walking, was immensely satisfying. We picked our way across the foot of a long spur leading into the valley we had chosen for our attempt to reach the watershed. The valley bottom was filled with the moraine residue of the receding glacier. That afternoon we reached a height of 4,700 metres on a scree shelf at the side of the valley, just above the snout of the glacier. A smooth, snow-covered glacier slope led up towards the col which was now only a couple of miles farther up the valley. The weather all day had been gusty and threatening with great clouds blowing in from the north-west.

In the event we need not have agonised about the climbing scientists' chances. Michael confirmed that the scientific team would have as their first priority the completion of their exacting work programme, and none of them would expect to climb Kongur as well. This was certainly a great relief to us, for it meant that there need be no untidy compromises and that the climbing team would be able to work as a completely balanced unit.

The following day we hoped to get over the pass into the next valley, so we started cooking before dawn, and set out in the early morning light across easy scree slopes on to the glacier itself. Although it was covered in snow, it was frozen hard and was at such an easy, smooth angle that it seemed safe to continue without a rope. Up to this point, Al and I had been going at about the same pace, but he now started to pull away from me. It was the eternal competition of climbers. Each walk can become an unspoken race, and this was one that I was losing. I decided to pace myself. After all, Al was nearly twenty years younger than I. He had stopped and waited for me about 150 metres below the col and now we went on at the same pace, picking our way over an easy little bergschrund and then plodding up hard snow to the col itself. There is always a tremendous excitement in reaching the end of a valley for the first time and seeing over the col to a new vista beyond. This was particularly so in this case, for it was quite possible that no one had ever crossed this particular col before.

On Clarmont Skrine's map the valley to the south of Kongur was marked as unexplored, for he had only surveyed the region to the east of the mountain. The modern Chinese map was almost certainly made from an aerial survey, though there were some metal triangulation points on the hills to the west of the Kongur massif. Our first glance was for the descent the other side. It looked formidable; much steeper than the route we had just climbed, on avalanche-prone snow dropping down on to a glacier that descended in a series of icefalls to the valley far below. Looking beyond, there was obviously a very complex valley and glacier system. The higher mountains were all veiled in cloud but on the other wall of the valley bristled a series of jagged black rock peaks which we assumed were part of the Shiwakte group, marked on Skrine's map as being around 6,000 metres. It was an immensely alluring, exciting view of a completely different character to the big rounded peaks of the main Kongur massif. These were technically difficult peaks that would be both challenging and fun to climb. But it was a long way down to the valley. There would be a certain amount of objective danger in the descent, and a long serious climb back up. In addition, Michael was obviously having trouble with the altitude and was a long way behind. We decided that we had better stay where we were, camp on the col that night and perhaps go for the 6,000-metre peak rising from the col the following day. At least from its summit we should get a good view of the southern aspect of Kongur. By the time Michael reached the col it had begun to snow. There was certainly no question of going on. We started to dig out a platform for our three-man dome tent, tucked beneath a little rock tower. It was a reassuringly sheltered position, safe from any threat of avalanche.

The storm raged throughout the night, the wind tearing at the tent and shaking down clouds of condensation crystals on to our sleeping bags. The tent was made from a single thickness of Gore-tex, a new material that both breathes and is waterproof. In theory it should have been the perfect material but in practice, in cold conditions, the water vapour from cooking and breathing froze on the inside of the walls before it had a chance of escaping through the pores of the material. As a result the problems of condensation were similar to that of any single skin tent. We didn't sleep much that night, and the following day the wind was as fierce as ever, though the cloud was broken and it began to clear later, giving some fine views of the peaks on the other side of the valley.

Al and I were keen to bag the six-thousander, which we christened Sarakyaguqi, after the nearest village. Michael was still having a lot of trouble with the altitude, unable to eat and very listless, but he never complained and didn't in any way suggest we should go back down. Although it was still windy that evening it was a fine clear night. Even though the peak we were going for did not seem particularly difficult, I couldn't repress that combination of excited anticipation and foreboding that seems to go with any summit push. I didn't sleep well and woke long before dawn to start melting snow for the first brew of tea. Al and I were away at first light, taking with us just fifteen metres of rope, a couple of ice screws and our axes. It was a wonderful morning, but out of the cloudless sky tore a savagely cold wind. The snow was wind-blasted hard and firm, or had been stripped off altogether to leave stretches of gleaming ice. The angle was quite easy so we left the rope off and just plodded on up through the clear air and driving wind. We were going at about the same rate, plodding steadily, going well for the altitude and our comparative lack of acclimatisation. The camp at the col was at about 5,500 metres and we had probably benefited from the two nights we had spent there. We took it in turns to go out in front, each aware of the other and his own enjoyment of leading. After two hours we came to a broad shoulder.

We sat down and rested and for the first time really gazed around us. The subsidiary peaks of the Kongur range had been immediately behind us. Big rounded hummocks, they partly concealed Kongur itself, but we now had a good view of its huge South Face, with its snow fields, sérac walls and rocky ridges. The top was rounded and it was as difficult as it had been from the bus on the way in to decide just which was the true summit. There seemed to be three, all of much the same height, linked together by a ridge or perhaps even a plateau. The way to the left-hand summit was up what seemed a comparatively easy-angled rock ridge. This led to a high snowy col and then another subsidiary hump, from which another broken ridge led across and then down to where it was concealed by the intervening 6,700 metre peak. With the knowledge of hindsight it is easy to put together the geography of the mountain, but this was our first clear view of the summit from the south and as a result it was very difficult to make an accurate mental picture of the shape of the mountain. Equally fascinating was the view of the Shiwakte peaks to the east of Kongur. Although dwarfed by the unwieldy bulk of Kongur itself, they had an elegant beauty that the larger mountain lacked. Al and I talked of attempting them when we got round to the north-eastern side of the mountain.

There was a bergschrund at the foot of the slope ahead and so we put on the rope, Al belaying me as I edged carefully up to its lip and pulled over on to the snow above. We then made steady progress up a short steepish slope that led out on to the final summit ridge. We were soon on the fine pointed top of our little peak, our first virgin summit in

OVERLEAF] *Looking south from the summit of Sarakyaguqi. The wedge-shaped peak on the right is an unclimbed summit in the Mustagh Ata massif. The prominent triangular peak on the horizon left centre is Karun Koh in the Karakoram, and to its left on the distant skyline, K2.*

Al climbing the North Ridge of Sarakyaguqi (6,200 m) with Kongur visible far right.

Central Asia. It was around 6,200 metres, of little consequence, and yet the satisfaction of standing there was immense. We had taken four hours to climb the 760 metres to the top, felt that we were going well and were able to gaze around us knowing that we should be able to snatch a few more peaks before the end of the expedition. This must have been the feeling Eric Shipton had when he wandered the mountains of the Shaksgam or explored the peaks around Everest. Technical difficulty seemed of little importance compared to the joy of finding one's way up an unknown peak, of gazing around and knowing that almost everything in sight was unclimbed and unexplored. Far to the south we could see a conspicuous triangular peak that for a moment I thought could be K2, second highest mountain in the world, but then I realised that it was too close and anyway K2 would be further west. Looking into the the haze of the west, in the far, far distance, there was just the vaguest shadow of another clear-cut triangle, higher than anything around it, the unmistakable shape of K2, which is surely one of the world's most symmetrical and beautiful peaks. We knew that Peter Boardman, Dick Renshaw, Doug Scott and Joe Tasker were attempting its West Ridge at that very moment. Closer to hand, Mustagh Ata dominated the western horizon, while to the north of it, mostly hidden by the intervening 6,700-metre summit we could see a distant range of snow peaks, little more than a white line on the horizon, which must be the Soviet Pamirs. From our viewpoint we could see across to Pakistan, the Hindu Kush of Afghanistan and into the Soviet Union.

We stayed on the summit for about twenty minutes before starting back down, leaping the bergschrund and then striding down the hard snow of the lower slopes of the ridge. Already we were making plans for the other unclimbed 6,000-metre peak, from which we would get an even better view of Kongur, and then there would be the exciting jagged summits of the Shiwakte group. We were in a veritable Aladdin's cave of unclimbed summits.

We got back to the tent at about midday. Michael was still feeling rough but we resolved to get down as far as possible that afternoon, which would help him to recover and enable us to get back to Base Camp the following day. That night we reached the bottom of the valley and set out the next morning for Base. It was a perfect morning with hardly a cloud in the sky. Al and I had shared out almost all the gear between us, but we were untroubled now by the weight, beginning to feel really fit and full of anticipation for the climbs ahead.

We had left the valley and pulled out on to the open hillside. Al had just stripped down to his running shorts, it was so hot, and from sheer exuberant high spirits broke into a run. His ankle seemed to keel over and he started to fall. His rucksack stopped him regaining balance and he fell heavily on his side on the hard-packed ground. He sat up slowly, nursing his ankle with both hands, face contorted with pain.

'I've really done it this time,' he said.

ABOVE RIGHT] *The mobile homes of Central Asia. The yurt in the foreground is rolled up ready to move to new pasture.*
BELOW RIGHT] *The Kirghiz enjoyed posing for family photographs.*

4
The lack of a Kirghiz phrase-book

Michael examined the ankle and confirmed Al's fears. The bones had been dislodged but fortunately had fallen back into place. Although some ligaments had broken, there was no fracture and no need for Michael to have to contemplate the disruptive business of sending Al back to Kashgar for X-rays. Already, however, the ankle had swollen to twice its size. There was no question of Al being able to walk on it and so we would have to get a yak to carry him. This meant one of us going back to Base Camp, explaining what had happened to Peter Chen, and then for Liu Dayi to go down to the Kirghiz village of Supas to arrange for a yak to come and pick Al up. The obvious course seemed to be for me to go for help while Michael stayed and cared for Al. We could see a little green hollow just below us where they could hope to find water and Al descended slowly on his backside while Michael and I ferried the rucksacks down. It was an idyllic spot for a campsite, with a spring just below them and a fine view looking out across the desert slopes towards the Karakol Lakes. They had enough food for a couple of days and in that time I hoped to be back with a yak to transport Al to Base Camp.

I left them at around midday. Soon the tent was just a tiny blue blob in the distance as I strode over the rolling ridges of the great desert plinth on which the Kongur massif rests. My feelings were mixed. I was worried that Al's ankle might take a long time to heal and this would end our chances of bagging all those attractive unclimbed peaks. But at the same time I couldn't help enjoying being alone in this huge, empty land. My perception of the ground immediately around me and of the great snow peaks in the distance became heightened. I stopped to photograph a clump of fragile dwarf iris, began to notice other flowers in this seemingly barren desert and became aware of the myriad of colours and shapes of the rocks protruding from and scattered over the desert.

I was heading for what I thought was the end of the Koksel Glacier, hoping to traverse it close to its snout to avoid having to cross the river that poured from under it. What from a distance looked an easy, open slope was anything but. The ground was seamed with ravines carved out of the desert by glacier torrents. There were unexpectedly valleys, crumbling cliffs and then, as I came closer to the Koksel Glacier, the sprawl of the moraine that formed a maze of boulder ridges and valleys, swamps of glacial mud, streams and pools. And then came the distant roar of the river. It was tumbling, brown and angry down the bed of a valley, carved out of the dirt-grimed ice and boulders of the receding glacier. Below me there was a way across, a bridge of ice spanning the torrent,

LEFT] *Kirghiz faces.*

Professional attention on the Pamir plateau for Al's injured ankle.

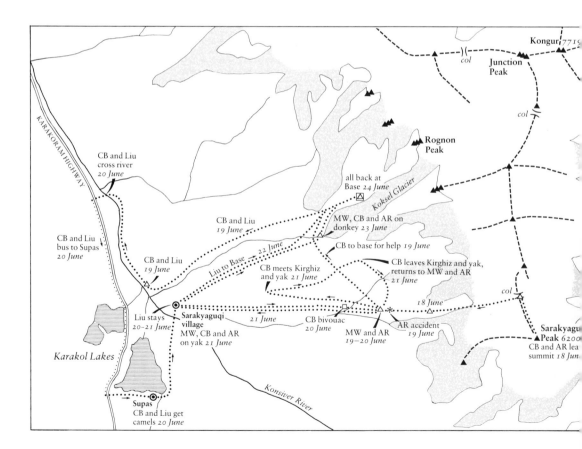

but to reach it I had to descend a ramp of old ice. If I slipped, I would inevitably slide down into the roaring waters of the river. I sat there for some time. I could always follow the river up to the point where it emerged from under the glacier but somehow I was attracted to the bridge. It was the way I had stumbled upon it, perhaps even the piquancy of the risk associated in trying to reach it. I started down, glad that I had kept my ice axe. I even cut the odd step in the gravelly ice and at last reached the bridge.

The moraines on the other side were interminable but at last I came out above the river valley on to easier ground and I recognised a cairn we had planted on the way in. Another hour's walking, and I could see our Base Camp nestling in its little valley, still and silent. As I came up to the cook shelter Liu came out and embraced me in his delight at seeing our return, but his face soon resumed its characteristically worried expression as I explained what had happened. I showed him on the map where I had left Al and Michael and we agreed that Liu and I should set out that afternoon for Supas to get a yak. There was no question of Peter Chen, our interpreter, coming with us since he was feeling the worse for altitude and not fit enough to keep up.

After a hastily snatched meal, we started off with Liu out in front setting a formidable pace. It took us a couple of hours to reach the top of the gorge formed by the Konsiver river where there was obviously a ford since the path wound down one side of the gorge and disappeared into the water to reappear on the far bank. But it was late afternoon and the brown frothy water looked all too daunting. It was definitely too high to cross that evening. We were now confronted by another problem, one of communication, for Liu could only speak one or two words of English. He turned downstream and headed for the crossing place that we had used ten days earlier on our way up. The waters here were smoother but the river was very much broader and obviously much deeper than it had been on the previous occasion. Liu indicated to me that we should stay the night on this side of the river in the hope that the level would be lower the following morning after the night's frost.

Lying in my sleeping bag I listened to the muted rush of the waters and tried to handle my fear. Twelve years before I had very nearly been drowned while trying to descend the upper reaches of the Blue Nile in a rubber dinghy. I was covering the story of the expedition for the *Daily Telegraph* and was tipped out of the dinghy when we went over a steep fall. I was caught in the stopper wave at its bottom and couldn't escape. It was like being churned around in a gigantic washing machine. Every now and then I'd get a breath of air before being dragged back down into the turmoil. Eventually I was thrown clear and able to reach the bank. But later in that same expedition, another team member was drowned in front of us while trying to cross a fast flowing river. Ever since that experience I have been instinctively frightened of water, and was dreading our attempt the next morning.

We got up as soon as it was light enough to see. There was a chill in the air and the river was still rushing past, swirling brown and menacing. I put my cameras in the top of my pack to keep them out of the water, took off my trousers, but kept on my training shoes and also my upper clothes. Liu did the same, looking grim and determined. He was bigger than I and certainly a lot more confident, so I was very happy for him to take the upstream position, where he would bear the main force of the flood. We gripped each other's arms and started out into the ice cold water. It lapped around our ankles and then raced up our calves, plucking and pushing, as we stepped hesitantly forward, feet trying to grip on the shifting stones of the river bed. It was now above our knees and we were barely a third of the way across. I could feel my legs being torn from under me. My whole being was concentrated on the other bank, but it seemed so very far away and the river was getting rapidly deeper. The water was now level with our thighs.

I shouted to Liu, 'For God's sake turn back,' but he was still struggling forward. We were now nearly half way across. Suddenly my feet were whipped away from under me. I was hanging on to Liu. He let out a shout as my weight, combined with the huge force of the torrent pulled his feet from under him. I lost my grip of him and was fighting to get back on my feet. I just managed to stand up, grabbed at Liu who was being swept past me, and his weight pulled me off balance once more. I lost my grip on him again, and was only conscious of my own desperate struggle to get back to the bank, of being tumbled over and over in the turbulent water, and then of being bumped and battered over rocks. I was in shallows, stumbled on to my knees, crawled, panting, gasping to the bank, and just lay there on the grass, racked by great gasping pants, which were followed by deep uncontrollable spasms of shivering. I was dimly aware of Liu Dayi a bare metre away, sitting on the grass, his head in his hands.

Once we had regained our breath we tried to communicate with each other by signs. Liu pointed down river. I assumed he meant we should walk down to the road bridge about fifteen miles below us. I had no desire to go back into the river. I shouted at him as incisively as I could, 'Bridge! Bridge!' Not that there was any point, since it was only a sound to him. He set off once again at a furious pace. I followed, still racked by shivering. The sun had not yet risen above the snow peaks to the east and it was bitterly cold. My spare clothes were also soaked, though, miraculously, my cameras had remained dry.

As we plunged down the valley, I could see the line of sunlight creep slowly down the hills on the other side. The valley soon opened out and the Konsiver now spread into a series of channels coursing down between spits of shingle. Liu Dayi headed for the river, and I realised with a dull sinking fear that he intended to try to ford it again, now that some of its force had been dissipated. We waded across a couple of shallow channels but were then faced with a much wider one. We tentatively took a few steps in but the bed shelved quickly and the waters were over our knees. I was in a straight blind funk, shouted at Liu, 'We go back,' and turned round at the same time to pull him back. Again I pointed down stream and shouted, 'Bridge!' I don't know whether he understood me, but we set out downstream once more. The sun had now crept above the peaks to the east; it still had very little heat in it and threw long, menacing shadows, but then as it gained height, its heat began to thaw out our chilled bodies and at the same time injected me with a little courage. I felt ashamed of my flight, angry with the river and my own sick fear.

The valley had now widened even further. The river was less menacing under the brilliant light of the sun. It was white and tumbling, almost playful. I called to Liu, pointed at the river, and headed for what seemed a shallow stretch. We picked our way from shingle spit to shingle spit, seeking out broken white water. We managed to find a route where the water never came above our knees and at last there was just one channel between us and the other shore. One more jab of fear to be suppressed; we gripped each other's arms and plunged in. The water plucked and tore at us for the last time; we were into shallows. Another couple of steps and we were on the far bank. We shouted and cheered, clapped each other on the back in our delight to have crossed this obstacle and to be alive and warm in the hot sun.

We stripped off our clothes, rinsed out the grit that had got into everything, and bathed our wounds. Both Liu and I were badly grazed from the battering we had. We chewed some nougat, the only food we had with us, and then set out to the road which was only a few hundred metres away. We were now about eight miles from Supas. We started walking but after about ten minutes a bus rolled past and stopped for us. It contained a survey team who were placing marker posts at kilometre intervals. Liu Dayi explained what had happened, while I sat on a pile of sacks and watched them talk. There were five men in the bus, from which the seats had been stripped to make room for the pile of marker blocks and a mass of tools. The surveyor, whom you could immediately identify from the ballpoint pens stuck in the breast pocket of his blue overall jacket, was Chinese, as was his assistant. The rest were Kirghiz or Uighur.

The bus, stopping every kilometre, made its leisured way towards Supas, past the Karakol Lakes, and then across a wide flat plain on which were scattered herds of horses and flocks of sheep. The houses of the village were in a series of clusters clinging to the crest of tiny hillocks. They gave the impression of mediaeval towns in miniature, each surrounded by its low mud wall. Beyond them were the offices of the work brigade and police post and the accommodation for the small group of soldiers which was also stationed at Supas. There was a beaten field that acted, no doubt, both as a parade ground and basketball pitch, where the bus came to a halt. A few soldiers, only identifiable because of the red stars in their caps, were lounging outside a hut. Within seconds of our arrival, however, a mob of youngsters was crammed round us, gazing with intense curiosity at the apparition of a fair-haired foreigner. We stood there for about twenty minutes, while people came and went. Liu Dayi was obviously telling our tale again, and was presumably waiting for someone in authority to turn up, who could actually make a decision. My lack of the language now became acutely frustrating, since I didn't know what was going on, was tired and hungry and completely impotent.

Eventually we were led by some of the soldiers to their quarters. This was just another single-storied hut with a small, bare-walled room opening on to the grassy lane outside. The only furniture were four wooden beds, made up with blankets. The beds were covered with a plastic sheet, presumably to protect them from leaks in the flat roof and the ever present dust. Four tin eating bowls hung on nails on the wall and an empty tin held some chopsticks. The possessions of each soldier were contained in a small box under each bed. We were motioned to sit on the beds and one of the soldiers, who was obviously a medical orderly, painted our wounds with a red antiseptic after which we were then given green tea in tin mugs. While this was going on there was a constant succession of visitors cramming into the doorway to watch the scene. One had the feeling that so little ever happens at Supas that anything even slightly untoward was a major event.

A big bowl of rice and another of mixed meat and vegetables were brought by one of the soldiers. After we had eaten this, everyone just sat around and chatted in a desultory fashion. There seemed to be a pleasant, easy relationship between soldiers and the local people and one soldier was helping a couple of young Kirghiz girls to plait a yak-hair rope. In the courtyard of the Kirghiz house opposite the entire family were sewing together the outer felt cover for a yurt. Strips of ornamental red felt were being incorporated along the seams. A young lad rode a big handsome horse over and obviously enjoyed showing it off while I took photographs. And so the afternoon dragged on. In many ways it was fascinating, but I was becoming increasingly worried about the other two whom I had left the previous day and increasingly frustrated that I could not understand what was going on. I realised that they would have to send for yaks from the high pastures, but the tempo of everything seemed so slow and timeless, that I couldn't help feeling more and more trapped by it all.

At last at about five o'clock that afternoon, some camels arrived outside our hut. I understood we were to go somewhere on these. They were Bactrian camels, the ones found throughout Central Asia, with two humps, and clumps of coarse brown hair alternating with bare scabby patches. They manage to maintain a strange dignity, partly from their stance and partly from the way their dark nostrils twitch disdainfully as they look down at you. We climbed on board, one person to a camel, and they rose sedately and set off from the village. At least we were going somewhere and were heading in the right direction. The gait of the camel was almost soporific. It was like being in a boat on a swollen sea.

We skirted the Karakol Lakes and then climbed a series of sand dunes by a well trodden track to breast the crest of a hill leading down into the wide open valley that divides the Kongur massif from Mustagh Ata. Through its bottom flowed a considerable river that joined the Koksel river a few miles further downstream. It was another cloudless day and consequently the water level was high, but the camels made easy work of it, cruising steadily through the broken waters.

The evening was beautiful, with a mellow light gilding the flocks of sheep scattered over the flat pastures. Smoke rose from a small bluff, an obvious sign of a Kirghiz encampment, and to our right, as we padded towards the smoke, was a Kirghiz burial ground where onion-shaped domes of whitened mud thrust up towards the deep blue of the late afternoon sky. We came over the bluff, and there below us was the encampment of Sarakyaguqi; a row of mud hutments and four yurts nestled into a little hollow between the high scarp of the desert foothills and the low bluff that we had just crossed. The flocks of sheep and goats were drifting back towards the camp and women were crouched beside the ewes doing the evening milking. We were beckoned into one of the yurts, offered the usual yoghurt and bread, and then the discussion began. Liu Dayi, who now also had a language problem since he spoke only a very little Kirghiz and the Kirghiz spoke practically no Chinese, was obviously involved in an argument that seemed to go on interminably. I gathered that the Kirghiz were not prepared to let us have any yaks. The frustration had been building up through the day and it now exploded. I jumped up, shouted at Liu that if the Kirghiz did not want to help us, I'd return to the others by myself, and started packing my rucksack. I wasn't entirely rational at this stage; my judgment was partly affected by fatigue, part by delayed shock from the near miss that morning and, even at the best of times, I have a streak of impatience when I cannot get my way. At the same time I was worried about the others and knew what it felt like to be left waiting when you are helpless. I thought that perhaps if I charged off that night, they would have no choice but to follow me with the yaks.

Whatever the motive, and however misplaced, it felt good to be master of my own

Kirghiz burial ground.

destiny once again, as I strode up an open sandy valley towards the mountains and the place I had left Michael and Al, the previous day. Liu, profoundly disturbed, was trying to persuade me to stay. I glanced behind me, and saw that he had followed me for a short distance, but had stopped fifty metres or so from the yurt. In his stance I could sense his exasperation at my tantrum, and began to wonder whether I was doing the right thing but by this time I felt committed. Chris Bonington, the Lone Ranger, was on his way.

There was a slight path going in roughly the right direction; I followed this in the gloaming, up through the narrow little ravine and then on to the open hillside. It went across a rounded spur and then down into the valley which eventually led up to the glacier and col which we had explored in the last few days. I could pick out the approximate place where I had left the others. It was still some miles away. The path led to a grassy field enclosed by a dry stone wall. There were some yurts pitched at the far end and a dog started to growl. I kept walking, giving them a wide berth. Someone emerged and called out, but I kept walking. It was now dark, but it was a clear night with a half moon and I could see just enough to keep going. The high snow peaks gleamed in the pale light, and the ground around me was a ghostly grey brown, but wherever there were shadows, it was an opaque black. I came to a ravine running down into the valley. It was in shadow, dark and menacing, and could have been as deep as the Grand Canyon. I could hear the sound of rushing water in its bottom, fierce and insistent. It was impossible to tell how much there was but the memories of the morning were too vivid. I dreaded venturing down into the dark shadows and so decided to stop for the night, got out of my

71

sleeping bag and huddled into it. Feeling vulnerable, alone under the immensity of a sky studded with countless stars, I picked out familiar constellations, felt reassured and through this content, to be here, by myself in the heart of Central Asia.

At first light the ravine was little more than a shallow furrow and the stream in its bottom, reduced through the cold of the night, held little threat. I took off my trainers and waded across. After a further hour's walk I reached Al and Michael's tent. They were still fast asleep, even surprised to see me. I produced some goodies, a supply of tea bags, some chocolate and cheese, and told them what had happened. I was beginning to realise that I had almost certainly done the wrong thing in rushing away the night before and therefore suggested that I returned to the settlement to see what Liu Dayi was doing to organise the yaks. So I started back down.

I had very nearly got back to the Kirghiz settlement when I saw a yak carrying two Kirghiz coming up towards me. I immediately assumed that this was the rescue party. There was no sign of Liu Dayi, but maybe he had decided to wait down below. And so I turned round and walked alongside them. It was a sight that could have come from a fairy story. In front was a wizened leprechaun of a man in a long black coat and a felt hat, white in the crown with a black brim. He had a hooked nose and little pointed beard. Behind him rode a young lad with a round, moon-like face. The old man made signs that

Michael and Al await transport, with Mustagh Ata in the background.

he would carry my rucksack, and held it in front of him as our little procession wended its way back up the hill. We stopped at the yurt, which I had passed the previous night, went through the ritual of yoghurt and bread, which I welcomed since I was now ravenously hungry, and then they settled down to a long chat. I contained my impatience, since I could at last see an end to the affair. Eventually we set off, the two Kirghiz riding the yak and me following on behind.

We had gone a short distance when I realised that they were not heading for the tent but instead were going towards the Koksel Glacier. Maybe they were going up to collect some more yaks to help get Al and our gear back to Base Camp? We seemed to be going in a gigantic circle, and as I plodded on behind them, doubts began to creep into my mind. What if they had nothing to do with our rescue? There was no reason why they should, and surely Liu Dayi should have been with them. Hell, I've messed it up again, I thought. I shouted at the Kirghiz, waved across towards where the tent was, but they took no notice at all and continued riding in the wrong direction. I therefore decided to leave them, recovered my rucksack and set off back across the desert towards the others.

Al and Michael were lying out in the sun, and whatever they thought about my wanderings, showed remarkable self-control by not mentioning it. Al's ankle was still very swollen and he was unable to put any weight on it, but he was cheerful and philosophical about his predicament. We spent some time surmising what could have happened but decided that our best course was to wait where we were. Sure enough, in the early afternoon a figure riding a yak appeared. Still no sign of Liu Dayi but this yak was definitely bound for us. It was ridden by a teenage lad, who gestured that Al should climb aboard. We quickly took down the tent, packed the rucksacks, and helped Al up on to the yak. He couldn't help feeling nervous. There was a saddle, but he was unable to use the stirrup for his injured ankle and this meant that his seat was both uncomfortable and very precarious, particularly when going down steep slopes.

We tried to ask the lad about Liu Dayi and also where he planned to take us. Was Liu still at Sarakyaguqi? This seemed the only explanation. Anyway, we set off, though to this day I am not sure whether it was the lad who decided which direction we should go, or whether, he, confused by all our unintelligible questions, thought that we had told him to go back towards the Sarakyaguqi. At any event when we reached it in the early evening, there was no sign of Liu Dayi, and the chief, who had negotiated with Liu Dayi the previous night, made it quite clear that we had done the wrong thing. This was confirmed by the little leprechaun, who rode past our tent later on that evening. He shook his head vigorously and pointed back at the mountains.

It was becoming increasingly obvious why the Kirghiz had been unhappy about helping us and what all the arguments had been about. They were on the point of moving on to their next grazing area. There was only one yurt still erected at the main settlement and it looked as if most of the goats and sheep had already set out. Michael and I made several visits that evening and the following morning to the yurt of the headman or secretary to try to explain that we needed a yak to carry Al up to Base Camp, but he obviously felt that he had done his bit, offered us yoghurt and bread, sat impassive as we tried to explain with sign language what we wanted and then just shrugged.

Our only consolation was the quality of the view we were getting of Kongur itself. We could now clearly see the summit pyramid and the way it was linked with subsidiary peak in front of it. This, combined with what I could remember of the view Al and I had from the top of Sarakyaguqi Peak, gave us a reasonable idea of the geography of the mountain.

We used a note book to draw pictures to try to illustrate the help we were requesting. One of the Kirghiz drew a picture of a donkey and, as far as we could see, he was offering us its services. It seemed most unlikely that the animal could get either across the Koksel river or over the glacier but we nodded our assent vigorously, and after a few more attempts at word pictures gathered that the donkey would be available the following day.

The next morning we woke up to find that the Kirghiz had left before dawn. It was as if no one had ever been there. The little mud houses were locked up; the yurts were gone. We sat outside the tent feeling lonely and helpless. Had our Kirghiz friend abandoned us? But there were some donkeys grazing on the pasture, so perhaps he was around somewhere. It was ten before he appeared, leading a very weedy donkey. Al was even more doubtful about this mode of transport than he had been about the yak. Once we had helped him on to its back, his feet were very nearly touching the ground. The donkey, however, was docile and we set out on what we hoped was going to be the penultimate stage of our Odyssey, though we were still not at all sure how we were going to manage the final stage across the Koksel Glacier.

We had been walking for about half an hour when we passed a solitary camel grazing off the sparse desert sage shrubs. It seemed quite young, and was obviously lonely for it

Picture language didn't get us much further. The Uighur, we later learnt, read 'Will you follow me?'

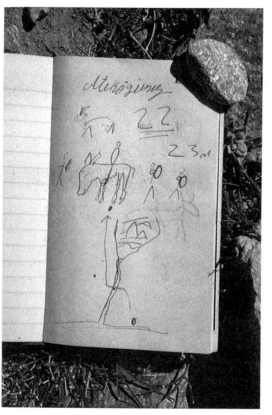

joined us, following at a distance of about twenty metres. We stopped by some boulders that gave the only shade for miles around. The camel wanted to join us, edging closer; the donkey felt threatened, bared its yellow teeth and set up an aggressive braying. The young camel, rejected, backed away, but followed us at a respectable distance as soon as we resumed our journey. The Kongur reconnaissance expedition was rapidly sinking into pure farce.

It took us about three hours to reach the start of the moraines which marked the beginning of the glacier. They were like the glacis of an eighteenth-century fortress, rising abruptly out of the iron-hard, sun-baked mud of the desert foothills. The Kirghiz indicated that this was as far as he could go. In gratitude to him, I offered him my blue fibre pile jacket, but he obviously didn't like it and pointed to Michael's black Cashmere polo-necked sweater. It wasn't so much that he had an eye for quality, but that he did not want something that would be conspicuous. Michael removed his sweater without a murmur. But our friend was not finished. He now turned to me, produced a little clasp knife – not an exotic Kirghiz one, but the kind that you would buy in Woolworths. He indicated that we should swap. Sadly, I surrendered my handsome Swiss Army pocket knife that had scissors, a saw, file, and even a tool for taking stones out of a horse's (or donkey's) hoof. Our friend was content, we all shook hands, and he led his donkey away, quickly disappearing from sight round a hummock.

A lonely camel attaches itself to our party.

Fortunately Al was by now able to put some weight on his foot and the next day made it back to Base Camp at a slow but determined hobble, using an alloy pole from the cooking shelter as a crutch. Liu Dayi was relieved to have his feckless charges reassembled again. Poor Liu, we learnt from Peter Chen, had developed a temperature after my abrupt departure and had to come back to Base Camp to recover, but not before organising the youngster with the yak. This was why we had missed him.

We slept in the next morning and were woken at about ten by a shout from above. We looked blearily out and saw an apparition of three camels and their drivers peering down at us. It transpired that this was a relief force, bringing up a substitute cook and a replacement for our interpreter, since both had complained of the altitude. Peter Chen was now perfectly happy, however, fully acclimatised and delighted to be able to spend the days listening to our collection of Western pop music – Carly Simon was his favourite. He also passed the time with a little hunting, using Liu Dayi's rifle, and his tent was adorned with the pelts of the unfortunate marmots he had shot.

He therefore elected to stay. Wang Yuhu our new cook was a most welcome addition to our little team. Very thin, and cheerful in a manic kind of way, he never stopped working. He was Han Chinese, had been born in Shandong province in Eastern China and had come to Kashgar at the age of eighteen to join his elder brother who was serving with the People's Liberation Army. At first he had worked on the land and then got a job as a cook in a factory canteen. He proved his ability immediately. Liu Dayi slaughtered our second sheep and that night we had a magnificent feast of mutton and fresh vegetables washed down by some bottles of beer with the delightfully appropriate name of Xinjiang Piwisi.

After a day's rest we began to make our plans. Michael had a thorough look at Al's ankle and, although he was impressed by the way that it had recovered, he warned Al that the ligaments were severely damaged. The wisest thing was probably for Al to go back to Kashgar and have it X-rayed, but if he stayed with the expedition and did only the minimum of walking it would probably recover on its own. Al decided to stay, though I could appreciate just how frustrating it was going to be, with this galaxy of exciting unclimbed mountains all around us. Selfishly I was disappointed as well, as I had really been looking forward to climbing with Al and perhaps bagging some of these challengingly steep peaks on the north-eastern side of Kongur.

Michael and I now decided to continue our reconnaissance by trying to find the best route up into the Koksel Basin and attempting to reach the col at the foot of the South Ridge of Kongur. We were going to take with us four days' food, since the yaks, which were going to carry all our gear down to the Karakol Lakes, were due to arrive on the 1st July. Already we had used up most of the time we had allotted for our exploration of the south-west side of Kongur.

5

The Koksel Basin

27TH JUNE–3RD JULY 1980

The pair of eagles soared, wheeling in and out of the crumbling towers and deep-cut gullies of the wall above us. Their effortless freedom contrasted with our own painful progress up the narrow alley we were following between the wall of the rognon on the side of the glacier and the glacier itself. We had been forced into this corridor by the serried crevasses and sérac walls of the glacier. A rock whined down from above, but we could not see where it was coming from or where it was going. There was nowhere to shelter as we edged our way across broken scree slopes above the dark cavernous hole of a crevasse. All the sounds were threatening; the rattle of a little avalanche of stones; the gurgle of running water from within the glacier; the creak and groan of slowly moving ice. The ice was no longer gleaming white; it was covered in grime and rocky debris.

There seemed an escape back on to the glacier by a rift in the ice. I wriggled up an ice chimney, jumped a gaping hole and, edging my way along the bottom of the crevasse, came to the other side of the ice ridge through which it was cutting. We had turned the worst of the icefall and a shallow valley, free of any wide crevasses, led up towards where the Koksel Basin began to open up. The surface of the glacier was still bare of snow, so there was no danger of hidden crevasses. Unroped we could each go at our own speeds. I tended to range ahead, ferreting out a route and would then wait for Michael to catch up. He was now going very much more strongly than he had on our first reconnaissance and was carrying the same weight as myself.

When we set out that morning we had talked of reaching the Koksel Col that day, but it was obvious that we had seriously underestimated the distance involved. It was now late afternoon and we had not even reached the basin. We decided to stop where we were. There was a little glacier lake which would provide us with plenty of water and we at least had the most serious difficulties behind us.

The next morning we followed a slight ridge running down the side of the glacier to a point where we could at last look across the basin towards the col. The summit pyramid of Kongur was hidden by the high walls of its outer rampart but the col looked readily attainable up easy snow slopes starting from the basin itself. A long, easy-angled spur led up from the basin towards the crest of the ridge linking Kongur with Kongur Tiube. It offered the possibility of a route to the summit and from its top it might be possible to gain a view of the summit pyramid. In addition it could make a good acclimatisation climb.

On the right hand side of the col towered the unclimbed 6,700 metre peak. I looked at it longingly, picking out a route through the ice falls of the face confronting us. Behind us, the Rognon Peak swept up in a shark's fin of ice and rock. Although we called it a rognon,

OVERLEAF] *The Koksel Glacier, our route was up the left-hand side of the moraine.*

strictly speaking, this was a misnomer since a rognon is an island of rock jutting out of a glacier. Our rognon was joined to the mountainside of Kongur Tiube behind it by a low, snow-clad saddle. There seemed an easy route down from this and we resolved to return by it to see if the glacier on the other side of the rognon would give us a better route. It could hardly be worse or more dangerous than the one we had followed the previous day.

The glacier was now covered in snow, the dark lines of exposed crevasses a reminder of the lurking threat of hidden ones. We put on the rope and started across, our feet sinking in a few inches at every step. We had been able to see a fairly direct line that led us through an initially heavily crevassed area and, as we came into the centre of the basin, the ice beneath seemed to be compacted and relatively crevasse-free. A small lake indicated that this was the case, but as the day wore on the sun became increasingly oppressive and the size of the basin ever larger. We still seemed a long way from the col. Finally we made camp on a wide shelf set near the middle of the basin at a height of 5,425 metres.

The following morning dawned fine and the surface snow was frozen hard, giving

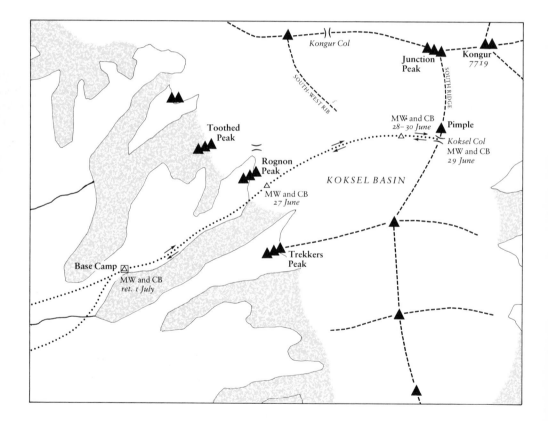

RIGHT] *The Koksel Glacier Icefall.*

delightfully easy walking, with crampons snicking into the crisp snow. It was about three hundred metres of easy angled ascent to the col. As we got closer we saw that the ridge of the 6,700-metre peak was truly spectacular, an incredible corniced blade soaring up from one bristling gendarme to the next. On the left, the South Ridge of Kongur had a steep ice and rock step which led up to a rounded subsidiary summit of snow which we dubbed the 'Pimple'. Beyond this a snowy ramp led up to what seemed a knife-edged rock ridge. We wanted to see beyond the snow ramp to check whether it connected with the easier ground that Al and I had seen from Sarakyaguqi Peak.

However as we approached the col, the most exciting prospect was the view the other side. Nobody had ever been here before and although we had seen the lower part of the glacier valley from farther down the range, there was still a sense of delicious anticipation as we breasted the last slope and worked our way above a narrow chute that dropped dramatically down the other side until we found ourselves on a platform above the col that seemed to hang over the glacier far below. Tendrils of cloud were reaching up the valley, rapidly covering the grey crevasse-veined river of ice. It was a view in monochrome, of whites and greys and blacks, the Shiwakte peaks, jagged saw-toothed black silhouettes already half hidden by cloud.

We caught only a glimpse of the South-East Face of Kongur, before it also became enveloped. It was enough to see how inhospitable it was with sheer ice walls alternating with avalanche-prone snow slopes. There seemed no route up Kongur from the south-eastern glacier. The cloud was now all around us and it began to snow. There was little point in staying any longer. We had seen enough. It had been a view that was both magnificent and discouraging. We dropped back down to our tent, hoping to return to the col the next day and climb the South Ridge, at least as far as the Pimple, and perhaps farther.

But this was not to be. We now encountered our first really bad weather, the cloud descended and with it the snow. We could only afford one day to sit it out, me on volume one and Michael on volume two of Elizabeth Longford's biography of the Duke of Wellington. It continued during the next night, and the following morning the tent sagged under several inches of fresh snow. We were in the middle of a cloud sandwich. It was time to retreat.

Fortunately Michael had brought his compass, and just before the whole Koksel Glacier filled with cloud, he took a vital bearing on the Rognon Peak. It was a total white-out. There were no features, no wind, no sound. Michael started off in front, and I followed keeping the rope between us taut. There was nothing to focus on except the silhouette of Michael's figure, constantly glancing down at the compass. Our progress was desperately slow, and, with nothing to measure it against, we did not seem to be moving at all. Our fear of hidden crevasses was heightened by this sense of uncertainty. A gaping valley appeared before us and we started to skirt it, before I realised it was little more than a shallow impression that we could cross. The snow on our left now began to steepen and our way was barred by a big open crevasse. I tried to visualise the basin as we

ABOVE LEFT] Retreating down the Koksel Glacier into a white-out.
BELOW LEFT] *Michael on the Koksel Col.*

had seen it on our way in, guessed that we had tended slightly too far to the right and were on the slopes leading up to the col between the rognon and the slopes of Kongur Tiube. We should be farther over to the left. I now went out in front and realised just how difficult and nerve-wracking it was breaking the trail. The shared danger and effort, increased both our respect for each other and confidence in each other's performance.

It took us the whole day to retreat from the glacier and at last in the late afternoon we reached the final moraine bank that led out of it, back on to the grassy shelf that ran below the rognon. There was a sense of light-headed release as we escaped the bewildering maze of ice and, as if to celebrate our success, the clouds rolled away and it turned into a perfect afternoon. Had we sat it out for a few hours, we would have walked down in perfect visibility, but that of course is something one can never know. We were rewarded however with a magnificent view of the lower part of the Koksel Glacier, dazzlingly brilliant in its mantle of fresh snow, fanning out into the brown of the desert, like a cloak, flung down before the majesty of Mustagh Ata on the other side of the void. The Karakol Lakes in the distance were a deep blue and the shadows of the high-flying cumulus chased across the varied browns and reds of the desert, making ever varied patterns.

The stress of the previous few hours enhanced the delicious warmth of the sun and the great open beauty around us. It had snowed down here as well, but already the sun had stripped most of it away, and in doing so had left the grass with a brighter, more resilient sheen. Just in the last week flowers had proliferated, a field of bright yellow buttercups, big pink daisies among boulders and everywhere the dark red primula.

We cleared our Base Camp next morning and set out with the yaks, but soon drew ahead. This time we were determined to keep close to Liu Dayi and with him around surely nothing could go wrong. Our little cavalcade was completed by our one remaining sheep. Left on its own it had become very lonely and therefore increasingly dependent on us for company. It obviously viewed Liu, who, incidentally, had acted as executioner, as the flock leader and followed him wherever he went. There was no need to tether him any longer. He simply followed along. One couldn't help getting rather fond of the animal. It had an aristocratic Roman nose, curled-back horns, a coarse shaggy coat of dark wool and a rear end that protruded in a way that robbed the poor creature of all dignity.

We followed Liu Dayi down beside the top of the gorge of the Koksel river to the crossing point that we had looked at when he and I had gone for help. When we arrived at its foot just before midday the flow was already fast, but it did seem passable. We settled down to wait for the yaks, and the afternoon crept gently by. Liu was obviously getting worried and kept peering through his binoculars at the empty hillside around us, but there was no sign of the yaks. And the level of the torrent was rising all the time.

It was now late afternoon and becoming increasingly obvious that the yaks had crossed the river farther up stream. We were in trouble again. Liu Dayi, Wang, Al and I had travelled light without either our sleeping bags or even spare sweaters. We had no food and no shelter. Michael, the veteran mountaineer, was the only one of us to observe the adage never to be parted from your sleeping bag.

But there was no choice. We would have to stay where we were. As night fell the temperature plummeted to around freezing point. Michael very gallantly offered Al his sleeping bag and the rest of us huddled round the fire of sage bushes that Liu made in the shelter of a large boulder. The roots would blaze up, scorching us for a few minutes, and then die down to a dull glow. I tried to sleep outside at first, using a rucksack to cover my bare legs, but it was too cold and soon all four of us were crammed into the tiny shelter. Michael then acted the magician once again, producing a half bottle of whisky. Liu Dayi rivalled this conjuring act by wandering off into the dark and reappearing a half hour later clutching a tin of oranges and one of Spam. Apparently he had left these in a cache on the way up. Like all bivouacs, the night wore on interminably but at last came a glimmer in the sky to the east and we were able to crawl out of our shelter and set out once more. During the night the river at the bottom of the gorge had been reduced to little more than a stream and Al was able to hobble across it without too much difficulty. It was good to be able to stride out once again, getting some life back into our stiff, chilled limbs. Liu Dayi even tried to bag a hare but without success.

We dropped down to Sarakyaguqi where we had camped a few days before, but it was now empty and deserted, just a cluster of mud houses standing by the empty sepulchres of the burial ground. In the clear light of the dawn, Mustagh Ata's giant bulk brooded over these ephemeral manifestations of man's presence. Liu Dayi led the way across the Konsiver river and the sheep stood hesitant on the shore, bleated a bit and then plunged in after him, was swept away, struggled to regain the bank, ran back and forth and then plunged in once again and, finding a shallower route, managed to get over. We followed, supporting Al on either side. There were some flocks of sheep grazing in the pasture on the side of the river and the shepherds offered us food, a wholesome stew of great hunks of mutton.

Another hour's walk and we were back at the Karakol Lakes. Peter Chen, who had ridden down on a yak, had got there the previous night. The party was united once again and later that afternoon the bus from Kashgar arrived. It brought our mail, fresh vegetables and a crate of beer.

We had completed the first part of the reconnaissance. In spite of our misadventures, which had an element of the ludicrous about them, we had learnt a great deal. There certainly seemed to be a route from the south-west side of the mountain, though we had not managed to find a single viewpoint from where the entire route was visible. It looked as if there were two possibilities; one from the Koksel Col either up the South Ridge itself or perhaps traversing the South Face to what seemed a gangway leading to the top; the other up the long, gently angled spur leading up to the crest of the ridge between Kongur Tiube and Kongur. This looked easy, but involved a long ridge traverse, mostly above 7,000 metres. Al, irrepressible as ever, was talking of the possibility of doing a complete traverse of Kongur and Kongur Tiube.

6
Northern cul-de-sac

4TH–21ST JULY 1980

The bus was loaded and we were nearly ready to go but we still had to persuade our sheep to join us. He had been prepared to swim a glacier torrent to stay with us, but a bus was just a bit too much. Our entire Chinese staff and the representatives of the Sports Federation from Kashgar were mobilised to get him aboard. Our journey took us back to the bleak police post in the bottom of the gorge at Gez Karaul. It was difficult to imagine this place being anything but an arid desert of sheer rocks and sun-baked mud, though the shapely spire of the 'Gez Matterhorn' beckoned as compellingly as ever.

We sat in the shade of the verandah sipping hot water and waiting for something to happen. Half a dozen rather mangy camels were brought down and the Kirghiz started loading our baggage on to them. We were obviously going somewhere. We followed the camels up a trail that crossed the glacier torrent by a rickety bridge and then wound up the steep side of the gorge. There was no clue as to what we were going to find at the top and when we came over the brow it was like stepping into a different continent. The track was lined with the entire population of the village of Gez, around eighty people. At the

Our sheep boarded the bus without enthusiasm.

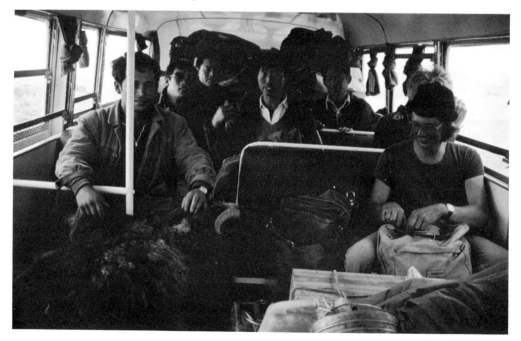

84

head of the line was the secretary of the work brigade, a small man with a little moustache and a perpetually worried expression under his white felt Kirghiz hat. As we approached, the whole line began to clap. We shook hands with the secretary and then went down the line shaking hands with all the adults while the children peered between their parents' legs or ran down behind the line, intrigued with these strange foreigners who were, perhaps, the first they had ever seen. This brought us into the village. It was obviously newly built, and was more spacious and ordered than the traditional hill villages I was accustomed to seeing in Baltistan on the southern side of the border. At its entrance was a scattered group of single storied buildings housing the school, a medical post and the work brigade offices. There were also some compounds and stores owned by the collective. The homes of the members of the work brigade were spaced neatly around a huge field of alfalfa that filled the centre of a wide shelf between gorge and mountain. The starkness of the lines of the little mud houses within their walled compounds was softened by the lines of trees at the side of the track and between all the houses. It was an oasis of green in the midst of a fierce mountain desert.

We were guided down the track to one of the houses which belonged to the secretary, though it was no bigger than that of any of the other villagers. An arched gateway led into a courtyard and before going into the house, the wife of the secretary poured water over our hands from a metal jug with a long curved spout and then a young girl, presumably her daughter, offered us a towel to dry them. Inside, there seemed to be just one big room, which was adequately lit by glazed windows, and had a raised sleeping platform on one side, and a kitchen platform opposite. Rugs were laid out on the sleeping platform and we all sat down cross-legged in a wide semi-circle. In the kitchen area, there was a brisk fire in an open hearth on which big metal pots were bubbling and steaming. It was all very light, clean and cheerful. It was obvious we were about to enjoy a feast, and it turned out to be one of the most memorable I have ever had.

It started off with plates of different types of wholemeal bread, all of which were oven hot and very tasty, accompanied by little bowls of mutton broth. I thought that this was probably the entire meal, since it was very much more than the standard Kirghiz gesture of hospitality of bread and yoghurt. I therefore tucked into three bowls of the broth which was quite thick and delicately spiced. A white liquid was then poured into a clean bowl beside each of us. It had a very fresh, fermented rather than alcoholic, flavour. This, we were told, was fermented mares' milk. It reminded me of the very best rice chang that you can obtain in Sola Khumbu in Nepal. It was deliciously refreshing and seemed harmless, but by the time I had drunk half a dozen bowlfuls I was beginning to feel decidedly mellow.

And the meal was by no means over. A huge bowl of boiled mutton was now put before us. The meat was on the bone in great succulent lumps. There was no question of knives and forks. You just grabbed a bone and tore the meat off it with your teeth. And while we were devouring the mutton the next course was being prepared. The wife of the secretary and some other helpers were making noodles, first kneading the dough, then rolling it out and finally chopping it into thin strips. This was boiled in a pot and placed before us though by this time we were full, to that magnificent degree when to eat more hurts, but the food is so good that you eat all the same.

The food, the fermented mares' milk, but above all the warm informality of the

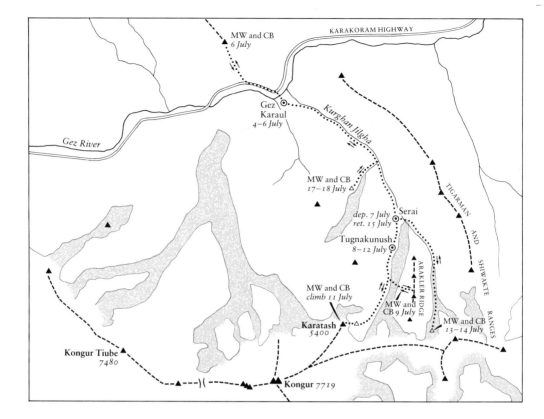

atmosphere made the meal especially memorable. After it, we set up our camp in a replete, drunken haze at the side of a small pool by a glade of newly planted willow trees on the very brink of the platform that overhung the gorge. We planned to spend two days at the village, using one of them to climb the north side of the Gez gorge to gain a viewpoint of the northern aspect of the range. We would then travel up the valley of Kurghan Jilgha to look at the eastern approach to the mountain.

Two guides arrived for us just after dawn on the morning of 6th July. One of them, a sharp-faced, slightly surly-seeming character was one of the cadre or management of the work brigade. With him was a youngster. We dropped down to the road and walked back up the way we had come for a couple of miles, going at a ferocious pace. I wondered just how long I would be able to keep up. Michael was having equal difficulty. The sides of the gorge seemed uniformly precipitous with crumbling terraced walls barring the way to what I assumed would be the upper pastures. Without a guide it would have been impossible to find a way. They led us up by the side of narrow gullies and across near vertical slopes of crumbling mud by tracks that were little more than furrows, until at last it all opened out into steep grass-clad pastures. The two Kirghiz stopped for a rest, but I could now see the route ahead and, impatient to gain a view of the North Face of Kongur and to get pictures while the sun was still quite low in the sky, I pushed on up the slope towards the crest of the ridge about 600 metres above. It was wonderfully exhilarating to feel fit and to be able to move fast and continuously in an upward direction. It took me less than an hour to climb the slope. I was now at a height of just under 4,750 metres and the entire northern aspect of the Kongur massif was laid out before me at a distance of approximately fifteen miles.

On the far left I could see the narrow valley of Kurghan Jilgha curl out of sight round the shapely tower of the Gez Matterhorn, at its foot the brilliant green oasis of Gez. But my eyes were drawn to the line of high mountains behind the Gez Matterhorn, which marched across the northern horizon, a great undulating wall, of which Kongur formed the highest wave, and was not so much a separate peak as part of this huge mass. From the south-west, the foothills had formed a gentle glacis leading up to the snow line, and even above the snow line, the angle had seemed to lie back, but here it was abrupt and fierce.

The glaciers from the north flank flowed very nearly down to the road, at about 2,700 metres. The wall itself reared abruptly from around 2,650 metres, giving a staggering height gain of over 5,000 metres to the summit of Kongur. I could see a route up a broken buttress that led into sweeping snow fields. It was challenging and exciting but not one by which to attempt the first ascent of a mountain. We gazed and gazed at the line of mountains through our binoculars. There were still so many unanswered questions. It looked so very different from the view we had had from the Karakol Lakes. What had happened to that distinctive, cap-like summit cone? Which was the highest point on the summit plateau? This was as puzzling from the north as it had been from the south. The westerly ridge leading up to the summit looked fairly straightforward. It was set at an easy angle and, although rocks in an intermittent cock's comb protruded from the snows, it looked as if there was snow for almost all the way. Perhaps this was the left-hand flank of the summit cone as seen from the Karakol Lakes? We could also pick out the subsidiary summit which concealed the bulk of Kongur from the west. It looked little more than a bump on the ridge.

Looking farther along, we could make out another bump and felt sure that must be the top of the long easy arête we had seen leading from the Koksel Basin. From this viewpoint, it looked as if it would be easy walking once we had reached the crest of the ridge, and we could remember that the ridge leading up to the crest was even easier. It was just a very long way at high altitude. But even that, from a distance of fifteen miles, did not seem so great. You could hide the whole of Kongur with an outstretched hand and under the bright sun set in a brilliant blue, cloudless sky it seemed little bigger than Mont Blanc viewed from the little peak of the Brevent. Indeed the height difference from valley bottom to summit was very similar. It is so easy to forget the insidious effects of altitude.

Our two guides had gone off on a mission of their own to pick up something left behind when they had last been here with their flocks of sheep. I was impatient to get back because an American expedition, two of whose members I knew, was going to pass through Gez at around midday on their way to attempt an ascent on skis of Mustagh Ata. So Michael and I did not wait for the two Kirghiz but plunged down the slopes towards the road. It was like an intricate maze, little sheep paths everywhere, with all too many of them leading to sheer drops down crumbling cliffs of mud. We ended up waiting for our guides to take us down the final stretch, and by the time we got back to Gez the Americans had been and gone. But they had left a very welcome crate of beer with Al. We were well pleased with ourselves. We had had the most comprehensive view of the mountain to date. In addition we had made a height gain of over 1,500 metres in just under three hours, a sign that both Michael and I were now getting really fit.

We were going to use camels for our journey round the eastern flanks of Kongur. They arrived the following morning and we settled down to wait patiently for the interminable process of packing, determined not to loose contact with our baggage at all costs. The entire village came to our campsite to watch the fun. At last we were ready and, sticking close to the string of camels, we set out.

We were forced, however, to leave our baggage train shortly after leaving the village. The camels waded the river that flowed down the Kurghan Jilgha, whilst we learned from Liu Dayi that there was a more direct route, too sheer for laden camels, along the side of the gorge. It was an exciting path clinging to the steep scree above the foaming torrent. They had brought a horse for Al to ride, but he declined the offer. Peter Chen, who believed in conserving his energy, took it over, ambling along the narrow tracks, with a sense of nerve that greatly impressed me. Our route took us through a precipitous cleft which then opened out into a sweeping valley. There was more grass and therefore,

Progressing along the Kurghan Jilgha by camel.

ABOVE RIGHT] *An oasis of green in the desert.*
BELOW RIGHT] *The instant camera was a great success.*
OVERLEAF] *Michael views the forbidding North Face of Kongur from a high point above the Gez gorge.*

presumably, a much higher precipitation on this side of the mountain.

It was an exciting thought that we were probably the first Europeans ever to walk up the Kurghan Jilgha, for Skrine had concentrated on the eastern end of the massif and Shipton had gone straight to the Karakol Lakes. Each bend in the valley brought exciting new vistas. The mountains were of a completely different character from the main Kongur chain. They were more like Alpine peaks, sharp and pointed, with rock arêtes and walls. The camels had now caught us up, and the Kirghiz urged us to take a ride. Perched on our steeds we rocked gently up the valley, gazing at the peaks that unfolded around us. They were not very high, compared to Kongur, a mere 6,000 metres or so, but each one of them would have given a challenging and technically difficult climb. Viewed on an Alpine scale, it was like riding up the Zermatt valley in the early years of the nineteenth century, when not one of the peaks had been climbed.

In the mid-afternoon we reached a point where the valley forked. A large meadow of grass, rich in flowers and clover, was protected by a dry stone wall. Some little flat-roofed stone houses merged with the rocks. We were later to discover that the place was called Serai. We stopped here for the night by a clear stream. Just above us in a shallow valley between the mountain slope and the moraine of the glacier was a solitary tree with a

Ancient religious cult symbols that have survived the arrival of both Islam and Communism.

ABOVE LEFT] *From the Arakler Ridge, the view south-east to the underclimbed peaks of the Tigarman range.*
BELOW LEFT] *Michael climbing Karatash, with Kongur in the background right.*

gnarled trunk and a broad spread of branches, but most intriguing of all, at the spot where the lowest branches spread from the trunk, were clustered the skulls of goats and sheep, garlanded with faded ribbons. They were symbols of an ancient pantheistic cult which had survived not only the arrival of the Muslim creed but also that of communism. It brought home how little the Kirghiz way of life had really changed; how the arrival of each alien creed had settled on these independent, rugged people like so many layers, to adapt a way of life but never to change it totally.

Just before dusk one of the Kirghiz who was looking through my binoculars, let out a shout and pointed to the mountainside opposite. High above, close to the snow line, he had picked out a small herd of Marco Polo sheep. Within a few minutes he had persuaded Liu Dayi to part with his rifle and the entire band of camel drivers set off for the hunt.

They did not find the herd of wild sheep, but just on the off chance of a kill they had climbed a good 1,500 metres, had bivouacked out with no more than their jackets to keep them warm overnight and got back to the valley bottom by eleven o'clock the following morning in time to take us on the last leg of our journey. In the event this proved to be barely a quarter of a day's march up the side of the moraine of the glacier flowing from the eastern flank of Kongur, to a wide grassy platform which provided space for a cluster of yurts. We set our Base Camp a few hundred metres above them. This was Tugnaku-nush.

The instant camera was once again a great success. Everyone wanted their picture taken, so I agreed to take one of each family, of which there were six altogether. The

We had formed a real friendship with Liu Dayi, relaxing here with Al.

womenfolk got out their best kerchiefs, some of them of fine lace, and also put on their jewellery – silver pendants, beads, and earrings. A few of them even tried some rudimentary make-up, putting flour on their cheeks. One little girl with a tame kid managed to appear in every single picture.

We were going to spend over a week at Tugnakunush and as a result saw more of this particular group than of any other in either the reconnaissance or the main expedition. There always seemed to be something for them to do and yet, at the same time, the tempo of life was a leisured one. Each night the flocks of sheep and goats and the small herd of yaks, which had grazed the grassy alps surrounding the camp throughout the day, were herded back to the immediate vicinity of the yurts. During the day, repairs were made to the yurts. Fresh felt was processed by a method of repeated soaking followed by rolling, wrapped in straw matting. Cheese was being cured for the winter. It was moulded into small spheres and placed to dry in the sun on a raised platform to keep it out of reach of the dogs. One night we were invited to the encampment for a sing song. The entire population was crammed into one of the yurts. Both the men and the women sang, taking it in turns to sing solos. It was very like a folk song club in Britain and the cadence of the singing was much more akin to European folk music than to that of India or China. The subjects were very contemporary; they were about fulfilling work quotas and the day to day life of the modern Kirghiz within their work brigade. The accompanying instruments were a balalaika-type instrument and also a mouth harp which the women tended to play. It had a particularly haunting and sweet tone.

We were a constant source of interest. Michael acquires an audience for his map reading.

Our trusty sheep had followed us all the way to Tugnakunush but its reprieve was now ended. I took myself for a walk when Liu Dayi slaughtered it on the second day and we all felt guilty as we ate succulent shish kebabs that night. We did not enjoy fresh mutton for long, however, for a dog stole the carcass and we had to eat tinned meat for the rest of our stay.

But our main preoccupation was discovering a route up Kongur and, in the process, to climb as many peaks as we could in the time we had left. The valley in which we were camped was a dramatic cul-de-sac. On the southern side of it towered the Shiwakte peaks, whose other flanks Al and I had seen from the top of Sarakyaguqi Peak and Michael and I from the Koksel Col. There was certainly no easy way up them or for that matter any easy or safe route over this mountain barrier. The end of the valley was terminated by steep ice and rock cliffs that abutted the eastern ridge of Kongur. The summit of Kongur was hidden. We were too close beneath it. Only on the northern side of the valley was there any let up. Broken slopes of scree and rock led up to a jumble of peaks that stretched out towards Gez Karaul. We chose as our first viewpoint the Arakler Ridge, at around 4,570 metres, on the opposite side of the glacier. From it we should be able to look up the valley towards Kongur and also, intriguingly, look out over the range of peaks to the east which Skrine had surveyed from the other side of the divide.

Since the crest of the ridge was below the snow line, Al resolved to come up with us. He had managed to maintain an amazing equilibrium, remaining his usual buoyant self and providing a very positive contribution to our discussion over plans and possibilities, even though he could not take an active part. He was making an accurate sketch map of the area based on the Chinese map and our own observations.

The view from the crest of the ridge was both daunting and intriguing. At the end of the valley a steep and narrow icefall led up into an avalanche-threatened upper glacier, which, in turn, led into yet another cul-de-sac, with a sheer head wall leading up to a high col between a subsidiary peak and the main mass of Kongur. The col itself merely abutted the flanks of the east ridge of Kongur, which seemed to mount at least two minor tops or perhaps shoulders before reaching the summit. It looked as if it would be hard and dangerous climbing almost from the very beginning. There did seem a reasonable route, however, to the summit of the subsidiary peak to the right of the col. We could trace a ridge line all the way from the bottom of the valley to the dome-like snow summit. From its top we hoped to get a close-up view of the North Face of Kongur.

We then turned our attention to the mountains to the east. The left-hand fork of the valley that was bifurcated at Serai was immediately below us. It led into another blind alley walled on all sides by steep, unrelenting walls of ice and rock. But on the other side of the valley a spectacular icefall led up to a level upper glacier from which swept a series of shapely summits. According to Skrine's map these were the Tigarman group and although they were only in the region of 5,000 metres, they were immensely attractive and seemed feasible for Michael and myself to attempt.

The following afternoon saw us plodding up the broken scree ridge at the end of the valley. We were on our way to tackle a snow dome to the north of Kongur called Karatash. We were determined to travel light, taking food for only three days, a tent, a length of rope and a few ice pitons. The slope proved to be both longer, steeper and very much looser than we had anticipated. We had only set out in the late afternoon and it was very nearly dusk when we reached the shoulder we were aiming for. We were on the crest of the ridge, just above the snow line at a height of 4,420 metres.

That night I set the alarm for three o'clock in the morning, hoping to reach the top before the sun had softened the snow. When the alarm went off I poked my head out of the tent; I could see a few stars through the cloud, but the weather was unsettled. Even so, we decided to make our bid for the top. Brewing some tea and forcing down a tin of sardines, we set off at 5.20 by the light of our head torches. We roped up straight away, but at first the going was easy up broken rock and fine scree on the crest of the ridge. After an hour the slope began to flatten out and we found ourselves on snow. But it had not frozen. It was wet and sugary and we sank to well above our knees. In the dim light of the head torch I could see the vague shape of a cornice up ahead. I moved up hesitantly, probing the slope ahead with my axe. Suddenly a hole opened out in front of me. I prodded the snow in an arc around me and there was nothing solid anywhere. I shuffled backwards, full of fear. I could imagine plummeting into that black void beneath. It felt as if it could go into the very bowels of the mountain, though my reason told me that this could not be the case, that I had a prusik loop attached to my rope and that I could easily climb out if I did fall. But cool reason seems all too inadequate against the blind threat of the dark.

I was back on more solid snow and could see a rock protruding, black and comfortingly stable. I stilled my panting, said something non-committal to Michael, and continued up the slope. We paused at the top of a shoulder. We were on the crest of the ridge once more, and could keep to the solid ground that marked the top. The light was now that dim grey between dark and dawn, when the beam of the head torch begins to be ineffective and yet it is impossible to see clearly. The sun was fighting its way up through banked clouds in the east, lighting the skies with a threatening glow. It tipped the upper reaches of Kongur, picking out the piled cornices and sérac walls in the golden light of dawn. But we were still in the shadows, as we picked our way along the fragile path on the crest of the ridge.

We were faced with a barrier, a smooth bulge of ice. It was, I estimated, forty degrees in angle, not steep by technical ice standards but daunting none the less. The pick of my axe and hammer penetrated half a centimetre or so as I worked my way up but we only had twenty-one metres of rope and I had to stop while still half way. Thank goodness I had a couple of ice pitons with me. I hammered one in, brought Michael up to me, and carried on. This time, when the rope pulled tight I relied on my stance, bracing myself on the ice and keeping the rope tight.

Another snow slope, a pull over a small cornice and we were on the summit ridge. A few minutes later and we were on top of Karatash. It was a superb viewpoint, looking across the huge expanse of the North Face of Kongur, but the view only confirmed what we had seen two days before. Kongur could undoubtedly be climbed from this side, but it was not a route for the first ascent of a mountain. It was so much steeper and more intricate than the approach from the other side. We lingered for a while, savouring the moment and the shapely beauty of the Gez Matterhorn which rose up in elegant symmetry to the north.

But it was time to go down. We started back and almost immediately got into trouble. The ice slope was too daunting for a descent and so I suggested we used the broken ridge

93

at its side. Michael went down first and reported that it was horrifyingly loose. It was just a pile of blocks perched crazily on top of each other. There was nothing to belay on to for nothing was solid and the shortness of the rope compounded our problems. We were now level with the foot of the ice slope but were separated from it by a shallow gully of polished ice down which rattled a steady bombardment of rocks, loosened by the morning sun, from the crest of the ridge above. We had no choice but to cross it. Michael started off but the rope ran out when he was only half way, in the centre of the line of fire. There was no belay. He just had to crouch on a boulder and take in the rope as I teetered on the front points of my crampons across the ice. The rocks whistled round his head as I traversed the gully above him, but he showed a surgeon's calm and self-control, swaying from side to side on his crampon points to dodge the bombardment and grinning laconically at me, as I scampered the last few paces on to the snow out of the line of fire.

The rest of the descent was straightforward and we got back to the tent just before midday. We were both tired, as much from the expenditure of nervous energy as anything else, and simply flopped into our sleeping bags and slept for a couple of hours before packing the tent and starting down the endless debris slopes leading back into the valley. It had only been a small peak of barely 5,480 metres, but it had had about it a threat of danger that was hardly in keeping with either its technical difficulty or size. It was perhaps the appalling looseness of its rock combined with the huge presence of the north flank of Kongur and I felt an immense relief when we descended the final scree slope and reached the valley bottom.

Michael and I made two more forays before leaving the eastern side of the mountain, one of them towards the Tigarman peaks and the other to the Gez Matterhorn, but each time we were thwarted by bad weather. We also spent a couple of days by the gentle meadow of Serai discussing the results of our reconnaissance and drafting our report. In this respect Michael provided the discipline of the scientist. I suspect that Al and I would quite happily have basked in the sun, gossiping and reading, and putting off the inevitable paper work until we got back to civilisation. In the event writing up our findings while they were still fresh in our minds, and before the diversions we would face on our way back, was invaluable.

We concluded that the approach from the east or north was obviously very much more difficult, longer and probably more objectively dangerous than one from the south-west. In the former case, the snow line and glaciers were very much lower and Base Camp would have been in the region of 3,650 metres – the same altitude as the Karakol Lakes. On the south-west side we could have our base camp at 4,750 metres and it would be little more than walking all the way up to the Koksel Col at 5,790 metres. There still seemed two possible approaches from the south-west; one by the Koksel Col, starting up the ridge and then inclining across the South Face to what Al and I remembered from our view from the Sarakyaguqi Peak, as an easy gangway leading to the summit; the other was up the long arête leading from the glacier basin to the crest of the ridge between Kongur and Kongur Tiube. At this stage it never occurred to us to attempt the crest of the ridge leading up from the Koksel Col.

After a lot of discussion we settled on the arête since it seemed technically easier and very much safer, being on the crest of a ridge almost all the way. During the course of the discussion differences in opinion came out. I was essentially pragmatic in my approach, realising how important it was that we did succeed, both on a personal level, because I wanted to get to the top of the mountain, and because of the sponsorship given to us by the Mount Everest Foundation and Jardine Matheson. This was not so much a sense of pressure from the sponsors but more a sense of responsibility bred from gratitude and friendship. Jardines had done very much more than just furnish us with the necessary money for the expedition. In Britain, Martin Henderson, the executive in whose care we had been placed, had become deeply involved in both the planning and the work of the expedition, and on our visits to Hong Kong we had been entertained so warmly that we had a very strong feeling that we did not want to let them down.

If it were necessary to fix some ropes, establish intermediate camps or even get help from our scientist team-mates, I was fully prepared to do this. Al on the other hand was more of a purist, said that he had never used fixed ropes or siege tactics and didn't intend to start now. For a while we became quite heated. Michael, very wisely had sat out during the discussion, though his views were the same as mine. As overall leader he most certainly wanted a successful conclusion to the expedition. I reassured him afterwards that I was certain Al would be amenable in the event to accepting whatever measures were needed to help achieve success. After all the smallness of the climbing team would limit any threat of overkill on the mountain.

By the time we left our camp at Serai, we had drafted a report and decided on the basic strategy for our ascent the next year. To prepare for an alpine-style push on Kongur we should first have to acclimatise by making a series of ascents of minor peaks. The scientists, therefore, would be able to monitor the progress of each individual's acclimatisation whilst fitting in with the schedule of the climb. Michael, Al and I had all contributed to the report, and this really summed up the way we had worked together as a team. Quite apart from what we had discovered about the mountain, the reconnaissance had been extremely important in the way that it had brought us together.

Before the expedition we had hardly known each other, were separated both by wide gaps in age and also background. In the course of the past six weeks we had come to like and respect each other and to discover that we could work well together. We had also built up a very real friendship with Liu Dayi, Peter Chen and Wang Yuhu.

We returned to Kashgar on the 21st July, were back in Hong Kong by the 29th and flew back to Britain via Japan on the 1st August. I was looking forward to returning to Kongur the following year, to the great empty sweep of the high Pamir plateau, to those intensely clear skies and, most of all, to the mountain itself. Although the photographs we had brought back showed a huge hummock of a peak which looked as if it would be little more than a long high walk, I had a feeling that Kongur had some surprises in store for us.

7

The team assembles

JULY 1980–MAY 1981

Michael Ward had decided on the composition of the scientific and climbing elements of the team before we set out on the reconnaissance. We both wanted Pete Boardman and Joe Tasker, and after finding they would be available, invited them to join the expedition. I had been expeditioning with both of them. Pete Boardman had been the youngest member of our expedition to Everest in 1975. He had gone to the top with our Sherpa sirdar, Pertemba, making the second complete ascent of the previously unclimbed South-West Face. He had gone on to climb the sheer West Face of Changabang with Joe Tasker. It had been a remarkable achievement in stark contrast to the huge expedition we had had on Everest. On Changabang there had just been Pete and Joe. They had planned to climb it alpine-style, bivouacking in hammocks on the face, but it had been too cold, too great a strain at altitude and they had resorted to siege tactics. Yet even this demanded huge reserves of determination and endurance. The climb, at the time in 1976, was probably technically the hardest that had yet been completed in the Himalaya.

In 1978 both Pete and Joe had joined me on K2. We had attempted the West Ridge but abandoned the attempt comparatively low down after Nick Estcourt was killed in an avalanche. In 1979 they went on to climb Kangchenjunga, the third highest mountain in the world, with Doug Scott, and then in 1980, while we were on the reconnaissance, had returned to K2 with Doug Scott and Dick Renshaw. They had first attempted the West Ridge, the route that we had tried in 1978, but had abandoned this a couple of hundred metres higher than our previous high point. Doug Scott had returned home but the remaining three had made two very determined assaults on the Abruzzi Spur, getting to within 600 metres of the summit, before being beaten by bad weather.

Pete Boardman has a surprising combination of qualities. When I first met him before inviting him to join us on Everest, I was impressed by his maturity, and yet this is combined with a real sense of fun and a touch of 'the little boy lost' manner, which he can use with devastating effect to get his own way. Perhaps it is a result of his upbringing; he is from a very close and supportive, comfortable, middle-class family background in Bramhall, the respectable suburb of South Manchester. This is combined with a great deal of talent, both physical and intellectual. He is a very strong natural climber with a romantic love for the mountains and the ability to express it in writing as is shown in his books *The Shining Mountain* and *Sacred Summits*.

As National Officer of the British Mountaineering Council, Pete revealed himself as a patient diplomat and a good committee man. Then after Dougal Haston's death in a Swiss avalanche, he took over Dougal's International School of Mountaineering in Leysin. He had packed a wealth of varied mountaineering into the last few years. In early 1979, he reached the summit of the Carstensz Pyramid, the highest peak of New Guinea, with his then girl friend, Hilary, who is now his wife, just before going to Kangchenjunga, and then that same autumn he led a small and comparatively inexperienced team on a very bold ascent of the south summit of Gauri Sankar.

Joe Tasker was an obvious choice for the fourth member of the team. He had an outstanding alpine background in the early 'seventies, when, with his climbing partner, Dick Renshaw, he had worked through some of the hardest climbs in the Alps, both in summer and winter. These included the first British ascent (which was also one of the very few ever ascents) of the formidable and very remote East Face of the Grandes Jorasses. In addition they made the first British winter ascent of the North Wall of the Eiger. With Renshaw, he had gone on to climb in alpine-style, the South Ridge of Dunagiri in the Garhwal Himalaya. It was a bold ascent by any standards, outstandingly so for a first Himalayan expedition. This led to Joe inviting Pete to join him on Changabang. They are very different in personality. While Pete gives an impression of being easy going and relaxed, Joe is very much more intense, even abrasive. He comes from a large Roman Catholic family on Teeside and went to a seminary at the age of thirteen to train to be a priest. By the age of eighteen he had begun to have serious doubts about his faith and left to go to Manchester University to study sociology. Inevitably perhaps, his period at the seminary has left a mark. He has a built in reserve which is difficult to penetrate, and at the same time he has an analytical, questioning mind. He is not prepared to accept an easy answer and will keep going at a point until he is satisfied that it has been answered in full. On our K2 expedition in 1978, I had barely had the chance to get to know Joe well, but I remember being exasperated by his constant questioning of decisions, particularly while we were organising the expedition. At the time I felt he was a real barrack-room lawyer, but on reflection realised that he probably found my approach equally exasperating. When it came to deciding who should go on Kongur, both the quality of his altitude performance and the way that he and Pete had struck up a really strong, long term partnership influenced me in recommending him to Michael, though I must confess that at this stage I was not at all sure that I really liked him.

I only knew one of the scientists whom Michael had invited. This was Charlie Clarke who had been doctor on our 1975 Everest expedition. In many ways he is rather suave. The son of a former president of the Royal College of Physicians of London, he went to school at Rugby and then on to Cambridge. Both talented and ambitious, he has managed to combine a successful career as a neurologist with several Himalayan expeditions. He combines considerable charm and political expertise with a massive capacity for work. His research interest is in the effects of altitude on the brain, particularly as shown in the back of the eye which is the only place that oedema and bleeding can be detected in the early stages.

We met the other two scientists briefly at the first expedition meeting held in London during the summer. Jim Milledge's father was a medical missionary in China when Jim was born. Jim himself is recognised as one of the leading specialists in his field which is chest medicine. High altitude research therefore interests him because oxygen lack is a common factor. With his wife Betty, who is an anaesthetist, he worked at the Christian Medical College, Vellore, in South India before returning to England because of the problem of educating their two children in the sub-continent. He has done a large amount of field work in the Himalaya and in the laboratory, and was, with Michael, a member of the 1960–61 Silver Hut expedition to the Everest region. He has done a great deal of winter ski-mountaineering and climbs regularly for pleasure. Jim has an open, almost nervous cheerfulness that conceals an obstinate tenacity, both in his profession and in the realms of climbing.

Edward Williams is a man of many parts and remarkable achievements. He was born in the Welsh border country where he first acquired an affection for mountains. His academic career began not in medicine but in physics. He was one of the youngest electrical officers in the Navy at the end of the war and then switched to medicine, training at the Middlesex Hospital. Edward is also extremely practical, can mend anything and is able to undertake long hours of hard physical work that many labourers would consider more than a fair day's toil. At fifty-seven he is fitter than many men half his age.

He is Professor of Nuclear Medicine, the only one in the U.K., at the Middlesex Hospital Medical School. His main interest on the expedition would be the effect of altitude on the endocrine system. With a jaunty greying beard and a quizzical gleam in his eye, he has a whimsical sense of humour which was a definite asset at Base Camp.

At this meeting Jim Milledge described the scientific aims of the expedition and exactly what would be expected of all members of the party:

We plan to study three areas of altitude physiology. First of all we want to look at the effect of altitude on two quite different hormone systems. The first is the renin aldosterone system with the (enzyme) angiotensin converting enzyme (ACE), all of which has to do with the regulation of fluid and salt in the body. We think that this system may be involved in causing acute mountain sickness, so that as well as looking at the effect of altitude on the whole group, we shall look to see if there is any relationship between the symptoms of acute mountain sickness, if anyone gets it, and their particular response. During the first few days at high altitude, the aldosterone level is reduced while the renin is rather variable and we have found that acute lack of oxygen reduced the level of ACE. We will be looking for these acute effects as we move up to the Karakol Lakes and Base Camp and then we shall see what happens in the longer term as we stay at Base Camp for six weeks or so. This study will involve taking blood samples before we leave and then at intervals during the time we are there, both on rest days at Base Camp, and also immediately on returning from higher altitude, and again after lying down for one hour.

We know that strenuous hill walking causes a retention of sodium which shows itself in puffiness round the ankles and eyes, caused by a retention of water. At very mild altitude in Switzerland we got much higher levels of renin, but the levels of aldosterone were about the same, as was the sodium and water retention. It will be very interesting to see the effect of the rather higher altitude on Kongur and particularly of the longer duration of exposure to altitude.

We shall also need to take blood from you when we look at the other hormone system called erythropoietin. This is the hormone which stimulates the bone marrow to produce more red cells, one of the best known effects of altitude.

The second area of altitude physiology we shall be looking at is exercise testing. In this case we shall be looking particularly at the difference between you climbers and us scientists. On previous expeditions in Nepal we have shown that Sherpas born and bred at high altitude differ in their physiology from lowlanders and this accounts for their tendency to be more efficient at high altitude. The question we want to ask is whether the physiology of climbers like yourselves who have been exposed to extremely high altitudes very often has become a bit like that of the Sherpas.

We plan to do control experiments at sea level, where you will exercise at increasing work rates on a treadmill, and we will measure the ventilation – that is the amount you breathe – the oxygen consumption, which is really a measure of the horse power you are putting out, and your heart rate. We will repeat this whole exercise test while you are breathing a low oxygen mixture to test the acute effect of lack of oxygen on your breathing and heart rate. We shall, of course, also do these tests on the scientists. We will repeat the tests at base camp in the open air and also while you are breathing air enriched with oxygen. In this way we can measure what we call the hypoxic sensitivity.

The third area of altitude physiology we would like to look at is particularly Charlie Clarke's responsibility and that will be to examine the blood vessels at the back of the eye, using an ophthalmoscope and the special retinal camera. He and others have found previously that people going quickly to altitude often get little haemorrhages from the vessels at the back of the eye and it is possible that what we see there reflects what may be going on on the surface of the brain, so again it might have a bearing on acute mountain sickness. In order to get a good view of the back of the eye we put in eye drops to dilate the eye which you may find a bit trying. The tests and blood sampling will all be done at Base Camp on the rest days between the alpine-style trips and, finally, after the summit attempt.

All these studies, but particularly perhaps the one to do with the salt and water hormones, renin and aldosterone, are of interest not only in working out what happens to climbers on going to altitude, but they may also give us information which can be helpful in understanding what is happening in patients who are short of oxygen because of heart or lung disease.

We were to have a foretaste of what was in store for us before our departure, since Jim Milledge wanted to do a series of initial tests to determine the base levels at which we started. In the months before setting out, the scientists tried out the various tests on themselves several times over to work out the system they were going to use, and then each of the climbers was summoned to the Northwick Park Hospital.

The hospital is a huge rambling erection of glass and concrete just outside Harrow. I was in the middle of a lecture tour when I went for the first set of tests and felt tired and unfit, having had too much to drink the previous night. What was worse, I had been warned that representatives of the press were going to be there to take some pictures which would help publicise the scientific content of the expedition. I was late arriving, had difficulty in finding a place to park my car, and then even more difficulty in finding the right entrance in this maze of buildings. When eventually I found Jim's office it was already crammed with photographers waiting for the 'star' athlete.

The trouble was, I was anything but a star. Very few climbers have a top athlete's physique or lung capacity. The requirement is different since, even in the case of Himalayan climbing, it tends to be a long struggle of attrition, of being able to keep going for weeks on end and of moving very slowly and steadily. I was perhaps especially sensitive since I was very aware that I was fourteen years older than the other three. I have never been a super athlete nor a brilliant natural high-altitude performer. I could keep going, but knew full well that in 1975, for instance, Doug Scott and Dougal Haston were going much more strongly than I was when it came to putting in a summit bid on Everest. How was I going to perform this time? I had not been to any great altitude since 1977 when Doug Scott and I reached the summit of the Ogre. On the way down, Doug had broken his legs and I smashed three ribs in a fall. This had led to the bone infection osteomyelitis. Eventually, I had to have parts of three ribs removed in the summer of 1978 and I felt that I was only really beginning to return to a good level of fitness during our reconnaissance of Kongur, but even then we had not been higher than 6,280 metres. And so, about to have my respiratory rate tested in public, I felt uneasy and defensive.

The laboratory was quite a small room, full of dials and electrical gadgets, with the testing device over by the window. It was a modern day treadmill consisting of a rubber mat running round two rollers. Both the rate at which it ran and also its angle could be adjusted. I was stripped down to running shorts, had a cluster of electrodes monitoring my heart rate fastened to my chest, and then had to stand on the mat. I now had a clamp placed over my nose and had to clutch in my teeth a mouth grip that led to a flexible tube which in turn was connected to a large empty plastic bag. This was to collect all my expelled air. And then it started, first with the mat rolling round at a very gentle pace, just

Chris submits to the treadmill at Northwick Park Hospital under the supervision of Jim Milledge.

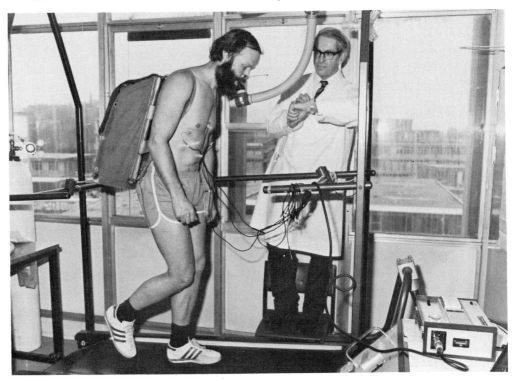

to get me warmed up. I was able to look and feel good, striding along to nowhere with the cameras clicking and flashing away. Fortunately most of the photographers were content with these pictures and rushed off to get them printed up for next day's paper, but one of them, from the *Daily Express*, sensed that there might be a better picture to come and insisted on staying. We now got into the serious part of the exercise tests. The speed of the endless mat was gradually increased, but it was bearable. I was quite pleased with myself. Not so unfit after all; must be the running I had been doing through the summer. We then came to the grand finale. A packframe carrying twenty kilos of telephone directories was set on my back; the movable mat was set at an angle of ten degrees and the speed was increased to a brisk five miles per hour.

'We'll just give you three minutes to warm up and we'll then start collecting,' Jim told me reassuringly.

By the end of two minutes I was approaching exhaustion. As I tired I crept slowly backwards on the remorseless mat until I was threatened with the indignity of being catapulted off it altogether. Tramp, tramp, tramp; my breath was now getting out of control, in great raucous gasps.

'I think we'd better start collecting now,' murmured Jim. He could see I wasn't going to keep going for very much longer.

The nose clips were clamped on, the gag shoved in my mouth, and somehow the speed of the mat seemed to increase. It was only a minute, but it seemed to go on for ever. I was now panting completely out of control, doubled over struggling to keep up with that infernal mat. And then it suddenly stopped. I slumped down, and could hear someone in the distance say:

'It was only three-quarters of a minute but I think we should have enough.'

And there was the click of the camera. The *Daily Express* man was well pleased that he had waited. I was not! My ego was definitely dented, but beyond that was a sneaking worry about how well I was going to perform on the mountain. Was I getting too old for it? Had my performance been permanently impaired by the damage to my ribs and chest?

We were all intrigued not only by our own performance but also how we had done in relation to the others. It was the eternal sense of competitiveness common to most people and certainly to all climbers. The results were predictable. Pete Boardman came out on top with the greatest oxygen intake per minute, closely followed by Joe, while Al, who had perforce been inactive because of his ankle, was just ahead of me. I was a little better than Charlie Clarke and then came the other three scientists. Martin Henderson of Mathesons was also very keen to try out the test since he had run for Cambridge and had been able to do the mile in just over four minutes. Jim gave him a test more suited to a runner, keeping the moving mat on the level but increasing its speed to simulate a running pace. Martin had a better oxygen intake than any of us.

Jim Milledge did his best to assure us that this was not a competition and that it need not necessarily reflect performance on the mountain. Even Pete's figures were well below that of an international athlete. In this respect it would have been very interesting to have tested Reinhold Messner, the brilliant Tyrolean mountaineer, who climbed Everest solo without oxygen in only three days. He has a pulse rate of forty and in his training schedule was making a height gain of a thousand metres in thirty minutes. This sounded more like the Olympic athlete's performance.

Preparations were going on apace. Our team had now crept up to ten. Michael felt that it was very important we should have a good English-born interpreter. During both our negotiations and the reconnaissance, even though the standard of interpretation had on the whole been very good, there had been occasional misunderstandings. With this in mind, Michael had invited David Wilson to join the expedition. He was a fluent Mandarin speaker with a good deal of Cantonese, working for the Foreign Office as Political Adviser to the Governor of Hong Kong. I also had met him in Hong Kong and had taken an immediate liking to him. Although his climbing experience was limited, he was a keen walker and had participated in an extraordinary game that I too had become hooked on. This was a kind of manhunt, invented by the historian George Trevelyan and the mountaineer, Geoffrey Winthrop Young, in the years before the first world war. It was in the days of academic study weeks in Wales or the Lake District, from which much of early British climbing had grown. The original game was a glorified hare and hounds with the entire Lake District as the field. The hare could easily have vanished in such a gigantic area, but to give good sport it was his rôle to show himself to the hounds, give a toot on a hunting horn and then to take off.

There were breaks for the two wars but the game survives, still supervised by the Trevelyan family. Today, the playing area has shrunk to the mountains around the top of Ennerdale and the hunt goes on for three days, though now the field retire for the night to a neighbouring guest house, rather than bivvy out as they did in early days.

I had only been on one hunt and had never been a hare, but just creeping around the top of Haystacks to ambush an unwary hare or racing in hot pursuit across Gable, I found it quite extraordinarily exhilarating. It was straight back to Cowboys and Indians in a magnificent setting with exercise as exhausting as you cared to make it. David Wilson, I soon learnt from others, was a legend in the man hunting game. He became a will o'the wisp character who would sound his horn in the midst of a fierce pack of hounds and then simply vanish, escaping his hunters by clever field craft and a quick pair of legs.

The team was finally made up with Jim Curran. We had always envisaged taking a film crew with us to Xinjiang. It seemed such a superb opportunity, since so little was known about the area and since no western crew had yet produced a film on this part of Chinese Central Asia. In addition a film would give our sponsors the kind of exposure that would justify the amount of money they had invested in us. Surprisingly, however, neither channel was prepared to commit themselves to sending out a full crew. We decided therefore to make our own film and began looking around for a suitable cameraman. A few weeks before I had been to a festival of mountaineering films at Kendal in Cumbria and had been immensely impressed by a dramatised documentary of the first ascent by Dougal Haston and Robin Smith of a climb called The Bat, on Ben Nevis. Robin Smith, who had a meteoric climbing career in the late 'fifties, wrote an article for the *Scottish Mountaineering Club Journal* called 'The Bat and the Wicked', which has since become a classic and greatly influenced climbing writing of the 'sixties. Jim Curran had been the driving force in making the documentary based on this article and I felt that his creative imagination could turn our story into something more than the standard expedition film format. He showed *The Bat* to Michael Ward and Martin Henderson. They also were extremely impressed and Jim was invited along. It only gave him a few weeks to get together all his gear, but somehow he managed.

Once again the main work of co-ordinating our preparations fell on Martin Henderson and his efficient secretary Pippa Stead. Joe Tasker and I got together the equipment while Charlie Clarke and Al Rouse worked on the food. At the same time the scientists were assembling all the specialised equipment for their research. Largely thanks to Jardines, with their many services, ranging from insurance, through travel to the supply of White Horse whisky, there seemed remarkably little to organise, certainly much less than on many other expeditions I had been on.

Throughout the preparation period we were all also busily involved in other things. The medical men had their regular jobs to keep doing. Joe Tasker and Al Rouse were off to Everest to attempt it in winter, while Pete and I were writing books both, co-incidentally, for the same publisher. Pete had been the blue-eyed boy for some time, having completed his first award winning book about his Changabang trip in a mere six weeks, well within deadline. He was being more ambitious perhaps in his second, trying to produce something different from the usual climbing and expedition book and, as a result, was now a year over deadline. It made me feel a little better since I also was a good year beyond mine. I was working on a study of post-war adventure, one that had already been frequently delayed by my pursuit of active adventure on the reconnaissance.

Joe Tasker only returned from Everest at the end of February. They had been stopped at a height of around 7,000 metres on the West Ridge by the bitter winter cold and winds. Joe immediately plunged into writing a book about the expedition and put us both to shame, completing it in under six weeks. Pete commented: 'Joe has gone to the top of the class in the publishing world now, but I shall reserve my envy until I see the results. However, if anyone mentions how quickly he's written that book, I'll vomit!'

All our equipment had been air-freighted to Peking three months before, so that it could be transported from there by train to Urumchi and then on by truck to Kashgar. This made our own departure feel even more unreal, since we had hardly had to think about the expedition for the past three months. On the eve of our departure there had been two receptions. One was at the offices of Mathesons, Jardines' subsidiary in England, so that we could meet the many people in the company who had helped make it so easy for us to organise our trip, and the other was at the Royal Geographical Society, given by the Mount Everest Foundation, who had initiated the entire project. Here a message was read out from the patron of the expedition, H.R.H. the Duke of Edinburgh, wishing it well, and hoping its mountaineering and scientific objectives would play a part in developing good relations between Great Britain and China.

Next morning we were off to Peking in a big British Airways 747. We were delayed for an hour on the ground before taking off and were compensated with free drinks that lasted all the way to Hong Kong and beyond, forty hours of non-stop drinking time, as we read, signed postcards to be sent from Base Camp to our supporters, and settled into the rhythm of being on an expedition.

8
The roof of the world

14TH–29TH MAY 1981

We may have been a ten man team of climbers and scientists attempting a 7,719-metre-high unclimbed mountain in the heart of Central Asia, but the crowd shepherded by Liu Dayi, who was still our liaison officer, more closely resembled one of the many tourist groups flying off to various corners of China. For our party had swelled still further. We had been joined by David Newbigging, Jardine Matheson's chairman, his wife Carolyn, and some of the people who had been closely involved with the expedition. Martin Henderson had flown out with us from Britain and we had been joined in Hong Kong by Tom Harley, a Lowland Scot like so many Jardines executives, who was the director who had been placed in overall charge of Jardines' involvement in the expedition. In addition there was Adrian Gordon, who had done an immense amount of work for us in Hong Kong, securing food and equipment. David Mathew from Peking was also coming along with us and had already done much to organise the itinerary of the 'trekking party' as they had come to be known. The final member of the group was Jim Boswell, a personal friend of David and Carolyn Newbigging. Jim, a lean and very fit American, was the oldest member of the entire expedition and one of the fittest. The trekkers were going to come up to Base Camp, spend a few days with us while we acclimatised, and then return to Hong Kong.

In addition, Mr. Shi Zhanchun was going to accompany us as far as Urumchi, the first time that the vice chairman of the Chinese Mountaineering Association had ever travelled with a foreign expedition. Pete wrote in his diary: 'This is so unlike normal expeditions – having sponsors along, making polite conversation much of the time, instead of descending to the usual basic crudities. It brings an invisible but nevertheless very real pressure on us, the climbers, to perform; to get up the mountain.'

Liu Dayi looked even more worried than usual, weighed down, no doubt, by the scale of his responsibility, as he coped with our prodigious pile of excess baggage and herded us on to the plane to Urumchi. He was helped by our interpreter, Zhang Xueshan, a slightly built youngster who was still studying English at university. He had a friendly manner and was very keen to help wherever possible. The very ease of our progress contributed to the feeling that we were not part of an expedition at all but were just another group of tourists.

We were swept along on our magic red carpet, through Urumchi, where we had more banquets, and on to Kashgar, where all the gear we had packed months before in Manchester was awaiting us. As deputy leader I was temporarily in charge since Michael

RIGHT] *Camp at the Karakol Lakes.*
OVERLEAF] *Base Camp, with the Koksel Glacier immediately beyond and Mustagh Ata rising from the clouds.*

Ward and Jim Milledge had gone to Shanghai to lecture. I felt rather like a holiday courier announcing the day's programme each breakfast time and trying to ensure that everyone was happy. There were organised visits to the Concubine's Tomb, carpet factories and a school. We watched a concert of local music which had some of the same performers as Al and I had seen in Urumchi the previous year.

Pete commented: 'Al's only two theatre visits in the year – in Xinjiang! What a life we lead.'

I had a lot to do at this stage, because I was also planning an expedition for the following year to the north side of Everest from Tibet. Some of the Kongur team were involved and Jardines were going to sponsor us once again. I had to sort out our plans and budget, and spent some time discussing the project with David Newbigging and Tom Harley.

Joe was amused by my hyper-energy, commenting: 'Chris with his high powered calculations and formulations impresses them all. He impresses me so much that I wonder how I've ever managed to climb a mountain without him!'

It is always very revealing, sometimes painfully so, when one's friends and fellow expedition members allow one to read their diaries.

We agreed to differ on quite a few topics. There were two schools of thought on the subject of training; those who believed in going out jogging and those who were fervent exponents of the art of 'horizontal training'. Arch priest of the horizontal variety was undoubtedly Joe. It never occurred to him to go out running. Lean and spare, he was still tired from his efforts on the winter Everest expedition and reckoned he needed rest rather than exercise before embarking on the climb. Al was in the same state and claimed that he couldn't run anyway, because of the damage done to his ankles, not just the previous year, but in previous climbing accidents as well.

Most of the rest of us were all into running at one level or another. Charlie Clarke and Martin Henderson had already been off on long runs around Peking. David Newbigging had been training hard in the preceding weeks, getting up early and belting up and down the precipitous paths of the Hong Kong hinterland before going to work. Jim Boswell had also been training, and there developed a very definite competition between this pair of tycoons. I have come to enjoy running, finding it an essential prop to remaining reasonably fit whilst pursuing the sedentary occupation of writing and also in an effort to keep up with climbing partners who seem to get progressively younger as I get older. I started jogging about five years ago as a necessary evil and have actually come, not only to enjoy it, but to find it a compulsive need.

Pete didn't go running whilst in Urumchi. Was this, I wondered, a gesture of solidarity with Joe and Al? But he did come out one evening in Kashgar, running with us through the chequerboard of dusty irrigated fields behind the guest house compound. It gave me a childish satisfaction to be much more running fit than he, though Martin Henderson strode ahead of us both with effortless ease.

The scientific programme had already been started with Edward Williams and Charlie

ABOVE LEFT] *Horsemen arriving at the* buzkashi.
BELOW LEFT] *Michael superintended the sheep ferry.*

Clarke giving all of us electro cardiograms and taking blood samples. The blood was then spun in a centrifuge run by a little Honda generator and the cells, thus separated, were placed in a cylindrical container called a cryostat. It was like a mediaeval alchemist's receptacle. Filled with a cocktail of carbon-dioxide crystals and nitrogen, it had a temperature ranging between $-195°C$ and $-80°C$ and would act as a super deep-freeze for the duration of the expedition. Charlie also checked our eyes for haemorrhages, photographing the pupil with a special camera. At this stage the two doctors were particularly hard worked for the other half of the scientific team, Michael Ward and Jim Milledge, was delayed by bad weather at Urumchi and had not arrived by the time we were due to set out for the Karakol Lakes.

During our stay in Kashgar the town had been enveloped in a blanket of airborne dust, but on the day of our departure, as had happened the previous year, it dawned a perfect morning, with superb views of Kongur from our bedrooms in the guest house. Everyone flocked out to gaze and take photographs. The expedition was beginning to feel more real as we piled into jeeps and a bus to drive to the Karakol Lakes. We used the same campsite by the side of the lake as we had the previous year, though this time there was a small village of tents. Our Chinese staff was also very much larger. The cheerful, slightly manic Wang was to be our cook once again but because of the greater numbers he was to have an assistant. He turned out to be an agreeable lad of Tadzhik descent, who had been born in the small town of Tashkurghan on the other side of Mustagh Ata but had spent most of his life in Kashgar and had now forgotten his native language. We also had a Base Camp manager, an employee of the Kashgar Sports Federation who was a basketball player. He was particularly anxious to learn English and took lessons from David Wilson. Our party was completed by two sturdy Chinese mountaineers who had the egalitarian title of high-altitude assistants. We planned to use them to help carry Jim Curran's film gear and also any scientific gear needed on the mountain. Because of the size of our Chinese contingent it was obviously necessary for them to have their own mess tent and although we had very friendly relations with them, it meant that we did not get to know them in the same way that we had on the reconnaissance when there had only been six of us and we had all eaten and lived together.

We had a dramatic view of Kongur on our first morning at the Karakol Lakes, through a window in a huge bank of piled, angry clouds. Our views, and consequently our photographs, of the mountain during the reconnaissance had been in almost cloudless conditions, for the mountain had either been totally concealed in cloud or completely clear. As a result the summit of Kongur had seemed small and innocuous, and the climb so straightforward we had even been worried that it might be so easy the ascent could be a bit of a non-event. Al had heard me at press conferences make the statement that I felt Kongur could have a lot of surprises in store. He had commented afterwards: 'That means we might have to use a rope.'

But it looked very different now; steep and threatening, and potentially dangerous. In the coming days Joe and Pete were to complain frequently of how little warning we had given them of how difficult the climb was going to be.

David Mathew had managed to gain permission for the trekking party to visit Tashkurghan. Very few Europeans had been there since the revolution. Some of the trekkers, however, were much more interested in exploring the hills around us, while some expedition members were longing to see Tashkurghan. It ended up with us splitting into two parties. Joe Tasker, Al Rouse and David Wilson joined four of the trekkers to drive to Tashkhurgan while Pete, Charlie and I were going to take David Newbigging, Jim Boswell and Martin Henderson on a short trek, in the hope of bagging a small peak.

The tourists took off on time but we were delayed both by the medical programme that Charlie had to complete and by the need to ensure we had a safe crossing over the Koksel river. My memories of nearly being drowned were still much too fresh. We had brought with us coils of thick polypropylene rope with which we could make a bridge and also a rubber dinghy, the brainchild of Charlie. We spent a pleasant day messing about in boats at the bottom of the gorge. Being early in the year the water was still quite low and you could wade it easily, which made our efforts seem a little ridiculous.

We could not find anywhere sufficiently narrow to sling a rope bridge to span the river so we decided to have a ferry, with a fixed rope across the river. The whole operation had become rather like one of those team initiative tests that the army revels in using to select future leaders of men. We certainly had plenty of promising candidates in the shape of the chairman of Jardines, its London financial director, and the head of the largest farming company in the world, not to mention us climbers. I think a selection panel could have had fun watching us as we tried to work out the best way of doing it. Pete commented:

Too many people with too little to do and Chris in a stentorian voice yelling instructions in a situation that would normally have resolved itself. I drilled a hole for an expansion bolt in a rock (for the first time ever) and Able Seaman Charlie clad in a wetsuit, wearing a life jacket, got in the rubber dinghy and paddled back and forth across the river. Eventually we worked a system.

When we got back from establishing the ferry, the Tashkurghan party had arrived back full of stories of what they had seen. They had certainly had a fascinating time. The drive to Tashkurghan had taken most of the day, skirting the lower flanks of Mustagh Ata and going within five miles of the Soviet border, where there had been no signs of military preparedness. The border is not even marked. David Wilson described the visit in a letter home:

Our two jeeps wound down over the passes to Tashkurghan in the late evening. No photographing to the right; that way lay the Soviet border. Photography allowed to the left; the mountains that way were not only beautiful, but apolitical. Tashkurghan – the Stone Fort – a name redolent with memories of the old travellers. It comes in all the books. The first significant settlement in China for those travelling north through the mountains of India to Kashgar. The most unwelcome posting in the Chinese Civil Service according to an unhappy occupant in the 1920s.

The ruins of the old fort are still clearly visible on a hill to the north of the town. As a strategic point – albeit well into China – Russian Cossacks had been stationed there until as late as 1904. Memories of this seemed dim but, on pressing, I was told that they had been driven out by a local patriot who had been rewarded with a rise in status of two ranks. Memories of the British were clearer. One old man reminisced about the consular post station which used to look after the mail being carried on horseback between the Consulate-General at Kashgar and the end of the Indian telegraph line about fifty miles south. Very few foreigners had visited the town in the past thirty years.

The old town is a huddle of stone and mud houses sheltering beneath the hill of the fort. Above this is now a post-1949 commune centre and frontier garrison-post with one wide, dusty, but tree-lined street and a small number of shops – remarkably well stocked considering how remote it was.

There may be nothing remarkable about the settlement itself. But the surroundings are superb. The fertile, well-watered valley is surrounded on all sides by snow-capped, jagged peaks. So dramatic that it looks like an artist's sketch or the cover picture for The Far Pavilions.

The real excitement started the morning after we arrived. A public holiday was declared. They were going to lay on a buzkashi. *Some claim this is the original version of polo in a wilder and woollier form. The 'ball' consists of the carcass of a goat with the head and legs chopped off. The game is a free-for-all with the objective of placing the carcass on an appointed spot. It was like a Central Asian Highland Games. Crowds started gathering in the early morning on an open space near the town. Most came on horseback, often two to a horse: the women in colourful Tadzhik dresses, the men more sombrely clad. Also a good number of soldiers from the small garrison; mostly from other parts of China and puzzled to know what was going on. One asked me about the rules of the game. I don't know why he thought I should know.*

Proceedings started with a practice game. About ninety horsemen of all ages lined up across the green grass. The master of ceremonies flung the goat carcass ball into the assembly and the practice started. Each time the 'ball' was dropped it would be picked up by a rider who had to lean down from his saddle until his arm was touching the ground. Others would barge and wrestle with him until they captured the 'ball'. From the scrum quickly developed the equivalent of a fast play by three-quarters, with horsemen stretched out for hundreds of yards across the plain in a long charging line. No boundaries. Spectators scattered as the horsemen charged towards them. An ambulance stood by. They said there were often quite serious injuries; but the day we watched people must have been on their best behaviour and nobody was seriously hurt.

While all this was going on we were entertained by a small group of girls, and the occasional co-opted and shy young man, doing the Tadzhik dances. Graceful hand movements with a backdrop of milling horsemen.

The game itself seemed almost tame in comparison with the scrums and mêlées of the practice. A small depression in the ground was appointed as the goal; the 'ball' was flung into the crowd; and play began. The best players were not the young bloods, but wizened old men who clung tenaciously to their horses and seemed to be double-jointed in their ability to stay in the saddle and scoop up the 'ball' from the ground. Finally, out of the jostling and charging somebody managed to place the carcass on the appointed spot and was declared winner. His prize: a roll of silk.

Next came a cross-country horse race. As in Mongolia, they used to race over miles of open country. But now the course is shortened to about a mile. Once again the horsemen came charging across the plain towards the spectators, silhouetted against the snow-capped peaks. We had been offered horses too, but none of us felt too keen to take part in such a fierce rampage over rough country. I ambled gently on mine in a small circle. David Mathew, more learned in the ways of horses, wandered over the plain as the horsemen charged around him. Looking at him in the distance with the hills behind, upright in the saddle and complete with straw hat and Old Etonian hatband, I couldn't help thinking that, for those with long memories, he would be a familiar figure. Tashkurghan is a place for memories.

Next day, 25th May, it was the turn of our trekking expedition, David Newbigging, Jim Boswell, Martin Henderson, Pete, Charlie and I, to reap the fruits of our Koksel gorge ferry labours. We set out up the valley between Mustagh Ata and the southern part of the Kongur massif, attaining a height of around 3,750 metres and carrying 16-kilo loads, enough at least to start the acclimatisation process and make up in small part for the lack of an approach march. When we camped for the night Charlie showed his strength as a natural host, producing a whisky sour mix for our pre-dinner cocktails and then preparing a magnificent menu of oyster pâté on wholemeal biscuits, turkey marengo, sweetcorn and mashed potato, followed by Wensleydale cheese, coffee and peppermint creams.

The following morning we climbed the hill above us. In their humpy, rounded form, these mountains reminded me of the Cairngorms. It was a long plod up compacted mud and then some snow slopes, but any illusions we might have had of making a first ascent were shattered by a tall metal survey marker on the summit. Even so there was a desolate emptiness about the peaks around that amply made up for their lack of dramatic steepness. The clouds were like huge mountains themselves, dark and menacing, crouching over the Kongur massif in a way that dwarfed the peaks beneath. The wind was blasting past, a grim warning of what it might be like on Kongur in a few days' time.

We got back to the Karakol Lakes the next day, to find that Michael Ward and Jim Milledge had at last managed to catch us up, and that Al and Joe had already set out to find a good site for Base Camp.

We were on our way once more the following day. Insufficient yaks and camels had arrived the previous night to take all our gear up to Base Camp in a single carry. We were therefore going to have to leave some behind to be brought up later. It was going to take two days to make the carry up to Base Camp, but some of us had decided to walk straight through, in the day, carrying tents and food as well as personal gear. Michael Ward and David Wilson stayed behind until all the yaks and camels had been loaded and then accompanied them to the river to supervise the crossing. The laden animals had no trouble in wading the river but the small flock of sheep, which was going to accompany us to Base Camp as meat on the hoof, received preferential treatment, with Michael ferrying them over, securely trussed, in the dinghy.

I had got away early and walked with Pete for much of the way. Although I had now been on two expeditions with him, we had never actually climbed together on the mountain, had only once shared a tent, and, as a result, hardly knew each other. We relaxed into an easy far-ranging conversation, which drifted over to the subjects of the book that I had just finished and the one that Pete was just completing. He was intrigued by the constant lifemanship play that goes on within an expedition, the jockeying for position in the pecking order of decision making and of day to day living; of getting the most comfortable place in a tent, of manoeuvring your partner into making the first brew, and so on. When he and Joe Tasker had been on Changabang, in an extreme climbing situation for months on end, this lifemanship had been constantly present; they had been aware of it, and had even used it as a form of light relief against the emotional pressure of being so totally dependent on each other over such a long period, much of which was at the very edge between life and death.

This confession of Pete's provoked me to an emotional outburst for I had noticed this lifemanship game on several occasions already on our trip. Pete and Joe would often hold back from simply mucking in to get mundane but necessary jobs done. I could remember a petty little incident that had irritated me at the time, when we had been having a working lunch at Martin Henderson's office in London and at the end of it everyone except Pete and Joe pitched in to clear up the debris so that we could get on with the meeting. They sat back and talked. There was a touch of the prima donna, and I suspected that, almost unconsciously, neither of them was prepared to be the first to get up and help. I tried to explain that, though such incidents are petty, if they get out of hand they can become divisive and therefore destructive in an expedition. It is probably a matter of numbers. When there are only two people involved, a balance is easily found, but once there are more, it is less easy. Pete partially agreed on this, remembering that on Kangchenjunga, when there had been four of them, the interplay of lifemanship had caused real stress. I ended up, though, as I so often do, apologising for the vehemence of my own outburst, admitting that it was probably because I was afraid of losing that particular game of social interplay and manoeuvring.

Ironically, the day after we reached Base Camp, when the yaks carrying all our gear arrived, I found myself guilty of the very same lifemanship on which I had lectured Pete. I made a beeline for one of the most comfortable tents to use as my personal home while at Base. It was noticeable that all four climbers had acquired the largest and most comfortable tents, though in this respect Pete had been slightly slow off the mark, and had the smallest of the four. He made up for this by securing a second tent later on.

Base Camp was in an idyllic situation, on the edge of a flat meadow of lush, at times waterlogged, grass, squeezed between the moraines of two glaciers. There were some big boulders at the side, and plenty of flat spaces both on the edge of the meadow itself and on the old earth-clad moraines that rose in a series of gentle mounds to the side. As a result we could pitch our personal tents haphazardly to have a little privacy and the view of our choice. At the head of the shallow valley was the shapely peak we had called the Rognon, with stony slopes leading up to the snows of its pointed tip. It was like a sphinx, sitting crouched with its two arms encradling the camp. As a result the view from the tents was limited to the immediate moraines, giving a sense of protective shelter, enhanced by the presence of the marmots, who would come and squeak and peer at us from their holes in the morning. The ground was covered in sparse grass in which were scattered little purple primulas.

You only had to wander a few metres from Base Camp up on to the edge of the moraine and the view opened out. On one side was the Koksel Glacier, a petrified sea of tossing ice reaching out into the desert. Beyond it on the other side of the wide, brown, dusty valley was the huge and solitary bulk of Mustagh Ata. Kongur itself was concealed by the Rognon, but looking away from the Koksel Glacier, the great snow flanks of Kongur Tiube loomed, wall-like, above the piled moraines that marked the northern limits of the meadow.

The summit cap of Kongur was hidden, not just by the bulk of the Rognon, but by its outer curtain wall as well. The summit seemed even more mysterious and remote than it had been from our camp by the Karakol Lakes.

We pitched our base tent, which was to become our communal living room, beside the meadow. In it was a powerful stereo cassette player, an essential for all modern expeditions, a boxful of paperbacks, stationery, some booze and a small tableful of snacks to which anyone could help themselves. With that and folding chairs and tables, Base Camp was truly luxurious. We even had a wooden thunder box, or toilet, one of the few items of equipment that has not changed in design since Sven Hedin first explored these regions at the end of the nineteenth century. It was certainly the loo with the best view in the whole of Central Asia. Our Chinese staff had their own mess tent, and there was a kitchen and another large tent for all the scientific gear. Our sheep spent the night in a pen, contained by large boulders and the screen originally designed for the loo, while hens scratched around the kitchen area and base tent for scraps of food.

There was a lot to do. The scientists had to set up their field laboratory and we were anxious to start getting acclimatised to the altitude. This entailed reaching increasing altitudes either by bagging some of the unclimbed peaks around us or in further exploration of the route itself. Jim Milledge and Charlie Clarke were preparing the skis they had brought with them, casting longing glances at the untouched snow slopes of the Rognon Peak. There was another attractive peak just the other side of the glacier, from which, with a bit of luck, we might get a good view of Kongur. At the same time this meant that we could give the trekking party a simple climb before they set off for home.

9
First forays

30TH MAY–12TH JUNE 1981

To reach what came to be called Trekkers' Peak, we had to cross the Koksel Glacier and on 30th May Pete Boardman and I found a route through its serpentine corridors and labyrinth of gleaming ice towers to the other side, where steep scree slopes led up towards the peak we had chosen. We climbed it the next day in a mass onslaught of climbers, trekkers and those scientists who could spare time from preparatory work on their projects. From below it had looked little more than a walk to the summit, but looks were deceptive, a feature we were soon to find of the entire range. The ridge narrowed into a knife edge of loose rock, forcing us to rope up. It would never have done for us to lose the chairman of Jardines. Above, the ridge broadened out into an easy angled slope covered by knee-deep snow. We were not yet acclimatised and were soon pausing every few steps for breath. Eventually eight of us, including David Newbigging, Martin Henderson and Adrian Gordon of the trekking party, reached the summit. It was a cloudy, windswept day, with fragmented, frightening glimpses of dark rock and sérac walls at the head of the Koksel Glacier. Behind these lurked the summit of Kongur.

That night we were all elated but very tired and glad to spend the next day pottering about Base Camp under a bright sun. The yaks and camels arrived the following afternoon after completing their second journey ferrying the food and gear from the Karakol Lakes. It had clouded over once again in the afternoon and began to snow, but now we had everything up at Base Camp. The expedition was at last self-sufficient, dependent only on its own efforts. Charlie, with his usual panache decided we should celebrate the occasion with a cocktail party and Liu Dayi turned one of the sheep into kebabs. Charlie wrote:

We were all very drunk by 12.30 and staggered off to bed through the snow. Little sleep with the booze and sound of snow pattering down on the tent, but thank God it arrived when it did and not a day or two earlier. About 6.00 a.m. my worry about the tents reached a crescendo which made me get up. Chris stirred so I called him. We staggered out to find nearly a foot of snow collapsing the lab. tent and weighing heavily on the roof of the mess tent – full of foul smelling, rancid Kirghiz tribesmen. They did not shift at all as we shook and bashed the snow off the roof.

The camels were extraordinary. Seated huddled, motionless, awake, smothered under mountains of snow. We photographed them by flash and still they didn't move. The yaks were like snowy rugs huddled half way up the hillside.

We had planned that day to try to find a better route into the Koksel Basin than the one

RIGHT] *Crossing the Koksel Glacier to Trekkers' Peak.*

up the Koksel Icefall that Michael and I had forced with such difficulty the previous year but the snow was so deep we decided to postpone it for a day. The weather was certainly giving the scientists a lot of problems. It was important for them to be able to take our heart rates (ECGs), blood pressure and blood samples as soon as possible after reaching Base Camp. They were also anxious to put us through the exercise tests. It is one thing to do this in a comfortably heated laboratory, quite another in sub-zero temperatures in a draughty tent. They had problems with all the electrical equipment: batteries would not work; Edward Williams had the centrifuge in bits trying to find a fault, and it was very painful for us, and even difficult for them, getting blood from our veins.

Even more serious, though, was the 'flu epidemic that was beginning to creep through the camp. Jim Milledge had felt ill when he arrived at the Karakol Lakes a few days before. He had probably picked up a virus infection while waiting for the plane in Urumchi. David Wilson was the first to catch it, getting a severe cold, and Al Rouse had been forced to abandon the ascent of Trekkers' Peak, he felt so ill. David Newbigging was the next to to go down, with a painfully sore throat. It was all he could do to stagger back to the Karakol Lakes on the 3rd June, which was the day the trekking party had to set off to return to Peking. We had thoroughly enjoyed having them with us, for they had given our company an interesting, broader dimension, but the very fact that it was now just the team at Base Camp, each person with his own specific rôle focused our attention on the mountain and we knew the real purpose of our expedition was about to begin.

That same morning Joe Tasker and I were going to try to find a route up the glacier to the left, or north, of the Rognon Peak, which we hoped would lead into the Koksel Basin. We had already observed from below that the glacier itself was very straightforward and the only question was whether there was an easy route down from the col at its head into the Koksel Basin. Jim Curran, accompanied by David Wilson, was also going to come up with us to film our exploration. It was a wonderful cloudless morning, and Joe and I gained height easily for about an hour. Then the moraine ridge merged with the mountainside and we had no choice but to drop down to the glacier. The going remained easy, for the glacier floor was level and seemingly free of crevasses. We didn't bother to rope up, each walking at his own pace. We were now at about 5,000 metres and I had to stop for a few minutes to relieve myself. Joe was about a hundred metres ahead, but once I started again, the distance between us inexorably increased. I tried to speed up, out of pride as much as anything else, but I just could not keep up. I allowed for the fact that I was a lot older than he was, but I reckoned that at this early stage of the expedition I should be fitter; after all I had been training throughout the winter. The doctors had even discovered that Joe was anaemic, so much so that they suspected he might have a parasite in his intestine. I tried to put on the pace but couldn't. By this time Joe was little more than a black dot in the middle of this broad highway of snow that stretched up ahead between steep walls of rock and ice.

Joe reached the crest of the col a full half hour in front of me. My only consolation was that I was still well ahead of Jim Curran, David Wilson and Song, one of the high-altitude

ABOVE LEFT] *Pete takes Martin Henderson across a difficult step on Trekkers' Peak.*
BELOW LEFT] *Our camels stood up to the snow rather better than some of our tentage.*

assistants. Beyond the col, it looked promising. You could see the pattern of crevasses, a series of cavernous moats stretching down towards the wide trough of the Koksel Basin. It was possible to pick out a lane all the way down to where it smoothed out. The summit of Kongur was now hidden behind its outer rampart but we could pick out the two possible routes very clearly. The snow slope swept gently up to the Koksel Col, and from there the ridge, in rocky profile, pointed up to the series of summits of what we came to call Junction Peak. It looked steep and difficult but relatively safe. The long snow arête, on the other hand, that stretched from the basin up towards the crest of the ridge between Kongur Tiube and Kongur, looked almost too straightforward, a featureless slog up an endless slope.

That afternoon we picked our way down into the basin, finding an easy route with only one little steep step down on to a snow bridge at the confluence of two crevasse systems. We walked a short way up the basin, but I was now beginning to flag, feeling unaccountably tired. We had achieved our objective anyway for we had found a safe and easy route into the Koksel Basin. The only slight risk was at the head of the glacier just

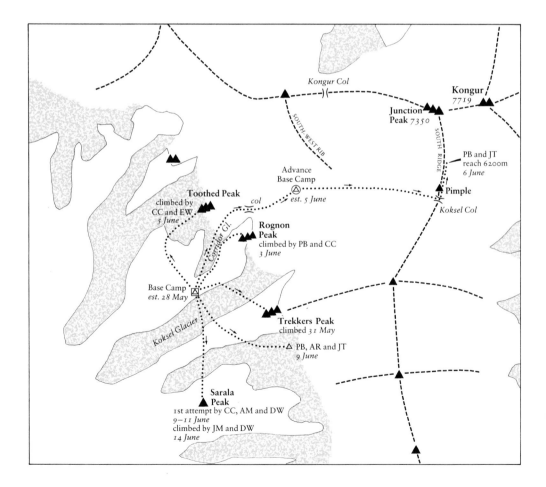

before the col, where it narrowed, with sérac walls banked high on either side. Blocks of ice scattered across the glacier were silent indications that if one of the séracs collapsed anyone on the glacier would be at risk. They looked very stable, however, and the danger area only lasted for a very short time. Because the glacier was long and narrow we called it the Corridor.

Once we started back, even though the first half mile involved a height gain of a couple of hundred metres, I seemed to get a second wind, and was going strongly again. From the top of the col at the head of the Corridor, Joe and I made fast progress, striding down and chatting about experiences on previous expeditions in a way we had never done before. It was through this that the reservations that I think each of us had about the other began to clear. We got back to Base Camp well content with our progress to find that Pete and Charlie had also had a satisfying day.

That morning they had set out to climb the Rognon Peak carrying skis, so that they could then ski down. The climbing had been straightforward, a long slog up a uniform snow slope, until it began to steepen near the top. They dumped their skis here and Charlie, slightly guilty because he was playing hookey from his scientific work, started ski-ing back down in a series of long, cautious traverses, but Pete was determined to reach the top, and set out by himself. He wrote in his diary:

I love mountaineering, it thrills me; gives me extra strength from somewhere to have a summit in my head. One short ice step – I cut steps. Out of sight the ridge narrows and I plod between the cornice and the steepening snow slope to the edge of the precipitous West Face of the peak. Slightly unnerved in the deep snow, I'm relieved to reach the top. Disappointingly not a good view of the Koksel Basin beneath Kongur – but I can see the mountain with its pyramid, as usual, in drifting cloud. I can also see the tracks of the others, far below me in the Corridor. A few photographs and I'm relieved to turn round.

Descent amazingly quick. I see a dot far below. Charlie is waiting for me. It's 1.30 p.m. Whoopee! I can do linked turns, even though the boots are not very supportive. It takes fifteen minutes to descend what took three hours to come up. This is the life. I am quite proud of the patterns I have made.

That afternoon Charlie got down to his research work using Pete as a guinea pig. Pete wasn't quite so happy about this:

Move into a darkened tent. Generator whirring, twenty minutes after anaesthetic and dilator put in my eyes. A new guillotine-type machine held in front of my eye. It's very dim and my forehead is propped so that I can't move. Blinding flash photographs, yellow and blue. The fuse box blows a blue flash and loud bang – very disconcerting.

Then a small needle put into my arm, syringe taped to forearm. I try to switch my mind off. This must be like being in hospital, a useful discipline for illness. Then he pumped some yellow green glowing dye into my blood, and a few seconds later it reaches my eyes through the blood vessels. He takes more photos. Winding down, with winding down drops. I have to wear dark glasses – can't read anything except large figures at a distance.

That evening there was an optimistic, excited feel in the mess tent. The scientists had

Ski tracks on the Rognon Peak.

ironed out most of the bugs in their machinery for carrying out the step test which the climbers were going to do for the first time the next day. We were then planning to move up into the Koksel Basin to have a closer look at Kongur. But I was still tired and went to bed early; I wrote in my diary:

I think I'm going to have to be very careful in safeguarding my strength. I've got to push myself to get fit, but I think I've also got to make sure that I really rest and relax, probably more than the others, to actually build up . . . I think the old demon age means that I don't bounce back as fast as the others. Also, I've got a really bad head cold starting.

I woke up at about three in the morning with fierce earache, stood it for as long as I could and then crawled out of my sleeping bag to ask Charlie for some painkillers. By morning I was feeling as ill as I have ever done, even worse than on the Ogre, when I had broken my ribs, had had no food for five days and probably had pneumonia as an extra complication. My head cold had now developed into a hacking cough and I could feel it creep down on to my chest. By afternoon Charlie confirmed what I already feared might be the case, that the 'flu had developed into pneumonia. He immediately put me on antibiotics and gave me some Valium, which allowed me a good night's sleep. The following day Charlie noted:

Chris has been very ill with a left lower lobe pneumonia, which, thank God, I recognised quickly. After thirty-six hours he has no temperature but he is very weak. I suppose it may knock him out for the climb but three could, I suppose, climb this mountain. I am sure we must be very firm about whether Chris goes back up, because in the light-hearted way this expedition has gone no one seems to be taking it very seriously.

116

It is salutory to think how very serious this illness has been and without treatment or alone at high altitude he might well have died if things had got worse.

I was certainly taking it seriously. It was now two days since I had contracted pneumonia; I felt a lot better but desperately weak and commented in my diary:

They're a bit non-committal about how long it will take to clear up but I suspect it is going to be about four or five days. I'm certainly not going up the hill until it is cleared. There just isn't any point. I'm obviously worried about my prospects of being on the alpine-style push and not getting to the top of the mountain but nothing more than that. I would very much like to climb it but if I don't, I don't. It's as simple as that.

I was able to get out of my sleeping bag after a couple of days but it was all I could do to walk the few metres from the base tent back up to my tent without several rests and I spent most of the day lying in the porch of my tent, reading, dozing or watching a family of marmots on the moraine bump opposite. They were equally inquisitive, popping out of their holes, standing on hind legs, sniffing and peering around them, with their whiskered little brown faces.

Meanwhile the rest of the expedition was getting on with the work in hand. On 5th June, the diminished climbing team moved up to establish an Advance Base Camp in the Koksel Basin. Jim Curran and David Wilson also went up to get some film. Next day the three climbers set out for the Koksel Col. Pete described the day in his diary:

A great day, and for the first time I get truly shattered! A day when I felt good from the beginning, when my alarm watch, tied to the neck string of my sleeping bag, woke me at 6.45 a.m. Last night it was so cold – a reminder that it is some time since I've been on a trip and camped on a glacier. It was a bit of a shock, but these days I can adjust readily and quickly to these things. I make the first few brews, two stoves roaring in my patch beside the door.

We set out just after nine. The snow does not seem deep, but the trail breaking is quite hard work – half an hour each, except for Al (still recovering from his cold; he coughs a lot of the time) who does about ten minutes at a stretch. Two and a quarter hours up the broad flat glacier to the Koksel Col. Séracs here and there, on either side. The suggested dotted line up Kongur [the route proposed on the previous year's reconnaissance and illustrated in the expedition brochure] looks easy but a very long way. The trail breaking would be hard and it could be difficult to find the way down in a white-out.

It's a long way to the Koksel Col, just to gain a few hundred feet above our camp but what a view the other side! Peaks upon 6,000-metre peaks stretch to the south-east, all unclimbed. What fun could be had there. They are probably all unnamed.

Al's had enough, so Joe and I climb almost directly up the South Ridge of Kongur. We put on crampons and climb through rocks on to an ice slope above a sérac. Meanwhile Al goes down to pass the distant figures of the film crew – Jim C. and David. The east side of the mountain is corniced and whipped like an Andean ridge. Its séracs are more alive also and fall into the eastern abyss as the sun touches them.

At first progress is rapid for the wind keeps the snow on the edge of the ridge in good

117

condition for cramponing, firm and hard. But then the altitude starts to hold back our steps and we count them before pausing for a rest; 60 at a time on the best conditioned snow, but dropping to 40 then 20, as we gained height.

Today I have the edge on Joe. But there is no competition. I encourage him. All I want to do is see around the corner, see around the ridge and look up the route for it is unlikely that we shall be up here again in the near future, before we have the first serious attempt.

The cornice is vast on the east side, though apparently stable. We rest on rocks well clear of the edge, nevertheless. We traverse up and down the Pimple – the little summit in the way. We stop and start, looking, discussing the route; pointing things out to each other. It's exciting, for it does not look too bad; it looks feasible even though the summit is hidden and complex.

Let's go on just a little farther, turn back at 3.00 p.m., no at 4.00 p.m. Just a little further, but at 4.00 p.m. the weather seems to be clagging in hopelessly – no view. We have reached the foot of the rocky part of the ridge. The mist closes in as we turn back. On the way up in the morning we picked out a direct route up or down from the Pimple, diagonally between the séracs, and we decide to try it on the way down. But after initial confidence we are soon lost; crevasses all around us, curving away on the convex slope, white cloud merging with the white of the snow. We cast around four or five times and each time the way is barred.

Eventually I offer to belay Joe; we undo coils and he descends the whole rope length, aiming at a deep cleft or bergschrund in the snow. He sits astride the brink; I come down, go on past him and through. The snow is frightening, unconsolidated, but the slope eases. We are on the glacier.

We plunge across side by side, breaking steps, towards the track. Joe's eyesight in white-outs is poor, but I can see the line of earlier tracks. We reach them, sip water, relieved. The weather as always is unpredictable and now the sun shines, the skies, except around the top of Kongur, clear. Golden sunshine for the weary miles down the glacier. A distant figure –Al coming slowly towards us, placing marker wands. It takes a while for us to meet. He's slightly negative, regretting, I suspect, not having come up with us. Jim C. films our return. We are almost too tired and dehydrated to sleep – too dehydrated to drink much from the little plastic whisky bottle we have brought up. But sleep, when it does come, is sound.

7th June: Today we planned to go up the original 'dotted line' to get a feel of it and investigate its snow conditions, but the constant snow fall pre-empts the plan, and so we have a lie-in. A long time before the need to pee drives us from our pits. Then we also soothe dry throats.

We seal up the tent doors, list the food and gear left there, tie up onto the same rope and plod off into the mist, with Joe out in front, missing the occasional wand. Below the short step through the crevasses, I put my foot through a monster hole. Jim Milledge visited the Koksel camp yesterday, alone, and we shout down the hole to see if he's down it. We carry on, Joe setting a cracking pace which perhaps was unfair on the others. But the other side of the col the weather seems clearer and we hurriedly unrope beneath a sérac. Al says he went on a week-long seminar at Cambridge about séracs. He likes to discuss and argue endlessly; perhaps he misses such talks from his

Cambridge days.
We stumble down to Base Camp in time for lunch. Chris looks pale, coughs and does not say much. I don't know what to say to him. He's on the mend but what a setback.

The climbing team were in Base Camp for just a day, busy with step tests, and then they set out once again, this time for one of the unclimbed 6,700-metre peaks to the south of Kongur. Base Camp was left very nearly empty, for Charlie Clarke, Jim Milledge, Edward Williams and David Wilson also set out to attempt a lower peak a little farther down the range. Only Jim Curran, Michael Ward and I were left.

The weather, however, was not kind and neither team got beyond the foot of their respective mountains. The following day everyone was back in Base Camp. I was now beginning to feel a lot better. Michael Ward had declared my chest clear of infection the previous day and I had managed to walk about ninety metres up the hillside behind Base Camp. We now began to reconsider our plans. The weather had been so much worse than the previous year and the mountain seemed more complex and difficult than we had originally envisaged.

12th June dawned fine and the four climbers met in Joe's tent to discuss future plans. I opened, saying:

'Well, I think it's more in your court, actually. What have you been thinking?'

'Just that we should get on the hill rather than climbing smaller peaks,' replied Joe. 'But there's the matter of considering what you're doing as well.'

'That really depends on what you want to do. If we had four or five days perfect weather, I suppose you could just go for the summit, even though it'd probably be pretty painful, but there's no way that I could.'

'I'm not ready yet,' said Pete.

'Nor am I,' said Al.

'One thing I'm shocked about,' said Pete, 'is the weather. It's just so terribly bad. We've had about four good days since we've been here which means it immediately gives the mountain a lot of seriousness. No matter what we do, it's going to be a hard job getting up it and I don't think we're acclimatising very well sitting here. Thinking about the other trips I've been on, you've got to really work for your acclimatisation, put a lot of effort in, and it doesn't seem that trying to do these six and a half thousanders, although they're incredibly attractive, is the way to do it.'

He continued: 'My initial thought is that we get a very good base up in the Koksel Glacier; we hump at least a week's food up there and we all go and live there. Every time we come down here it wastes two days down and back again. I know it's nice to be cooked for and that, but at least we will be acclimatising better up there. If the weather's bad then we can establish a camp on the Koksel Col – we can do that in snowfall, but at least we'll be working and doing something and not just ticking over.'

Al added, 'I don't mind particularly the style we climb the mountain in. The thing is that whatever you do you accept it as being that and don't pretend it's anything else. If you want to keep climbing it in alpine-style, one way of doing it is to go up one route and prepare it to some extent, then go up another route and try it. If you fail on the route you're trying, you've got a route prepared and you can go up to the top. On the other hand, you still haven't spoilt your chance of doing it in alpine-style.'

The discussion now revolved around practicality versus ethical considerations. Pete, Joe and I favoured establishing a secure base in the Koksel Basin, using our Chinese assistant to carry some of the food we would need for a prolonged stay and then making reconnaissances of both the South Ridge leading up from the Koksel Col and also the long South-West Rib leading up to the main ridge line. We also wanted to mark both these routes. Al was still concerned with the ethical question, saying: 'You're using porters and fixed camps. You certainly couldn't claim in any way that it was alpine-style.'

'I think that's a load of shit,' replied Joe. 'You can get the train up to Grindlewald. Is it alpine-style if you use the train or téléférique?'

'I just don't feel it's satisfactory for other people to carry my gear, that's all.'

'Well if I've put a lot of effort into climbing a mountain I don't find it unsatisfactory at all.'

I tried to clarify what we were arguing about: 'Am I right in interpreting that what we intend to do is use the HA assistants to get our Advanced Base established in the Koksel Glacier, but not beyond that?'

'Yes, that's right, not beyond that,' said Pete.

'You shouldn't have written in the brochure that we were going to try the climb alpine-style, in that case,' Al said.

Exasperated, I replied: 'Quite honestly Al, I just don't remotely see what you're getting so steamed up about. If we're making our launch-off point the Koksel Basin, that then is the start of the climb. We had yaks and camels to carry our stuff into Base Camp. Surely it's just a matter of semantics. One of the HA assistants has already carried a bundle of marker wands into the Koksel Basin anyway.'

'O.K. O.K. Forget it. I'm not at all bothered anyway.'

We now got down to specifics, discussing when to start out and what to take with us. There was also the question of my own participation.

I knew there was no way I could get to the summit in the next week but I had a clear set of lungs again now according to Charlie, and would hope to build up my strength while we followed our new recce plans. So I was ready to set out with the others, even if I trailed behind a bit at first. But at all events I was determined not to be a hazard to the other three or slow up their progress.

We then went on to talk about pairing off for the climb. Al pointed out that Pete and Joe knew each other so well that as a united pair they might dominate the decision making process. He therefore suggested that since he and Pete probably knew each other the least, they might as well pair up. This seemed a sound decision and so after a little more general discussion I went off to find Michael Ward so that we could explain our plans to him. We spent the rest of the day sorting out rations and gear for our sortie the following day.

ABOVE RIGHT] *Finding a route up the Corridor.*
BELOW RIGHT] *Looking up the Koksel Basin.*

OVERLEAF] *Climbing through the crevasses in the Koksel Basin.*

10
Choosing a ridge

13TH–22ND JUNE 1981

The ground was covered in snow even at Base Camp when we set out on 13th June. Determined to get a good initial lead on the others, I started first, setting a slow rhythmic pace that I hoped I would be able to keep up throughout the day. I was carrying around eighteen kilos of personal gear with a little food as well, though I had off-loaded as much as possible of my share of the communal load on to one of the high-altitude assistants. I didn't have any ethical scruples as I knew I was going to have to take it easy in the initial stages.

I made good progress for the first couple of hours before the others, who had left Base Camp quite a bit later, inexorably began to catch up and then overtake me. I was the last to reach the col at the head of the Corridor. It was a perfect cloudless day and the sun was beating down upon us. We sere sinking up to our knees, sometimes thighs, in the fresh snow that had fallen in the past few days. Trail-breaking had become a wearisome chore, which Pete and Joe shared between them.

It was late afternoon when we eventually reached the site of Advance Base Camp, and the two high-altitude assistants, who were returning to Base Camp, had dumped their loads half a mile short. The next morning started fine and whilst Al and Pete set out to break trail towards the Koksel col, Joe, Jim Curran, David Wilson and I dropped back to pick up the loads left by the Chinese the previous night. We then started the long plod up towards the col. Joe commented on how much harder it was than on the previous occasion. We were now sinking down with every step, even when following in the tracks of the front pair. Once again I was going so slowly that David Wilson and Jim Curran were able to pass us. Joe was delightfully relaxed about it all, quite content to conserve his energy and wander along at my pace. We camped on the col which meant we had had a short day, something I felt I urgently needed.

Next morning it was the turn of Joe and myself to go out first, climbing the steep snow and rocky buttress that guarded the bottom of the South Ridge. It was not technically particularly hard, but it demanded concentration. After a good night's sleep, I felt that I was going more strongly than the previous day, while Joe had a bad headache. As a result our performance was now more matched and I was able to take my full share of trail-breaking. Although Joe had been this way before, it was new ground for me and had all the stimulus of being so, as we picked our way from the top of the buttress towards the Pimple.

It was just two in the afternoon when we reached a broad col between the Pimple and the long shelf that led to the foot of the steep section of the South Ridge. We stopped there

Advance Base Camp with the South Ridge outlined against the sun.

to wait for the others and it was only three o'clock when they caught up with us. Pete was in favour of pushing on farther up the shelf to the high point that he and Joe had reached the previous week, but I was very happy to stop where we were. It was a good, safe campsite and I didn't want to overstretch myself. Joe, whose headache still troubled him, was also happy to stay, while Al sat on the fence, simply saying that he would go along with the majority. After arguing around the subject we stayed where we were, putting up the tents and lazing through the afternoon. Pete, Joe and I had brought books with us, and were happy to spend the afternoon reading, but Al had not. This was partially to save weight – 'If you're doing an alpine-style push you can't afford to carry books up the hill.' But it was also because of his temperament. Al loves to chat and argue, to reminisce about previous expeditions or climbs, wild times in North Wales and adventures in South America. Joe and I could hear the monologue in the tent next door with an occasional response from Pete. Joe and I spoke comparatively little, even when we didn't have books to read, but the silences were comfortable and we seemed to be settling into an easy

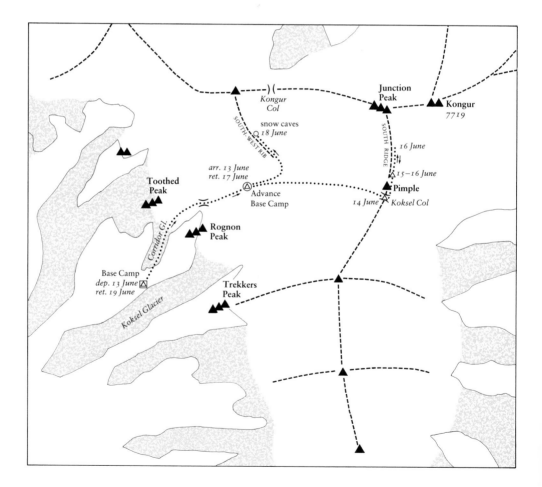

partnership. I was doing most of the cooking, partly from choice since I found that it helped to pass the time and partly because I felt that Joe was probably going to have to do more than his share of the work when we were actually climbing. Whilst I woke up early naturally, Joe was at his worst in the morning and was delighted to be served brews of tea when we started to get going each day.

The following morning I woke at six when it was still dark. The light of a full moon was fighting its way through the clouds, so I shouted to the others that it was a fine morning and lit the gas stove. But the weather, ever unpredictable, had closed in by dawn and it was snowing with almost nil visibility, so we dropped back off to sleep for another couple of hours. Perversely, it then showed signs of improvement. It was still cloudy, but the ridge above was beginning to break through. By this time, however, our initial drive and enthusiasm had slid away. We argued round what to do, to carry the damp farther up the shelf or to push on, travelling light, and then return. Pete finally decided it by getting dressed and climbing above the col by himself to see what snow conditions were like. He shouted down that it was safe and we followed, Al joining Pete out in front and moving cautiously one at a time, with Joe and I following unroped in their steps. It took us two hours to reach their previous high point. Everything was covered in fresh snow and we were now at the foot of the steep section. The ridge soared in a dramatic knife edge, with a rocky cock's comb of pinnacles about thirty metres above us.

Pete wallowed on steep, deep snow-covered rocks, while I cast off to the right and found some hard snow which gave better purchase and started up this tentatively. Pete soon overtook me, however, and continued up over broken ground to the top of a shoulder. We had now been going for about three hours. I was tired and still anxious to conserve my energy. Pete wanted to go on farther to get the feel of the ridge. We sat around and talked it out, deciding to go back down. We also discussed the merits of the ridge. Once again, Al was the odd man out. The three of us were enthusiastic about the South Ridge, partially for reasons of safety, fearing that the other, the South-West Rib, being less steep, might be more avalanche prone, and also on aesthetic grounds as the South Ridge seemed more exciting and sporting, with the possibility of some interesting technical climbing. Al had his doubts and wanted to look at the other ridge before making a final decision.

We therefore resolved to return to the Koksel Basin and investigate the other arête. Getting back down next morning proved a mild epic in thick cloud and a bitter driving wind. Joe and I set out first and quickly lost the correct line, even though we were using a compass. Steep slopes dropped away below us and it took us some time, aided by a fortunate break in the clouds to realise we were going straight down the steep flank of the Pimple into the Koksel Basin. We eventually got back on route and descended to the Koksel Col, from where we could see two tiny dots slowly moving up the Basin. These turned out to be Jim Curran and Edward Williams who were carrying some more of Jim's film equipment up to the col. It was an arduous task for the snow was now even deeper, but both of them were delightfully cheerful. Edward displayed an infectious joy at just being amongst the mountains. He wasn't bothered about reaching any summits, but was simply glad to be there and to be able to help in any way that he could.

We got back to the camp in the early afternoon and spent the rest of the day brewing tea, discussing plans for the next day and eating. The idea was to climb the South-West

Climbers in the Koksel Basin.

Rib. In part this was a sop to Al, but it also meant we could gain some altitude and see whether this was a good line of descent. This was Pete's idea. Pete was the forceful one at this stage in his own gentle kind of way.

The rib was little more than a long uphill walk, but the snow got progressively deeper and consequently the trail-breaking became more laborious. I tried to take my turn but could only manage a limited amount and Al had a bad cough and was going barely better than me. Joe also did his share but undoubtedly Pete did the bulk of the trail-breaking.

By late afternoon we had reached a slight shoulder at about 6,300 metres. We were still a long way from the top of the rib, which seemed to stretch above us endlessly. Cloud alternately engulfed us and then opened out to allow tantalising glimpses of the surrounding mountains. The Rognon was now far below us, and we could gaze over it at the Karakol Lakes in the distance. The larger was a brilliant turquoise, the other, a muddy blue. Beyond them were brown and shaley hills dusted in snow, that stretched to the far horizon. We were looking into the Soviet Union, whose border was barely thirty miles away.

Behind us, through breaks in the cloud, we had momentary views of the barrier formed by the mountain that still hid Kongur's summit cap. We dug out platforms for the tents and while Joe settled in I ploughed slowly across the slope to see round the corner of the ridge to the slopes leading to the col on the main ridge between Kongur and Kongur Tiube. I was pleased that I still had the energy to do this and was rewarded by a brief sight of the col. It seemed quite close, over comparatively easy angled slopes. But then the clouds rolled in once more. To the west, dark threatening clouds were riding over the foothills; the weather was as unsettled as ever. The discussion that evening revolved around whether to traverse the slope to the col next day, or keep to the crest of the ridge and cross higher up. The slope was easy but then so had been the slope on K2 when Nick Estcourt had lost his life when it slid away in a huge avalanche. For some reason we did not understand, despite the very high snow fall on the mountains there seemed very few avalanches. There were hardly any tell-tale snow cones at the foot of slopes one would expect to be constantly swept by avalanches. Even so Pete, who combines caution with boldness, was worried and wanted to follow the ridge line as far as possible. Joe pointed out that the ridge had so flattened out that there was barely any difference between the slope and the crest anyway.

We could leave this decision for the time being since we still favoured the South Ridge and the next day simply hoped to reach the top of it to gain height for acclimatisation and a better view of the route. We settled into our sleeping bags and began to prepare the evening meal, well content with the day's progress. Then, in the early evening it began to snow in earnest with a steady pitter patter on the tent. Pete was immediately concerned, writing:

I start thinking about the angle of the slope, the build up of snow, what could trigger an avalanche: put my penknife in my top pocket, have it handy in case I have to cut myself out of the tent. Bloody weather; we're very vulnerable here on an open slope thousands of metres high, above and below . . . An argument drifts across from next door – Joe doesn't agree with our plan. Oh well, I wonder sometimes if he really enjoys climbing and why he does it . . .

In fact, what Joe could not see the point of was slogging up an endless snow slope sinking in to his thighs at almost every step. Pete, particularly on this trip, had so much stamina and strength in reserve, that for most of the time he was well within his physical limits. But both Joe and Al were undoubtedly run-down from their experience on Everest just a few months before.

As the snow started pattering on the tents once more we became uncomfortably aware again of our vulnerable position. Joe began telling me tales of his and Pete's experience on K2 the previous year. They had spent eleven days slowly working their way up the mountain, were nearly out of food and fuel, but were within two days of the summit. They had pitched their tent below a rock wall, confident that it would deflect any avalanches, but that night they had been hit by a storm. An avalanche thundered straight over the wall and the tent was very nearly swept off its ledge down to the glacier thousands of metres below. Dick Renshaw, the third member of their team was hanging in space, supported only by the fabric of the tent, and Joe was buried in the snow, wrapped in the suffocating shroud of the nylon tent material. He only saved himself from death because he had had the presence of mind to keep his penknife handy and had been able to cut himself a small hole to breathe through. He had lost consciousness all the same. They had had a desperate descent and the fact that they survived at all was a tribute to their skill and determination.

We could hear the murmur of voices from the tent next door. Pete was telling Al the same story. It was hardly reassuring in our position. If the slope did go, we were part of that slope. By this time it was dark but none of us slept; and then at eleven I saw a light go on next door:

'What are you doing?'

'Digging a snow hole. It's too bloody dangerous in the tent.'

In digging a snow hole they would at least be beneath the slope, so that if there was an avalanche from above it would probably sweep straight over them. Joe and I stuck it out in our sleeping bags for another ten minutes. It was warm and comfortable inside the tent. We could hear the wind gusting outside. But there is nothing worse than knowing that your partners are going to be safe when you are still at risk, and so, with hardly any discussion, we wriggled out of our bags, put on boots and outer clothing and crawled out into the howling dark, to start digging a snow cave.

It took three hours to dig the caves. Pete described his:

We have embarked on a fairly ambitious double entrance style, because we thought Chris and Joe would join us, but they, much to my pique, decide to dig their own. It's difficult to empty debris since the slope is only 30° in angle: also no shovel. Axe a bit long but on the whole we enjoy this digging. I feel like a Welsh miner following a rich seam. Fortunately the digging is easy, because strangely there is no layering, no crusting. I try to discipline my work plan, kicking away the debris, diligently. But I am working like a dervish; the tent nearby is becoming buried. It's two-thirty before we are finished. The others using a one entrance system are ready before us.

Only one person of a team could dig at the snow face, while the other crawled behind and cleared and kicked away the blocks of snow. Joe and I had made for ourselves a cave that was just big enough for the two of us to squeeze into. By the time we had finished we were hot and sweaty, our outer clothes damp with the snow we had been crawling in. There was only one way to dry out, to use one's body heat inside the sleeping bag, but it was a chillingly cold process.

The entrance, blocked with rucksacks to keep out the spindrift soon became sealed by snow, and insufficient fresh air seeped through. The following morning when I woke I had to clear an air hole and even then it took several matches to light the gas stove, there was so little oxygen in the atmosphere.

We were up first, and I crawled out to find the others. The tents were still standing but the other snow hole took some finding. I eventually located a tiny air hole and dug away until a cavernous entrance appeared. The others were also struggling with their stove.

Pete commented wryly:

Chris crawls in, shouting much too cheerfully something about delivering the post. The stove flickers into more life, but Chris can't stand the fetid atmosphere for long and crawls out again. They are more ready than we, talking of going up the ridge. Chris as usual not quite with it about snow conditions, although agrees we did the best thing, playing safe during the night. Joe apparently thinks that a metre or so would have to fall before we were in danger. But they were sensible to do what Al and I did – they'd have been a bit daft if they got the chop and we didn't.

Al and I still have to have three brews (including soup) and some jam and crackers, and to pack before emerging. I worried unnecessarily that Chris and Joe would leave without us, making a lightweight foray up on to the ridge, or making a dangerous traverse across to the col. Chris sometimes announces his plans so dogmatically and emphatically – though he is easily influenced and does change his mind quickly . . . But they do wait for us, as we pack and crawl into the sunlight.

The day had started fine and I think my enthusiasm for pressing on had been more from a sense of duty than inclination. I wanted to be, and to be seen to be, keen on pushing out the route and yet at the same time wanted to conserve my own energy, until I had built up to the same level as the others. But even while Joe and I waited for them to get ready, the weather began to deteriorate with clouds, starting with a few wisps in the clear blue air, rapidly building up into dark galleons, sweeping over the desert hills towards us. It wasn't long before it was snowing again.

We couldn't make up our minds what to do. If we weren't going up, I was all in favour of going straight down. Joe, who had never been that keen on going up anyway, agreed with this view, while Pete tenaciously wanted to hold on in the hope of being able to gain more height the next day. Al sat on the fence saying, 'I'm easy either way.'

And so we went down, ploughing through snow that was frighteningly deeper than on the previous day. Its very depth indicated that we had probably made the right choice. Even so we made fast progress and were back at the camp in the Koksel Basin in the early afternoon. The tents were sealed and silent, but in the mouth of the store tent we found some letters that Michael had left the previous day. One was to the entire group congratulating us on our efforts and the other was for me. In it Michael wrote that David Wilson and Edward Williams had told him that, though I was going surprisingly well after my illness, I was not nearly as fit as the others. He asked me to consider very carefully whether I should join them on the bid for the summit.

It was probably a subject more easily covered in writing than in conversation and I could appreciate and understand his concern both as a doctor and leader of the expedition. At the same time though, it was like a douche of very cold water at a moment of elation at the end of our first foray on the mountain. I felt I was building up my strength and knew that I would choose to pull up well before I became a drag on the others. I showed them the letter, which probably was not very fair of me, for they had little choice but to reassure me, but I think that their reassurance was genuine. They cheerfully declared me officially well and said I could start demonstrating it by breaking trail on the way back.

I managed it about half way to the col, setting up a smart pace. We made good time, wading through the fresh snow, to the col and then, still in white-out conditions, down the Corridor towards Base Camp. But it was now subtly different. The snow was wet and slushy beneath our feet. Rivulets were running down the surface of the lower part of the glacier, and in the moraine valley at its side water was rippling and tumbling between the scree; there were dashes of green and specks of purple, as primulas peeped from the fast thawing snow. We would no longer have a water problem at Base Camp. The summer had arrived. The field, which had been a drab brown with grass desiccated and dry, was now a brilliant green with the stream, brimful, snaking down it.

At Base Camp the others flocked out to greet us. They were relieved to see us, worried by the weight of snow fall. They also had good news. Jim Milledge and David Wilson had made the first ascent of Sarala Peak, a subsidiary summit of Sarakyaguqi Peak. There was plenty of food, and drink, and good company with whom to exchange stories and plans. There was also blood to be given, exercise tests, reports to write and, most important of all, mail to receive. This arrived with a crate of beer on our last day at Base Camp. Neither Pete nor I had letters from home. In a way it was worse for Pete than me. His wife Hilary was also on an expedition in the Kulu mountains of India. She had sent a postcard to Joe, which had arrived, but the much bulkier letter that presumably she had sent to Pete had taken longer. We were both subdued and a little depressed that night.

We spent three days resting and getting ready. We had been in the area for nearly a month, and it was high time we made a serious attempt on Kongur.

ABOVE RIGHT] *Climbing up onto the Pimple above the Koksel Col.*
BELOW RIGHT] *Joe crossing the Pimple with the South Ridge rising left and the summit pyramid beyond centre.*

OVERLEAF LEFT] *Chris and Joe on the col below the South Ridge.*
ABOVE RIGHT] *Descending from the South Ridge, the Koksel Basin in the background.*
BELOW RIGHT] *Camp on the South-West Rib, with the Rognon Peak beyond.*

11
The South Ridge

23RD–26TH JUNE 1981

Those seven days at altitude in bad conditions took a fair amount out of all of us, and even after four nights at Base Camp I personally could still have done with another week's rest. Pete was expressing cautious optimism:

I look forward so much to the climb ahead. This feeling of well being comes with spring like warmth. If we do get up the hill this time, I wonder if it will feel like a real expedition? I suspect not. And I have other ambitions here beside the summit of Kongur – to see so much, to be here, among such a remote unexplored range. Few people have had such a chance during this century.

Yet once we started the next day, it was all right. There had been a couple of day's fine weather and the surface of the snow was frozen hard into an easy highway that we could stride up. It took us a mere three hours to the camp in the Koksel Basin. Jim Curran and

Al, followed by David Wilson, coming up to the head of the Corridor.

LEFT] *Two tiny tents on the shelf where the South Ridge steepens, the summit pyramid beyond.*

Al and Pete crossing the Pimple on the first summit attempt.

David Wilson had set out a couple of days earlier. They were planning to ensconce themselves on top of the Pimple, so that they could film our ascent of the South Ridge, and that day they had walked up to the Koksel Col. They were an improbable pair; Jim, crumpled, battered, self-deprecating of his own efforts in a series of jokes or stories at his own expense, compared to David Wilson, clean-cut, clean-shaven, and very self-confident, with the manner more of a man of action than a diplomat. Jim smoked about twenty cigarettes a day with his head stuck out of the tent entrance because David could not stand the smell. They were now established on the col.

We got away early on the morning of 24th June, once again making fast progress on firm snow to the col, where we found Jim and David just emerging from their tent. With the fine weather had come a bitterly cold, driving easterly wind, from which we had been sheltered in the Basin, but which was blasting across the col, blowing great clouds of spindrift with it. We gave David Wilson some letters from home and also our own letters for him to take back to base when he and Jim returned which would be well before we did. Then it was on up the mountain, to get a camp as high as possible at the foot of the South Ridge. We quickly reached the site of our previous camp on the other side of the Pimple. The tent we had left up was partially buried by snow but had withstood the hammering it must have had surprisingly well.

We brewed up and discussed whether we should gain some more height that afternoon. This time we were unanimous and decided to press on. It was at this point that Joe realised that he had not given the letter he had written to his girl friend, Maria, to David Wilson. He promptly decided to go back with it, hand it over and then catch us up – true devotion at over 6,000 metres. While Joe cut back over the Pimple, Al, Pete and I plodded up the now firm snow crest of the shelf leading up to the steep section of the ridge. It was a magnificent afternoon, with light friendly cumulus clouds riding high over the lower peaks, and the view to the south ever opening out as we gained height.

Pete commented: 'I enjoy myself – one of those rare cherished hours when I actually am filled with joy – old fashioned word I know – and feel it all through myself. Chris I think, shared it.'

I did. The previous sortie had been a struggle, each step hard earned but now I also felt good, when each step was a pleasure, when the feeling of crampon snicking into snow, of the drop beneath, of the wildly corniced ridge behind and those countless unnamed, unclimbed, unexplored mountains stretching to the south, gave a sense of delicious anticipation of the days ahead.

Meanwhile, Joe had climbed back over the Pimple to find that David and Jim were still a long way behind us. He dropped down the slope, meeting David first, and offered to help him with his load, but David declined. Joe then lost even more height to go to Jim's help, carrying his rucksack all the way to the crest of the Pimple. Our film team were installed in the orchestra stalls.

There was a postscript to this story. Jim Curran and David Wilson went down a couple of days later, having seen and filmed us vanishing over the crest of the South Ridge. They got back to Base Camp in time for the mail run down to the Karakol Lakes. Two of the Chinese staff took down the rucksack full of mail but unfortunately they were not brilliant boatmen. By this time the Koksel river was in full spate and had risen so high that the cable we had left stretched above it was not dragging in the water. In trying to pull themselves across in the dinghy, they managed to capsize it, and in their struggle to get to the bank they lost the rucksack containing the mail – a small loss to pay for their narrow escape, but it meant that Joe's dash down the mountain had been in vain, as was all our letter and post-card writing.

But we knew nothing of this, and were already immersed in a world which was at the same time, both tiny, with just the four of us totally dependent on each other, and yet vast with the great vault of the skies overhead, in the heart of these mountains of Central Asia. That evening we stopped near the end of the shelf, just short of the point where the ridge steepened. Joe caught us up before I had even finished digging out the platform for the tent. We all had a sense of excited anticipation as we settled down for the night. We made a good start the following morning. Pete and Al were away first, climbing unroped up to our previous high point. Joe and I followed. The angle now steepened, the ridge soaring with a sharp snowy crest to a rocky gendarme that barred the way. Pete described it:

Al arrived and took over the lead up a steepish snow slope for a while. It was loose and unconsolidated, with a tricky bit across a bergschrund. We are taking it in turns to film – Joe is handling the film this time, moving into position, enjoying himself. We're aiming for a prominent gendarme that seems half way up the ridge. I wonder if the snow slope on the right is connected to the main Kongur ridge – large séracs and intimations of an abyss indicate that it isn't.

Wonderful weather. If only it'll last. Clear sharp lines of distant horizons stretch towards the Wakhan Corridor, the Pamirs, the west and to the south-east, a chaos of white summits and valleys lost in their jagged edges.

Clouds, as on mountains all over the world, rise up as the day progresses. Al, and as usual traverse-loving Chris, want to go onto the snow slopes out to the right, but I'm a rock hugger. I take over the lead for Al is a cougher today.

Sometimes the ridge gives rocky, fun scrambling, sometimes I climb around pinnacle gendarme blocks on sugary soft, collapsing snow. Glad I have a long axe – it's only disadvantage is in the close fighting of a snow hole. But I like my axe, it feels part of me.

And at last the gendarme; no alternative but to pass it on the right. I belay on a knife blade in a vertical crack, and place an ice screw as well. (Al investigates an angle piton, but the flake behind which he hammers it, expands.) Gosh, it's a real pitch; real ice climbing. Hope these Salewa clunk click (clip on, strapless crampons) don't let me down. Not here.

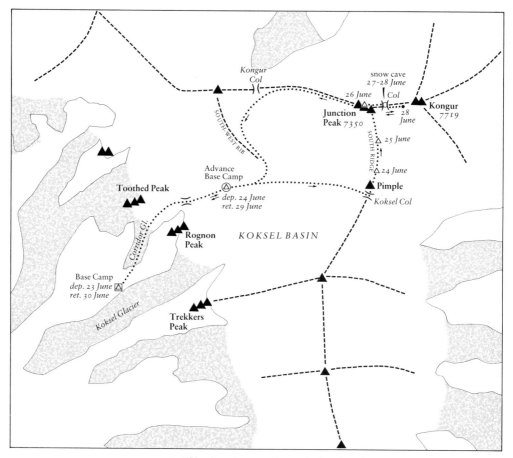

RIGHT] *Al leading the steep ice on the South Ridge.*

Carrying a sack, at this altitude, I have no choice. I cut steps. At first, white airy ice, and a couple of swinging chops suffice. But the farther away, the harder the ice. A proper thrill; real climbing this; none of that fearful unease in the pit of the stomach born from the gratuitous risk of avalanche-prone snow slopes. The step cutting, going diagonally, tires my right arm. We have cut our ropes down to two, 36-metre lengths; they seem to run out quickly and Al yells at me to belay.

This is the sort of climbing I've missed. Reach a little rock buttress, clear away gravel and little stones, and put in two angle pegs, hard banged.

Al arrives and takes the next lead. Pleasant thoughtful moves with a lay-away on an icicle and a good sharp incut around a protruding rock, quartzite, I think. I take over the lead, only a few steps and we're on the snowy arête.

Joe and I followed. The angle now eased, but as a result the quality of the snow deteriorated. Not only was the trail-breaking hard work, but the risk of avalanche was with us once again. Pete stayed out in front, writing:

A long lonely trail break into the late afternoon, begins. Trying to spot nuances, shades in the snow, to show the safer areas to climb. The rocks of the South Ridge, which we'd hoped would offer a safe route, are too far to the left and too steep, bristling with overhangs. Little bulges of ice offer the promise of havens of security, and very, very slowly I plough my way towards them. Below and beside them they offer firm nevé, but on top there is usually a hole. At the second ice bump, I try to place an ice screw, but my first placement must have stripped its thread. Still the stop, with a dubious ice axe belay, at least offers an excuse for a rest.

Backwards and forwards, zig-zagging between these ice bosses, calculating coldly the safest route. I cross to rocks I've been aiming for on the ridge. Good to be on secure ground, but I soon see that this is not the top of the South Ridge. There is a foreshortened snow slope above that will take an age. But it's nevé on this first part of the upper ridge and I move quickly, bringing Al up.

The nevé crust eventually disappears and it's back to trail-breaking. I have done far more trail-breaking on this expedition than on any previous trip; becoming tired; swirling thoughts, nearing hallucinations, fill my head. Neither Al nor the others offer to lead.

We were happy to follow in Pete's wake. He was going so much the strongest and, anyway, never asked any of us to go out in front. Joe seemed happy to let me set the pace out ahead of him, as I plodded up the track left by the front pair. I was making just about the same pace, in their good set of steps, as Pete was out in front, breaking trail. We hardly had to think, just one foot in front of the other, lulled into a false sense of security from the very existence of the trail.

For Pete it was different:

Worried about stability, I keep a full rope length between Al and myself. The crust on the left is constantly collapsing, the angle about 45°, I decide to look over to the right. Gosh, what a steep slope, but over there is the main Kongur ridge, the final Kongur pyramid and the col at its foot. No, no cornice to frighten me here, and I cut a slot in the ridge for a view, shouting to the others to have a look across when they reach it.

What a situation. It seems safest, if hardest work, to carve a slot up the exact crest of the ridge, pulling away soft bottomless snow with kicking feet and clawing mitts. Above, the slope steepens into a cornice, far away, seemingly never coming nearer. I save my deadman for the last pitch, pulled deep into the snow. But I needn't have worried, for the final steep snow is hard and only my lack of breath and panting gasps hold me back. Wonder if Jim's filming me from back on the Pimple. I pull over and wave my axe in the air, a wild free primitive gesture.

The crest provided a perfect campsite, not as flat or large as a football field, but it felt like that after the continuously steep, threatening slopes we had toiled up throughout the day. It was certainly the first spot where we could put a tent. Even so there was a lot of digging to make platforms large enough. It was as if we had climbed the prow of a gigantic ship and were now perched on its forecastle, with the superstructure barring both our way and our view of Kongur itself. The afternoon cloud swirled around us, giving tantalising glimpses of snow peaks and the dusty hills of the Pamir plateau. The crest of Kongur Tiube was now visible; no longer a shapeless whaleback, it was transformed into a fairytale peak, a stately snow ridge sweeping up to its pointed summit, a banner of cloud clinging to its corniced northern flank.

We were tired as we bundled into the tents, crawled into sleeping bags and began the slow process of cooking. Brews first, but our dehydrated bodies were like blotting paper, our thirst insatiable, as we alternate mint tea with ordinary tea and then some soup. But it all takes time, to melt the snow, bring the water to the boil and then start all over again. It was already dark. We were longing to sleep, but we must eat.

The main dish each night consisted of a dehydrated meal. They all sounded delicious and were full of variety; beef stroganoff, lasagne, chilli con carne; but after a time they all tasted exactly the same, bland and processed. That night neither Joe nor I could face the panful of pale brown porridge that was meant to be meat balls in gravy but had as much taste as polystyrene. We threw it away barely touched. There was nothing else to eat and anyway we were too tired. Our gain in altitude was probably a contributory factor, for that day we had climbed from around 6,400 metres to just over 7,300, a height gain of more than 900 metres and the first time on this trip that we had been to such an altitude.

We all woke late the following morning. The crest of the ridge was between us and the rising sun, and I could not bring myself to shove an arm from out of my sleeping bag until its cheering rays had hit the tent. By this time we were hungry, but there was very little for breakfast, just more drinks of heavily sugared tea and coffee, and a handful each of meusli, powdered milk and dried fruit, moistened with warm water. We did not dare break into one of the main meals until evening for this would have reduced the number of days we could spend on the mountain.

It was eleven o'clock before we were ready to start – a superb clear morning with only a few tiny fluffy clouds clinging to the peaks in the far distance. It was the turn of Joe and myself to go out in front and break trail. Joe led off round a shoulder of the ridge and a broad col was just below us. Above it the crest of the ridge rose in rocky crenellations and, both from what we could see, and from our memory of what it had looked like from the arête we had climbed a few days before, it seemed easiest to traverse the western slope of the ridge. We started across and, as we set out on the slope, with a dramatic suddenness cloud seemed to appear from nowhere, and what had been a bright, apparently harmless sunny day, was transformed into murky threat. The snow on the slope was deep and unstable and felt steep enough to slide away. We took what belays we could and moved one at a time, trying to pick out the best line through the shifting cloud. Broken rocks loomed above; we debated where we were and whether to gain or lose height as we skirted rocky buttresses.

There was a notch in the ridge above, and I headed for it; a scramble up a little gully and I found myself on a broad flat col of wind blasted, hard snow. We were soon all gathered there, discussing what to do. We had brought with us a copy of the expedition publicity brochure which had a series of pictures of the mountain in it and we now huddled over it, arguing about where we might be. But in the driving cloud it could only be guesswork and we finally decided to stay where we were until the cloud cleared. At least it was a safe spot. Joe and I put up our tent and all four of us crowded into it, lit the stove, made a brew and whiled away the afternoon chatting about a wide ranging series of topics, from climbing politics to other expeditions we had been on and personalities we had known.

Outside the wind gusted and the cloud blasted past without a break. Pete, the pusher, finally admitted that the weather was not going to clear and resigned himself to erecting his own tent. Joe and I crawled into our sleeping bags, relieved at being able to stretch out and settle down for the day. By this time we were ravenous and later on that afternoon started cooking. Having missed one meal, even dehydrated meat balls in gravy with green beans could be exciting, but I had made it a little too watery and decided to thicken it up with some mashed potato powder.

Al had sorted out all the food we were to take on the hill and to reduce weight to the minimum had thrown away as much packaging as possible, decanting the food into small plastic bags. We had little bags of milk powder, salt, sugar, lemonade powder and mashed potato powder. Unfortunately, however, we had not troubled to label them and we had packed them badly anyway, just stuffing the lot into a big bag which was now a hideous mess of loose bits of chocolate, muesli, sweets and other items of food that had escaped from their original containers.

I dug out what I thought was the mashed potato, licked my finger and shoved it into the powder so that I could taste some. It seemed to have a neutral kind of flavour, so just to be sure I asked Joe to try some as well. 'Tastes all right to me,' he endorsed, and so I poured the lot into the pan of bubbling mixture. It didn't thicken at all and after another few minutes I passed the pan and our sole spoon over to Joe so that he could have the first few mouthfuls.

He took one. His expression changed from one of quiet anticipation to nausea as he lunged to the tent entrance, and spat out the entire mouthful. 'That was lemonade powder you put in. Try some.' And he handed the pan over to me. It was appalling, but it was vital that we got some food down and I therefore forced down about twenty

RIGHT] *Al followed by Joe and Chris. Behind the South Ridge stretches a range of unclimbed peaks.*

OVERLEAF] *The camp on the top of the Pimple from which Jim Curran filmed our ascent of the South Ridge.*

Joe, left, and Pete at the Notch where we stopped to plan the next move.

Lost – Al consults our expedition brochure.

LEFT] *Crossing the avalanche-prone slopes on the west side of Junction Peak.*

mouthfuls of the mixture before admitting defeat and pouring most of the contents away. This was the second day that we had had very little to eat.

That night the wind built up to a crescendo. Joe, who was on the windward side took the brunt of it, for the material of the tent was belled in against him as if it was only him that was holding it down at all. There was little question of sleep with the constant rattle of the tent fabric and the roar of the wind tearing past. The others were in an even worse state.

Pete describes it:

We didn't pitch the tent corners properly and it's now threatening to take off. We spread our limbs around the corners. Think calmly Pete, you've come out of this kind of situation before. But the tent is shaking, stitching creaking, and I know from Kangch that only one thing has to go and then the tent crumbles and the world falls to pieces and you have to fight for your life. A tent can actually be blown away with people inside it by a strong gust . . . if it gets that strong on this mountain . . . I pack things into stuff bags, link them all together with a karabiner. Fortunately these boots are easy, fast to get on. Sleeping bags stuffed in. By 6.00 a.m. we are all ready – if the tent collapses, we will scuttle behind a boulder and shelter until 7.00 a.m. dawn.

12
The sting in the tail

27TH–29TH JUNE 1981

Joe and I dropped into an uneasy sleep just before dawn and were only woken by a muffled call from the tent next door, telling us to have a look outside. I peered through the hole of the ventilator to get my first view of Kongur from this angle. It was a sobering sight, a wedge of snow-veined rock towering through a gap in the clouds. Suddenly, it looked very remote, very big and very hard. It was the first time that we had really considered the summit pyramid at all. The views in profile we had had from both north and south had shown the ridge to be at an average angle of around 25°. Even the view we had had from the South Ridge two days earlier had not alarmed us, since our concentration was entirely absorbed by the slope immediately in front of us. We had somehow brain-washed ourselves into thinking that the South Ridge was the challenge and once this had been solved, we had almost climbed the mountain.

As we struggled to take the tents down and pack them in the buffeting wind, we continued to have glimpses of the pyramid through the driving spindrift. It was a fine morning with hardly a cloud in the sky, but visibility was still poor because of the wind-driven snow. Pete and Al got away first, plodding over the hummock immediately above the col on which we had camped. By the time we reached the rounded summit that was the highest point of the ridge and an unclimbed peak of over 7,000 metres which we named Junction Peak, the wind had dropped a little and we were able to get a clear look around.

To one side was the broad easy ridge that curved round to the col which was the lowest point between Kongur and Kongur Tiube. Easy angled slopes led across to the crest of the arête we had climbed only a few days before. Looking at it, this was undoubtedly the easiest way to the summit we were now standing on, though it was quite a bit farther in distance. Al had been right in wanting to take this route rather than the one we had just followed. We could now see down into the north side of Kongur, into the deep-cut gorge fully 4,260 metres below, which we had followed on our way in. There was the Gez Matterhorn, its top far below us, dwarfed by our own great height, and yet retaining a fragile elegant beauty that tugged at my own desire; if only Michael and I had managed to climb it the previous year. Would I have the chance again? Across the gorge was Chakragil, a fine pyramid of snow, lower than us, but none the less dominant in its isolation, surrounded as it was by plunging ravines. To the north-west was a distant line of snow peaks, little more than a dimpled line of white dividing the brown of the desert and the deep blue of the sky. This was the Tian-shan range, merging at its extreme western end with the Pamirs. Could that be Pik Lenin and that Pik Kommunizma, probably 160 miles away?

OVERLEAF] *Our first close-up glimpse of the summit pyramid from the camp on the Notch.*

But it was Kongur that dominated everything, and was the focus of our gaze and aspirations. Its shapely mass blocked out the view to the east. It was very similar to Gasherbrum IV at the head of the Baltoro Glacier in the Karakoram range in the symmetry of its wedge shape. It was like an unexpected mountain piled on top of the mountain we had come to climb, and psychologically we were barely prepared for it. The slope dropped easily to a broad col, from which rose a gently ascending knife-edged ridge of rock and snow, that led to the base of the summit pyramid. We dropped down the slope; easy walking this, to just above the col. We had had enough of tents and resolved to dig a snow hole, scouted around for a suitable drift and eventually settled on one. The wind had now dropped a little and we had all afternoon in which to dig.

The most awkward part is starting the hole, for only one person at a time can work, hunched awkwardly in the start of the burrow, to keep the entrance small. It is only when he has carved out sufficient room to sit in that it becomes easier. Then his partner can crawl behind him to clear the snow as it falls from the sweeping cuts of the adze of the axe. The process speeds up when there is room for two at the snow face and soon all four are working, two digging and cutting, two clearing.

It took us three and a half hours to dig a cave big enough for the four of us, but when we all crawled in with our rucksacks, we quickly realised that it was not big enough, and piled gear to one side to make the chamber even larger. We even had cooking alcoves and shelves for our mugs and food. Most important of all, we were now all together so that we could talk things out as a team.

Pete commented: 'It's a cosy life here, not the same undercurrent of competitiveness as when we were in tents.'

Cosiness is a relative concept, for the temperature in the snow hole was −10°C, but there was no wind, no flapping and banging of tent material with the constant threat of one's shelter being torn to bits. It is silent within a snow cave, no hint of storm or sun outside. We stuffed the entrance with our empty rucksacks, leaving a narrow space at the top for air, but by morning it was blocked by spindrift. As usual I was the first out, driven on this occasion by a full bladder. It was another cloudless day with a brilliant blazing sun, but out of that sky came tearing an icy, clutching, pounding wind, that bit at the face, tore at the clothes and pummelled the senses. I fled back into the cave and gave a weather report. But what to do? Pete wanted to press on at all costs, noting in his diary:

An early morning of prevarications and too much talking. We should take our sacks, move on, dig in. But Chris and Joe, unnerved by their no meal on the mid-crest camp, now fussing about weakness and vulnerability due to cold and lack of food. It might be windy, yet this weather is the most settled from the sky signs that we have ever had. Good weather inevitably means strong north winds blowing from Central Asia.

Joe and I were worried by our low intake of food, and even more so by the little we had left – only three main meals and two cylinders of Gaz. We were now a long way from

RIGHT] *Dropping down to the col below Junction Peak.*

home with a 150-metre climb back over Junction Peak before we could start down, either by a completely unknown route, which we would never find in bad weather, or the way we had climbed up, which we knew would be both difficult and dangerous to descend. Looking at the route ahead it seemed by no means certain that we would find either sufficient snow to dig caves or platforms for the tents. It seemed fairly unlikely that a tent would stand in this kind of wind anyway. We argued round the subject and eventually decided to make a dash for the summit from the cave, travelling without rucksacks in the hope that the going would be easier than it looked. But it was getting late already; it was eleven o'clock in the morning, with sunset at around 9 p.m. – just ten hours to climb at least 600 metres of difficult, unknown ridge.

Joe and I were first away, cramponing across the wind-polished ice of the col and climbing up a short snow wall that led to the crest of the knife-edged ridge. The snow was hard packed but, most important of all, the wind now dropped; we were in the lee of the summit pyramid. At first we traversed below the crest, on increasingly steep slopes of hard snow. This was fun; it was real climbing. The slope fell away giddily beneath our feet to a snow shelf networked with lurking crevasses, about 3,000 metres below; then beyond that another drop to the glacier about 3,000 metres lower.

A gully led up towards the crest. My turn to lead. This was front-pointing territory, ice picks digging in reassuringly as I kicked upwards, stopping just short of the crest where the snow began to deteriorate. Joe moved through, traversing just below the wafer-thin top on frightening, sugary snow that had no substance. We moved one at a time, sharing the lead, running out the full length of the rope, round rocky projections, over small ice towers and cornices. It was intriguing progress. Fatigue vanished in the fascination of finding a way and the tension of constant risk. An easy whaleback of snow led to the first serious obstacle, a fang of rock that barred the ridge. Joe was belayed at its foot.

'Do you want me to lead it?' he asked; a gesture which was in no way condescending for we had reached an easy relationship based on mutual respect and a real liking for each other. I was frightened by what I saw, but a combination of pride and even more a desire to share fully in our effort forced me on.

'No, it's O.K., I'll have a go at it.'

I collected pitons and slings and pulled up on to the sheer rock wall. There were big shelf-like holds for my mitted hands and clumsy cramponed feet; fear bubbled within me, as I glanced across and down steep rocks to snow slopes that plunged to the glacier thousands of metres below. I was now on the north side of the ridge, and I tried to escape the steepness by traversing on to rocky slabs but there were no holds, no cracks in which to hammer a piton. I was forced back on to the arête, steep and dizzy, but a metre above was a rocky spike, a haven on which to focus, to put a sling on, and reduce the frightening potential of a fall. Gain a bit more height, another peg runner and I could traverse across the wall steeply, but on good holds, into a little scoop.

ABOVE RIGHT] *Al crossing Junction Peak, with Chris and Joe behind on the Notch.*
BELOW RIGHT] *Crossing Junction Peak, Al and Pete ahead, Chris following.*

OVERLEAF LEFT] *On the knife-edged ridge, Al with Chris and Joe on the rock gendarme behind.*
RIGHT] *Chris climbing the rock gendarme, belayed by Joe.*

I was now six metres from my last runner, with no positive holds, just bridged across delicately. It would be serious if I fell but fear had fled, driven out by concentration and the joy of climbing. A little shelf, led awkwardly towards the top of the gendarme and I put in another piton runner. A few more metres and I'd belayed. I knew a pleasure and delight I had hardly experienced up to then on the climb. Until that moment I had been struggling to keep up, had taken a passive rôle, even when leading on comparatively easy ground, but now I'd stretched myself to my own limit, and basked in Joe's muttered approval as he joined me on the stance.

It didn't even matter much when I found that the lead was for naught. Joe climbed a few more metres to the edge of the pinnacle, peered over the top and called back, 'We'll have to go back and find a way round the bottom. There's a bloody great drop here.'

And so we returned; tensely reversing our route while Al dropped down and round, finding a good traversing line at the top of the frighteningly steep snow slope at the foot of the pinnacle. By the time we caught them up, they had reached a col just beyond the gendarme that I had climbed, but short of our next obstacle. Pete was already half way up it, picking his way confidently over sugary snow lying upon shaley rock that had the texture and substance of sand. He vanished round a small buttress and soon the rope was pulling at Al, who shouted that it there was no more, it was fully run out. But Pete could not hear and kept on pulling. Was he belayed or was he still climbing? The most difficult and precarious moves were at the beginning. If Al slipped, would he have pulled Pete with him? He yelled again but there was no reply, just the insistent tug of the rope. He set out, cursing, and I followed just a few metres behind, belayed by Joe who had tied himself to a crumbling bollard of yellow schist. At least I had a trail to follow.

It was easier than the rock gendarme but much more frightening. There was nothing to hold on to if you slipped and I was uncomfortably aware of the consequences of even a short fall. A broken ankle would have been desperately serious so far from base.

Joe and I caught up with the other pair of the top of the gendarme. This was the last one before the summit pyramid, but the day had now fled away. It was late afternoon, with no chance of reaching the top. The pyramid, grossly foreshortened, looked grim and threatening, with buttresses of black rock veined in snow; but at its foot there was a snow gully.

'You could get a snow cave there,' said Pete.

'If there's enough snow,' I replied.

'There's sure to be. It'll have collected everything from the rocks above. We could go for it tomorrow. Hell of a pity we didn't bring our sacks along today.'

None of us replied. It was time to get back anyway. The return went quickly; familiarity breeds confidence. We kept the rope on but climbed together, perfecting the route, found short cuts where possible, were even able to rest on the col and absorb the magnificent view to north and south of desert and snow peaks bathed in the warm yellow of the late afternoon sun. That night we did not speak much of future plans but Pete had set his alarm watch early and was the first to wake and clear the entrance of the snow

ABOVE LEFT] *Returning along the knife-edged ridge with Junction Peak in the background.*
BELOW LEFT] *Chris climbing the second rock gendarme.*

145

hole. He reported that there was no cloud though there was still a lot of wind, and then the discussion, at times acrimonious, began. It slid around, shooting off at tangents; Pete wanted to press on, Joe, Al and I were less certain. I felt that we were short of food and, even more seriously, short of fuel, but here there was a disparity. Pete and Al had three Gaz cylinders left, Joe and I only had two. Pete felt that we had been extravagant in our use, whilst he and Al had conserved their fuel throughout. I was undoubtedly defensive, both because I was counselling caution and also because I felt guilty at having used too much fuel. As a result I was aggressive, accusing Pete of being sanctimonious. This set the argument off at a tangent and ended with me apologising for losing my temper.

Pete noted:

Raw opinions and arguments and some insults. If only we knew where the summit of this mountain is – if it is the top of the pyramid (which seems the most likely) or the next top, or the next, we have to be prepared for so much. Yet I feel that Joe, and perhaps Chris, just can't say what they mean.

Last night I felt full of bounding optimism, but now I feel that hope gradually eroded, deflated; I don't think the food has been that bad, that meagre, but Joe and Chris say they are very much weakened and Joe has felt vulnerable and drained by the cold and inadequately clothed against it. Joe, it emerges, and Chris want to go down and so does Al, so there is little that I can say.

Outside the spindrift blows a mad maypole first in one direction then another; it doesn't look possible to make much progress this morning; it would be a waiting game. And yet are we over-estimating the difficulty of the final pyramid? Surely, beyond our high point yesterday, there is just a ninety-metre or so step and then it's a Crib Goch spur upwards, broad and mixed to the top, or supposed top?

If all four of us had a different attitude, would this be a different story? Chris is older, though not wiser! Yet he's a friend and we are not waging war on the mountain. I tell Joe he is being negative and he resents this a little and uses the word again and again, picking it up as I intended and as is his habit, in a circumambulatory way, even dragging in my guiding technical pretensions.

Joe saw the argument differently, writing:

The answer seems obvious to me – go down. A suggestion about going down germinates and Pete, predictably, counters it. He wants to go on. I try not to say too much in these situations. I feel that I put so firm an argument that it engenders instinctive opposition, so I let it work itself towards the end I think best.

Finally I tell Pete that I resent the charge that I only produce negative arguments and he rounds on me with, 'That one word really upsets you,' and changed it to 'reactive arguments'. I told him that he seems keen as a guide to criticise other people's knots and belays but shows little mountain sense or estimation/appreciation of the people he is with.

And so the argument went on and through it, I believe we reached the right decision. We were still physically fit with a reasonable reserve of endurance, but our shortage of supplies made us vulnerable to a change in the weather. Had we been caught in a bad storm, retreat would have been very difficult, perhaps impossible, yet we had barely enough to sit it out. I felt that in going down for more supplies we could return to our high point very much stronger than we were now. Selfishly perhaps, I also knew that it was unlikely that I would bounce back sufficiently fast if we made an abortive attempt and were then forced to retreat. Pete finally resigned himself to agreeing with us. Although the discussion was fierce at times, the respect and real affection we had for each other was not eroded. This in many ways was the beauty of the size of our team and the style in which we were climbing, that the argument could be aired and that a consensus could eventually be reached.

We set out on the return at about ten in the morning, starting with the exhausting plod of 150 metres back up Junction Peak. From the top there was no doubt about the route. The way down the main ridge line towards Kongur Tiube was like a broad high road. The snow was firm, hardened by wind and a few days' fine weather, and we were able to stride across the broad shoulder leading from Junction Peak and then down a steep bluff which eventually led to the col, the lowest point between Kongur and Kongur Tiube. A long traverse led from this through deep, exhausting snow, to the crest of the arête we had climbed so many days before. We passed the marker wands we had left to locate the snow holes we had dug in that night of panic, and then plunged on, down and down the long easy rib.

As we neared the bottom we saw a tiny figure leave Advance Base Camp and come to greet us, no doubt expecting to hear of success. After all the weather had been perfect for the last three days. They could know nothing of the driving wind and bitter cold of the high mountain ridges. We had been out of sight, out of touch. As we came closer we could see it was Michael Ward. We all felt guilty, dreaded having to break the news to him.

'Go on Chris, you're climbing leader. You'd better justify your title. You tell him,' someone said.

And I did. Neither Michael's face nor voice registered any disappointment and he immediately asked for all details. We told him as we walked that last few metres back to Advance Base, where Jim was waiting to film the conquering heroes on their return. It was now getting late. It had been a long, hard day, and so we stayed the night in the camp, returning to Base the next day.

The following morning, the cloud had rolled in and once again it was grim and grey. As it happened we had made the right decision. Better be down here in the Koksel Basin a short easy walk from Base Camp than high on the summit pyramid of Kongur.

Back at Base Camp David Wilson, Jim Curran and the scientists had not been idle.

Michael has the next chapter to describe what was going on.

13
Eggheads and superstars
by Michael Ward

Most men would prefer to share their sleeping bags with their wives or girlfriends. On an expedition this is rarely possible and other occupants may be boots, a stove, water bottle and food. With scientists however the priorities can be different, and so it was on Kongur, as Edward Williams, that practical perfectionist, shared his sleeping bag with a test tube of blood. The reason was simple. We wanted to find out if the prolonged decreased pressure of altitude caused a change in the shape and therefore the properties of the red cells. These cells were preserved in a special fluid that under no circumstances should be allowed to freeze, so he carried the tube with him all the time, as the human body was the only constant source of heat, watching over it like an anxious mother with a delicate baby until the cells were safely examined in the United Kingdom by electron-microscopy.

The addition of a major scientific project to any mountain expedition increases the work load fourfold and imposes its own disciplines and tensions. This adds to both the interest and the difficulties, particularly when the members of the party are each of a single-minded disposition and well used to individual authority. To complicate matters, each man's obsession was a little different.

The ascent of any mountain over 7,600 metres imposes a physiological 'experiment' of a subtle complexity on the participants, of which they become aware only with the onset of illness. Prolonged exercise following a quick ascent to altitude produces many changes and these we wanted to study, using new techniques. Most important, we wanted a group of super-fit climbers, able to work at the most taxing attainable levels. The exploration and ascent of Kongur was conceived as two parallel and complementary projects needing an unusually ordered structure, precise advance planning and complete co-operation.

Each stage dealt with a different stress factor. First there was the rapid ascent in hours, and without any exercise, from 1,200 metres at Kashgar to the Pamir plateau. This sudden exposure is common now to many trekking parties and it would be an excellent period in which to assess hormonal changes governing blood function and fluid shift. It meant that within one hour of arriving at the Karakol Lakes we had to be able to take blood, centrifuge it, and put the plasma in the cryostat. Over the next few days a daily questionnaire about symptoms had to be filled in and further blood taken.

The next phase was the jump in altitude to Base Camp. Only on this occasion we would be taking exercise. From Base Camp, parties ascended to increasing altitude for a few days and then returned. Our original plan had been to use this acclimatisation period for a thorough exploration of the surrounding peaks. But the best route on Kongur itself had proved difficult to assess, so this time was spent on the problem of the route. Throughout this period serial exercise tests, hormonal estimations and other investigations were carried out.

After what we hoped would be a successful ascent we would descend in perhaps three days or less from Base Camp to Kashgar. All the mechanisms switched on by exercise and altitude would be turned off rapidly and we would monitor these.

Three stages of this progress would be well controlled – the ascent to the Pamir plateau, the ascent to Base Camp, and the descent from Base Camp to Kashgar. The six week period at and above Base would be much more flexible. At one time I had thought of carrying out studies in the Koksel Basin, but after a lot of discussion we decided to make no attempt at any scientific work here, and were very glad. One pitfall is to try and do too much with the result that not everything is done thoroughly. Another point was the weather. In the basin this could stop work at some vital period. At Base Camp we could still continue despite bad weather, and our facilities there would ensure the best calibre of work. Finally, because the route on Kongur was still uncertain, the combination of science and mountaineering above Base Camp could easily lead to stress and conflict, as the Koksel Basin was too high for a real rest.

The exercise tests were the most complicated and time consuming of all our work. In practical terms what this meant was exercising individuals at different rates (and therefore oxygen uptake) from rest to the maximum possible at different altitudes. This whole project was the responsibility of Jim Milledge. We started in the United Kingdom nine months before the expedition left for China. There were two main reasons – the first being that we had to get sea-level values and at the same time the technique had to be honed to as near perfection as possible. The second factor was that it would bring the members of the party together and enable them to understand the reasons for the extra labour, and it would make them familiar with the technique. The natural competitive instinct ensured that each member of the team co-operated to the full. Each experiment lasted between one and a half and two hours, and involved a series of fairly complex actions. If for any reason a reading was not made correctly, a tap not turned at the exact moment, a stop watch inaccurately read, or the subject failed to co-operate, the whole morning and afternoon's work would be wasted. Three people, one subject and two experimenters, would be very fed-up. We did, in fact, do many trial runs on ourselves before asking any of the four climbers to take part.

At Base Camp Charlie Clarke took retinal photographs. This was done in a darkened tent. A dye, fluorescein, was injected into an arm vein and any leakage from the retinal vessels could be photographed. This investigation also started months before hand at St. Bartholomew's Hospital. It required great patience and co-operation on the part of subject and investigator.

In some of the blood tests and the exercise studies we could get answers within a day or so. This raised our spirits immensely. It was very much harder for Edward Williams who was masterminding the hormonal work without having any idea of what results he was getting. The serum disappeared into the cryostat to emerge as a set of figures six months later in the United Kingdom. Because any errors that emerged could not be corrected, all this work had to be extraordinarily meticulous.

Perhaps the man best equipped to understand the stress Edward worked under was our cameraman, Jim Curran, who, in his very different field, shared exactly the same problem – the need to produce top quality professional work under the most difficult conditions with no margin for error.

The social centre of Base Camp was a simply vast tent in which we ate and talked. Its erection nearly defeated the considerable mathematical, scientific, business and moun-taineering expertise at our disposal, and took most of one day. Even now I am not certain that it was put up correctly, and it had to have ropes run over the top to keep it from flying all over Asia. Also bits did collapse in the heavy snowfalls. We also had a scientific tent and a cook tent into which no one except Wang was usually allowed. The Chinese also had a smaller mess tent which seemed more stable than ours.

We each had individual living tents and, of course, tables and chairs. All this was a necessity not a luxury, as it is impossible to produce work of calibre without being reasonably comfortable. We worked by the sun, and very often snow and wind delayed our start. However the snow would thaw and by the time it had all would have been arranged for an exercise test. This was conducted in the open near the science tent. It meant stepping on and off a step of measured height at a rate set by a metronome, and breathing into a bag whilst connected to an ECG machine that measured heart rate. Often part of the procedure was carried out in a snow storm. Luckily snow did not affect any of the apparatus and melted on the subject's body. The real difficulty was the chemi-cals used for the analysis of oxygen and carbon dioxide in the Scholander apparatus that had been carried lovingly and carefully by Jim Milledge from Northwick Park. The scientific tent in which he carried out this painstaking, finicky and essential analysis had to be well heated and lighted. Even so, it was a considerable feat of skill and determi-nation to reproduce accurate results. It also took a long time and consumed much nervous energy. All this took place after the actual exercise had been completed, so one session would take four to five hours in all from start to finish and involve three people at least.

All subjects submitted themselves on an entirely voluntary basis, and if they felt too tired they postponed the session. Towards the end, we let people work maximally under their own compulsion rather than against a metronome, and we got higher rates of work by this method. This is because we were all very familiar with judging our own physical performance. Most mountaineers have a very good idea of how long they can work at, say, making steps in knee-deep snow. They know they can always do eighteen steps, sometimes nineteen, occasionally twenty, but never twenty-one at a stretch.

Most of the apparatus had to have some repairs carried out and Jim and Edward were most expert. The generators were our source of power and they worked sturdily through snow, wind and cold, needing only occasional care. My memories are of Edward seated quietly on a box in the snow, his face frozen partly in concentration and partly by the wind, his beard snow-flecked. Whirring in front of him is the centrifuge and on one side the humming generator. At his back is the genie's bottle. The cork is removed and out pops a foaming spectre of liquid nitrogen fumes assuming a hideous shape. In goes the tube of serum and on goes the cork and the genie is back in his frozen home.

Jim wore a hat with its peak sometimes forward, sometimes aft and often askew. His main problem was the Scholander which really did need the gentle touch. Encased in a bath of water, the entwined tubes of glass containing mercury and other ingredients were shaken gently by a motor. The meniscus rose and fell, but not always correctly. Then Jim would try again. All was delicacy and finesse until the results were reproducible.

Charlie communed a lot with his retinal camera in a darkened tent, the occasional blinding flash lightening the gloom. The dye injected into our veins emerged as fluoresent greeny yellow urine and added an odd touch of colour.

My own preoccupation was seeing that everything worked and everyone was happy. I knew that we had within our grasp a great prize and not just in climbing a peak. But the weather and the complexity of the Kongur massif were very taxing. It was really a question of persistent application. Another worrying factor was the health of Liu Dayi. He had abdominal pain for a long period and there was a slight possibility that surgery might be needed. Luckily all passed off, but I felt for a period that I should not be away too long from Base Camp.

Our reading ranged from Leslie Charteris to Kenneth Clarke on Leonardo da Vinci, and Jeffrey Archer. One author whose mood and tempo seemed to suit me was le Carré. It takes me time to go forwards and backwards with his characters, to remember the nuances and to see how he weaves his intricate plots.

We could cover a lot of country by carrying a tent one day's march beyond Base Camp and some of us took the opportunity to climb a number of small surrounding peaks. Sarala Peak to the south of Sarakyaguqi Peak (climbed by Chris and Al on the reconnaissance) repulsed Charlie, Jim, Edward and David Wilson at the first attempt with some really filthy weather. However David and Jim climbed it on 14th June and had reasonable views of the country to the south and east and a jumble of unknown peaks and glaciers. One of the summits of the Rognon Peak above Base Camp and of Toothed Peak beside the Corridor were also climbed.

During the first attempt on the summit of Kongur Jim Curran and I were at Advance Base Camp in the Koksel Basin. We saw the party climbing up into the clouds on the South Ridge. I knew the mental strain of being cut off by a mountain from base, but also the calibre of the members of the team. What worried me more was that neither Chris nor Al were completely fit, in that they had lost stamina through illness. However, when they returned, driven back by the weather and the obvious difficulty of the summit pyramid, though they were tired, no one was physically or mentally worn out. In fact they seemed to me to be annoyed more than anything else. At Base Camp they could rest and recuperate properly. Joe and Pete even managed to do exercise studies.

Charlie Clarke now discovered that whenever he went above a certain altitude he suffered from a splitting headache and vomiting. Probably he had developed an intolerance to altitude, which has been recorded very rarely. Because of this he did a major part of the plant collecting.

The Herbarium at the Royal Botanic Gardens, Kew, had no specimens from this part of Central Asia, so I had promised the director, Professor Patrick Brenan, that we would obtain as many as possible. None of us could claim to be in any way even an amateur botanist, but we were given a pamphlet of easy instruction, field note books and presses.

It was extremely rewarding. Once we started really looking for flowers, lichens, grass or moss, it was surprising how often we found them. A superficial glance would reveal nothing except sand, stone and bare multicoloured rocks, yet tucked away in minute moisture-containing niches we would find a flower. We even found a water weed lying on a brackish pool left by the melting snow. Inevitably we came to recognise the common flowers. Walking with eyes directed to the ground is usual in mountains, and it gave us great pleasure to recognise our old favourites, and to discover new ones. The passage of weeks also enabled us to recognise the slight warmth of summer which made our surroundings much greener. Certain moraine hollows near water were luxuriant with grass and flowers. Yet a few inches away all was desert dust and bare stones.

Every morning a group of ram chukor swooped across the camp soon after the sun rose, uttering their characteristic cry. A number of other birds boldly visited our tents, and on the Karakol Lakes, which may well be a staging post on a migration route between Central Asia and the Indian sub-continent, we saw an even greater variety.

Far from being a barren waste, the Pamir plateau seemed to support a considerable variety of plant life, which would be more abundant if there was better irrigation and the winters were not so harsh. In addition, the nomads' flocks eat every young green shoot.

The weather was totally unpredictable. In most mountains there is usually some sort of pattern. Here we could find none other than learning to expect the unexpectedly virulent on every occasion, and then be thankful that it was no worse. Perhaps the closeness of the Taklamakan desert and the high peaks on the edge of the Central Asia plateau had something to do with this. The weather dominated everything we did. Kongur seemed to produce its own brand, the clouds sitting on it like a cap and enveloping the whole massif.

So it was with hope, but no certainty of success that we watched the climbing party set off on 4th July. When we saw them next they would have much to tell.

Chris takes up the story again.

RIGHT] *Joe in foreground, and Al and Pete beyond, hunting for the entrances to our former snow caves.*

14

A long plod

4TH–8TH JULY 1981

We had just three days at Base Camp, eating prodigious Chinese meals served by Wang, who worked, almost single-handed, to feed us throughout the expedition. He was one of those cooks who would barely let another into his kitchen. In this respect I think his assistant had a very easy time.

I certainly would have liked more rest. Although I had felt superbly fit on our return – we made it from our Advance Base in two and a half hours – once back in my tent, the stress and fatigue of the past week took their toll and I felt listless and washed out. Then there were the scientific tests; I did not mind giving blood for I could lie down while doing that, but I was not prepared to undergo the more extreme exercise tests. I had a slight cough, but beyond that I felt that I was going to need every tiny bit of energy and strength that I had for our final attempt. I was a miser, conserving the last farthing of my meagre resources. Al, who had a very bad chest cough, felt the same way, though Joe and Pete, more richly endowed in stamina, went through the full régime.

There was no question of delay, for not only was the season beginning to run out, but we were soon to be faced by competition from the Japanese expedition who were to attempt Kongur from the north. We knew they had permission to move into their Base Camp at the foot of the north side of the mountain on 14th July, but they had been in the area for nearly as long as us, climbing on Mustagh Ata to gain acclimatisation. The day after we returned to Base, David Wilson and Charlie Clarke, who had gone down to the river to sort out the ferry, came back with news that the Japanese had climbed Mustagh Ata and were on their way round to the north. We certainly had to get back on the mountain as quickly as possible. We had already learnt just how unreliable the weather was and how difficult that final pyramid might be.

We left Base Camp on 4th July. Jim Milledge and David Wilson had agreed to help us on our first day out of the Koksel Basin, carrying part of the load we were taking back up the mountain. We had left as much as possible in the top snow cave and, as a result, were planning this time to take a full ten days' supply of food with ample Gaz cylinders so that we could sit out any bad weather before launching our attempt on the final pyramid.

Our three days' rest had been marked by cloud-filled skies. There had even been a dusting of snow at Base Camp, a sure sign that we were in the right place. Perhaps we had at last got in phase with the weather, for the morning of the 4th dawned fine, and the 5th was a perfect cloudless day. Michael Ward and Edward Williams had gone out a day

ABOVE LEFT] *Looking out of the snow cave at the summit pyramid.*
BELOW LEFT] *Inside the snow cave below Junction Peak.*

PREVIOUS PAGE] *Pete and Joe breaking trail towards Junction Peak.*

ahead to rescue the gear, including our ski sticks, that we had left on the Koksel Col when we had set out on the South Ridge.

This time we were going to return by the South-West Rib which we had reconnoitred two weeks before and descended after our first attempt. Our decision, though, was not unanimous. Joe still clung to the South Ridge route as being more direct and safe, but once again the democratic process worked and we talked it round until he agreed to go along with the majority.

But a lot of snow had fallen in those three days. The Koksel Glacier and the crest of the ridge were covered in a thick mantle of fresh snow, that made trail-breaking even more exhausting than in the past. All four of us took turns out in front, arriving at an agreement that we each broke trail past two of the marker wands we had left on the route. There was an element of chance in this since they were not set at even intervals.

Pete, Joe and I were using ski poles, finding them a great help both in the way you could build up a slow rhythm in which arms were sharing the work with legs, and also because

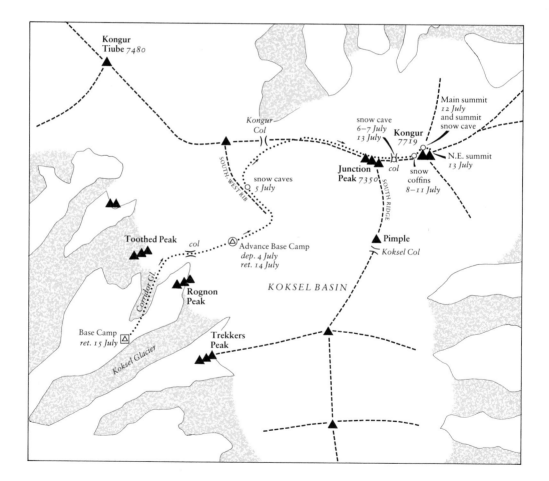

when resting you could sag on to them. Al had never tried them. He seemed to be against them in principle, feeling they were extra, not strictly necessary items of equipment to be taken up the mountain; that everything must be pared down to the bare minimum for an alpine-style push. But I had come to like my ski poles, and sagged on them every few steps to steal a rest.

And the slope seemed endless, longer, if that were possible, than it had been the first time we went up. We were hoping to get all the way to the col on the crest of the ridge, and then the next day cross Junction Peak and return to the snow cave. Jim Milledge and David Wilson came with us for about 600 metres, but the strain was beginning to tell on Jim and he decided it was time to return. David seemed to be going as strongly as any of us – better than me, I couldn't help thinking, wryly. Perhaps it's he that should be going for the top.

We shared their load out amongst us and sacks that had felt heavy before, now felt unbearable. We were probably carrying about sixteen kilos each. And the plod went on. My turn to be out in front. Fifty steps at a time. I counted them, each time my right foot sank into the soft, clogging snow. I managed the first fifty, paused for a rest, leaning on my sticks, the others waiting patiently just behind; then another effort; I only managed forty-eight that time; I glanced up and the marker wand with its tiny flag seemed no closer, and so it went on, a grinding monotonous agony.

'I'm never going to make it back to the snow cave; I'll end up being a burden on the others,' I muttered to myself, something I hated the thought of. I turned to Pete as he came up to take over the trail-breaking.

'Look Pete. If you think I'm going to hold you up, I don't mind going back now.'

'Don't be bloody stupid. You'll be all right. You're not holding us back anyway. It's good to have a bit of rest at times.'

And I kept going, ashamed of my weakness, but immensely heartened by the warmth of Pete's response. It was four o'clock in the afternoon when we reached the shoulder in which we had dug our snow caves on our early reconnaissance. The marker flags were still in place indicating where the entrances were meant to be. I had been thinking for some time of our plan to reach the col. I knew that I was getting near my own limit, but beyond that, straight logic seemed in favour of stopping at caves we had already dug rather than going on for a further four or five hours through deep snow, and then having to dig a fresh cave late into the night.

I put my case. Predictably, Pete was in favour of pushing on to the col, feeling that if the weather did break during the night, the slope in front of us was probably the most dangerous of all, and that therefore we might not be able to cross it. Once on the col, however, we should be able to get back over Junction Peak in almost any conditions and sit out any bad weather there. It was a perfect evening, however, and it seemed unlikely, even on Kongur, that the weather was going to break that night. Joe agreed with me and, as so often happened, the decision was reached not so much by agreement as inertia. We began to unpack and scratch around in search of the entrances to our snow holes.

Pete and Al found theirs quickly, but it was some time before Joe and I did. It's quite amazing how elusive a cave can be, even when it is marked by a wand. When we did find ours, there was still some work to be done, for the roof had sunk in the preceding three weeks and needed digging out. Nonetheless, there was considerably less work than there would have been had we started from scratch.

Joe and I had settled into being a closeknit team. Pete noticed this, commenting in his diary: 'I think Chris is just a little scared of Joe. Certainly, I've never heard him use "the tone" with him.'

'The tone' to which Pete refers is my tendency to get autocratic every now and then, particularly in the early mornings, when I can be very self-righteous. I certainly never used this with Joe, but I don't think it was so much a matter of being afraid as the case of the partnership that had developed over the climb.

Joe and I woke first the next morning and were away in front of the others. As usual I started off strongly, but on this occasion, determined to husband my resources, we agreed that Joe should break trail for two hundred paces at a time to my hundred. We had been going for an hour or so before I noticed that I seemed to be covering as much ground out in front as he was.

'How do you count your paces?' I asked.

'Each time my foot touches the ground of course,' was the reply.

I couldn't help laughing. I'd been counting mine every time my left foot sank into the snow and so we had been doing exactly the same amount of work. In a funny kind of way it was a fillip to my ego, but one for which I was to pay a high price later on. The others caught up after a couple of hours and took over in front. The snow was much deeper than when we had come down a few days before and we were sinking up to our thighs at almost every step.

We reached the col at around 12.30, had a brew and something to eat and then set out once again. Pete described me subsequently as a 'four hour rocket', and there was quite a lot of truth in this. I had gone well for the first four hours, but now was definitely beginning to flag. Pete and Al, with Pete doing most of the trail-breaking, were out in front, followed by Joe and me. The route that had seemed so quick and easy on the way down, now seemed interminable. The weather also was beginning to change. Clouds appeared from the blank blue sky, settled on the ridge above us, spread over the peaks to the south, and then engulfed us in a driving swirl of windswept snow.

We plodded on through the near white-out, climbing the steep step in the ridge, and then on to another. My own fatigue sapped my will and, as I caught up with the others on the crest of one of the slopes, I slumped into the snow and told them that I thought I had gone far enough for the day, suggesting that we broke the journey up into three days instead of two, and that we'd all be so tired the next day we'd need to rest anyway. But this was the wrong suggestion and it was Pete who encouraged me into keeping going, telling me that we were very nearly there, and that we didn't want to have to dig yet another snow hole.

So we carried on in the tearing wind, Pete out in front, picking a route, peering into the driving snow, trying to interpret the dark shape of rocks on the crest of the broad-backed ridge. He had to take responsibility for the constant risk of cornice or avalanche, while we plodded behind him, taking his judgment for granted. I was walking in a daze of fatigue, regretting my momentary weakness, now determined to keep going somehow, and through this getting a second wind. We passed a marker wand, only just protruding from the snow. We were on route. A short way beyond we reached a conspicuous tooth of black rock which we had named the 'Matterhorn' on the way down. We now knew

On the shoulder of Junction Peak, Joe and Chris, seated, take a rest in the blizzard.

exactly where were were. It was Al who suggested that we should change partners. Wracked by coughing, he was going as badly as I, and had done very little trail-breaking on the way up. Pete, as a result, was beginning to show the strain of being constantly in front.

As they set out on a general compass bearing across the broad shoulder that we knew led to the summit of Junction Peak, the wind tore a gap in the clouds and the summit pyramid of Kongur, from this angle a perfect triangle of snow-plastered rock, came into view. It looked very remote and was quickly veiled once again. Like a will o' the wisp, it was tempting us from the safest route; it seemed so easy to strike across towards where the col and snow cave must be, but this would have taken us over crevasse-strewn, avalanche-prone slopes. We had no choice but to climb Junction Peak, a weary 152 metres of ascent, before we could drop down on the other side to the haven of the snow hole.

Although they were breaking trail, Pete and Joe were going faster than Al and I. They vanished and then reappeared in the swirling cloud; their tracks were being blown over already. All we had to do was keep them in sight, but they had to find the route. Pete wrote:

It's not that far away, but this is proving to be a hell of a day. I'm looking hard for a submerged marker flag. See a black crease in the snow, and walk towards it. Black rocks and cloud below me. I'm standing on the cornice above the South Face! Quickly shout to Joe and step back. And then see, much lower down, the flag that marks the point where we can descend to the snow cave col.

Joe and I traverse right, looking for wind creased snow, which will be safer. It's a relief to reach the rocks just above the snow cave. And yes, the flags are over there. It's 9.00 p.m. and I shovel away the spindrift that has built up over the entrance. On a quick inspection the snow cave seems intact.

Al and I reached it about twenty minutes later. We were soon all crammed inside in a confusion of part unpacked rucksacks, loose snow, the foam mats on which we would sleep and a clutter of food, some left from our previous effort and some brought up freshly. We were all tired, but relieved and content that we had made it to the snow cave with enough food and fuel to sit out a storm and still have a reasonable chance of going for the summit.

Our rations had also been improved in one very important respect. This time we had brought with us some packets of spices, chilli and garlic powder plus some fresh onions. The bland dehydrated food well laced with chillis became quite palatable and the fire of the spices was even warming. That night we did not discuss any plans for the morrow, we were too tired, but I certainly was praying for one day of bad weather so that we could have a rest.

Pete commented in his diary:

At least we've passed all those potential avalanche slopes and are stuck up here until our adventure has gone one way or another. Come to slowly, with Chris waking us up as usual at 7.00 a.m. Somehow Chris always seems to be the first to suggest staying; Joe doesn't ever need much persuading and Al says he doesn't mind either way, but in a way that isn't convincing since he seems so ill.

Chris has pronounced it a bad day, but when I crawl out to have a look, it doesn't seem that bad to me. I wonder if Joe was like that on Everest – determined but quiet, when right at the end, his silence became his undoing and he found himself almost on his own, because the others had found little encouragement or optimism expressed to spur them on. Al has said he thinks Joe inhuman. But whatever the case, neither Joe nor Al look out this morning; they seem to think that my opinion and Chris's – two poles – are enough.

Perhaps I'm being the devil's advocate, always pushing to go forward, particularly when confronted with arguments to slow down. Would I really be that capable, if some one took me up on the challenge? But it is, after all, a rest day and who knows what it would have been like out there, since we never left? And inside here, a tomb-like quiet, with no knowledge of what's going on outside.

Once again, we reached a compromise decision, which I think was probably for the best. It certainly was from my point of view, and I suspect might have been for all of us, even Pete. We spent the rest of the day brewing up, chatting and also deciding on plans for the summit push. Pete was convinced that there was enough snow in the gully at the foot of the summit pyramid to dig a cave, and was in favour of abandoning the tents, heading for it the following day and then going for the summit, hoping to get another snow cave near the top where undoubtedly there was more snow. I was not convinced that there was going to be enough snow in the gully and mooted the possibility of taking tents to the end of the ridge. After some discussion I gave in quite quickly, relishing the idea of carrying the extra weight no more than the others. We were going to take with us four days' food, the bare minimum of climbing gear and rely on moving fairly quickly.

I was still worried, however, about the gully and, jokingly, the morning that we set off for the summit, recorded an interview with Pete:

CHRIS *It's the morning of the 8th July. Pete, am I right in assuming that you are staking your entire mountaineering reputation on the fact there's going to be a snow hole in the gully at the end of the long ridge? Mr. Boardman, can we have your comments.*

PETE *There is a precedent which is when Shackleton crossed South Georgia. He could not be certain if there was a route across, but he came out all right in the end. There comes a time in a climber's life when you have to take chances, have to go for it; leave the tents, take a shovel, and* HOPE . . .

CHRIS *But Shackleton had no choice and we have.*

15
Snow coffins

It was very different from the last time. Deep snow plastered the knife-edged ridge that led to the foot of the summit pyramid. Joe went first, ploughing through the deep snow just below the crest of the ridge. He commented:

It was the most gripping lead I did on the entire climb. It wasn't difficult ground but it was really worrying and dangerous in the context of avalanche. I was wading through waist-deep snow and it took me about an hour to go three hundred feet. I had to stamp down every step before I dared put my weight on it. I was quite frightened but thought 'Chris is belaying me; he's on the ridge and can always jump down the other side if the slope avalanches away.'

I just kept on going and I suppose it was because I was so exhausted that I didn't look back and just focused my attention on keeping going. I thought the rope was getting longer and longer, but even so it was a shock when I looked back and saw that Chris was walking along behind me in my track and that if the slope had gone, then both of us would have gone with it. There would have been no question of a rescue.

He came to the foot of the first step in the ridge and found a secure belay at last on a rocky spike protruding from the snow. I led through, up some rocks covered in snow and then across another snow slope. I couldn't get too close to the crest for it was corniced, and yet the slope I was on, was both steep and terrifyingly insubstantial. No matter how much snow I dug away, there seemed to be no solid bottom to it. It was like a great mass of candyfloss, as much air as substance. I struggled up to a notch in the ridge, poked my axe into the snow and looked down through the hole I had made to the glacier some three miles below on the north side. But I had to pull myself up on to the lip of the cornice. The snow here was at least more solid than the slope beneath. If it did collapse Joe should be able to hold me; I would go down the other side of the ridge from where he was sitting crouched below. I tried to distribute my weight as widely as possible, kneeling on the snow, shuffling gently along and at last I reached a rock, hauled up on it, and slumped down the other side. I pulled in the rope and Joe came up and led through. We moved slowly, cautiously one at a time along the ridge. We were even slower than we had been the previous occasion, for not only was it very much more dangerous with its jacket of fresh snow, but we were now heavily laden with our four days' food, sleeping bags and spare clothes.

RIGHT] *Deep snow plastered the knife-edged ridge that leads to the foot of the summit pyramid.*

OVERLEAF LEFT] *Chris leading through the deep snow on the knife-edged ridge, belayed by Joe.*
RIGHT] *A menacing cloud build up rolls in behind the rock gendarmes.*

Half way along the ridge we let Pete and Al move ahead and they continued past the rock gendarme, edging along the top of the snow slope where it clung to the precipitous rock. Pete managed to hammer in a couple of pitons to safeguard the traverse. Even so, it felt frighteningly precarious. The snow-clad gendarme beyond was as unpleasant as ever with loose snow lying over loose rock, but more worrying than this was the weather.

A huge wall of turbulent dark cloud was inexorably rolling over the dusty foothills from Russia, swallowing Mustagh Ata and sweeping on to Kongur Tiube, whose bulk seemed to be holding the huge wave for just a little. It was more, much more than the standard afternoon cloud and bad weather. It had a gigantic ominous majesty that surely heralded a serious storm. By the time Joe and I caught up with the other two, Pete was already in the bed of the gully where we hoped to dig a snow cave. We had brought with us one of our ski poles, stripped down to act as a probe, so that we could find the deepest bank of snow, but we hardly needed it here. Wherever we searched there was no more than a metre of soft snow before reaching ice or rock. We cast back along the ridge to see if there was enough snow for a cave in any of the cornices clinging to its crest, but were disappointed.

A drift of old snow about three metres deep is the ideal thing in which to dig a comfortable, four-man cave. In this case there seemed only one solution; to dig what were little more than tubes between the ice or rock and the surface of the snow. Pete and Al had already started digging in the middle of the gully and so Joe and I burrowed in slightly to one side and below them. All too quickly we hit ice. It is possible to dig into ice but it is a long and wearisome business, and so we spread out in each direction to dig a tube in which we could each lie. This meant carving out the snow as close to the surface as we dared. In my direction I quickly came to rock on the inside. I had no choice but to hollow out the snow towards the surface. On Joe's side there was ice rather than rock and he cut away a fair amount but even so his outer wall of snow was fairly thin. By this time it had begun to snow and flurries of spindrift were chasing down the rocks above us and pouring down the gully into our newly hollowed holes. It only took us a couple of hours to burrow out our caves. I could barely sit up in the tube that I had dug and had to be careful not to lean against the walls of snow. My head was level with the entrance which we blocked with rucksacks. It quickly became choked with spindrift and we were sealed inside. Joe's feet were just about level with my nose, his head at the end of the tube, away from the entrance. This meant that I would have to do all the cooking, but I had been doing most of it anyway.

We cooked a meal and settled down for the night. Inside there was no hint of what the weather was like outside, but when I poked a hole through the entrance the following morning, spindrift poured down through it. It was snowing and we were in cloud. There was no means of communicating with the others; we just settled down for a day's wait, hoping that the following day would bring fine weather. It was very difficult to prevent snow getting on to the sleeping bags, but in this respect we were saved by the Gore-tex material with which they were covered. Though not totally waterproof, it is certainly

ABOVE LEFT] *Joe in his ice and rock snow coffin.*
BELOW LEFT] *Study in outrage, after Pete has stepped through Chris's coffin lid.*

much better than any other material on the market and has done as much to help lightweight alpine-style attempts on high mountains as any other technical advance. The greatest problem is remaining dry in extreme circumstances. Once one's sleeping bag is soaked, body warmth and then strength drain away with an alarming speed.

Through the day, the outer walls of the snow holes slowly collapsed in upon us. It reminded me of the story by Edgar Alan Poe, where one wall of a room slowly, almost imperceptibly closes in, to crush the occupant to death. I was becoming positively neurotic about being suffocated, poking air holes through the snow with my ice axe. Joe, meanwhile, was stoically silent. He had a capacity for sleep that I envied.

Our second night in the 'coffin' was more fraught than the first. My end was in the final stages of disintegration, with the snow of the roof pressing down on my face. The atmosphere was so badly polluted by carbon dioxide that the stove would barely light and burnt with a dull glimmer. The following morning, when I peered outside, the storm was raging unabated. My own hole was now untenable and I had to resign myself to digging a new one. That meant getting dressed, packing my now damp sleeping bag away in the rucksack and crawling out into the storm, to dig a fresh hole on the other side of the one occupied by Joe.

I found Al already outside about the same business. This time I found ice and spent most of the day hacking away at it to ensure that I had a better snow cover on the outside. Joe was also enlarging his hole and we were cutting towards each other hoping to make it into a single chamber, but were thwarted by a large rock. All we could do was dig a narrow window at one side of it, through which we could communicate and pass food. This also became the kitchen with the gas stove sitting just below my feet.

The day dragged on, punctuated by the occasional brew of tea, until at last it was time for supper. We had reversed rôles and Joe was doing the cooking. It was to be beef stroganoff, the best of the dehydrated meals, suitably titivated with chilli powder and fresh onions. It smelt delicious. It was very nearly ready and my mouth was already beginning to water in anticipation. I sat up and, as I did, my feet must have eased forward, striking the stove and upsetting the pan over Joe who was lying below. His mitts, down suit and sleeping bag were covered in a sticky pulp of beef stroganoff. I was horrified, both by the loss of our supper and the appalling mess I had created, but what impressed me most of all was Joe's self-control. He did not say a thing.

But that night he wrote in his diary: 'Chris thought that I was incredibly controlled because I didn't say anything and just started clearing up. It wasn't control! I couldn't find words sufficient to express the venom I felt towards him at the time.'

We managed to salvage a quarter of a panful of the stroganoff and consoled ourselves with the fact that we were not using up too much energy. Even so the cold was beginning to bite. My clothes were damp from my excavations that morning and it took a long time to dry them out. In addition the sleeping bag was becoming progressively damper, both from the snow that inevitably spilt on to it and crept underneath it on to the Karrimat, and also from the damp clothes I was trying to dry out.

But there was one glimmer of hope. Although it was impossible to tell what was happening outside once our entrance had been sealed with spindrift, the altimeter was an indication of weather changes, for it worked on the barometric principle and therefore any seeming change in altitude indicated a change of pressure. That evening the altimeter showed a significant drop in height which denoted an increase in atmospheric pressure, which in turn should mean an improvement in the weather.

I therefore willed myself to wake before dawn, gave Joe a yell, for only he could reach the stove, and we started to brew. I delayed opening up the cave to the very last minute, for the tiniest opening led to an avalanche of spindrift, but by eight in the morning we had had a couple of brews and a cupful of muesli and were ready to start. I got fully dressed, packed my rucksack and opened up the entrance. A gust of wind-blown snow poured in, but I crawled out all the same, to find that the weather had improved. We were in deep shadow, the ridge above us denying us the sun, but there was a certain amount of blue sky overhead though the mountain tops were all covered in cloud. More serious, there was a bitter savage wind which gusted clouds of spindrift down the rocks above. There was no sign of the others' snow cave, just a uniform snow slope. I did not dare move around for fear of stepping through their roof. I shouted, and eventually, just in front of me, the snow broke away to show a cavernous hole, out of which Pete's voice wafted up, sepulchral. We talked over the situation and decided to give it another day.

I then returned to my tube to settle down to another twenty-four hours of inactivity. There was a womb-like quality about the snow slot; the complete confinement, the silence, the lack of all the conventional stimuli. There was barely anything on which the eye could focus other than the dappled patterns of light that picked out the axe strokes on the roof of the 'coffin'. Joe was out of sight, the other side of the rock, silent, no doubt asleep. We talked very little, and when we did it tended to be on the practical matters of day-to-day survival.

'How about another brew, Joe?'

'We've just had one. I'm trying to get some sleep.'

My mind wandered, lethargic, drifting from dreams of mammoth breakfasts to making pictures from the light patterns. Time slid by surprisingly easily in this limbo world.

And then came an interruption from the outer world; Pete's voice from outside, muffled, but insistent. 'You got the shovel, Chris? Shove it out will you.'

I could hear his feet crunching into the snow, getting closer to my safe little tomb and shouted out, 'Keep away from the bloody hole; I'll give you the shovel.'

But his footsteps seemed to be getting nearer and nearer. My own reactions were slowed up. I could have pushed the shovel through the snowed up entrance, and Pete would then have known where our cave was situated and got what he wanted, but somehow I never thought of that. I think I resented my peaceful isolation being disturbed and dreaded having anything to do with that cold and bitter outside world. As I shouted into the sound-absorbent snows, Pete was now nearly on top of me.

And then, crash! A boot came smashing down through the roof a few inches from my face. The snow poured in. I got a glimpse of Pete's embarrassed, concerned face, but it made little difference as I erupted with all the pent-up frustration, discomfort and fear of the past two days, hurling at Pete a string of abuse that had best remain unprinted. I followed this with the shovel that I hurled out of the hole . . . and then as always, chastened by my loss of control and relieved no doubt by the tension I had released, I apologised for my outburst.

Pete replied: 'If it makes you feel any better, Al did exactly the same thing to me yesterday and I used the same words on him.'

Pete returned to his hole and for the rest of the day I could hear the steady tap and thud through the snow as he enlarged his home. I was left with the problem of mending my roof and in the end managed to block the cascade of spindrift by wedging my rucksack with my ice axe against the hole, and stuffing blocks of snow I had carved from the inner walls around it.

I contemplated the damage; my sleeping bag and foam mat were covered in snow. I spent another hour painstakingly brushing the snow away, but everything was that little bit damper and the cold was insidiously chilling deeper. I sank back into daydreams interspersed with thoughts about our prospects. We were now getting low on food and had only one more main meal left. This meant that we really did need to make the ascent the following day. I kept checking the altimeter throughout the day and it was steadily losing height; in other words the weather was improving.

That night I found sleep difficult, partly because I was now so cold that I had periods of uncontrollable shivering, and partly from excitement tinged with forebodings at our prospects the following day. But each time I looked at the altimeter, it was still slowly losing height. I called out to Joe to start cooking at six in the morning when it was still dark. Two brews and a very small cupful of muesli and dried fruit later, the snow of the roof was glimmering a light grey. The dawn was upon us.

I probed a spy hole through the snow with my ice axe and peered through it. I could see the spindrift cascading down past it and the sky seemed grey. The weather was as bad as ever, and yet this time we had to go. It was the morning of 12th July; both our supplies and our resistance to the cold were very nearly at an end. We could not sit it out any longer. And so, I packed my sack, stuffing the wet sleeping bag into it with the scant remains of our food, and hacked away the snow at the entrance to make a hole the size of a picture frame. As I did so, my spirits soared. The narrow view through the spy hole had deceived me, for outside the sky was clear; the shapely summit of Chakragil on the other side of the Gez gorge was bathed in brilliant sunlight. It was still bitterly cold and windy and we were chilled and weakened from four nights and three days in our snow coffins, but it was the best we could hope for.

16
Going for the top

12TH JULY 1981

I felt a wild, exuberant joy at the prospect of escaping from inactivity and the excitement of the climb ahead. I shouted at the blank slope under which Pete and Al were hidden. Some snow crumbled away and Pete peered out. They also had been brewing up for some hours. Joe was still in the bowels of his hole, and I stamped up and down in the snow, impatient to be away. It was nine o'clock before we were all out of the holes, with our rucksacks packed with sleeping bags that were already beginning to freeze in the bitter cold of the outside air. We gathered in the nick between rocks on the col, pausing for a second before the commitment of the climb. I suggested to Pete that he started out on the ridge. Was it a courtesy, or perhaps a little jab of fear, a holding back from the steep ice-clad rocks above.

Packing up ready for the summit push.

Pete started up, climbing blocks of rock plastered in snow on the crest of the ridge, a fragile stairway to the base of the pyramid. We debated where to go. Joe was in favour of going straight up, Pete and I were for doing a high traverse round the left, which is the route we took. This was real climbing, steeper than the North Face of the Matterhorn, more like the North Wall of the Eiger in winter. Frozen snow clung to crumbling rock. It needed care, stepping delicately from one rocky hold to the next, precariously balanced on crampon tips.

Pete led round a shoulder, hammered in a piton belay and it was Al's turn to lead, up an open scoop of hard snow into a little rocky niche. Hard awkward climbing at sea level, but this was at around 7,315 metres in a bitter wind shaded from the encouragement of the sun. Joe and I caught up with Pete, the three of us sharing a small ledge, while Al eased himself into an open rock groove, hammered in a piton for protection, and then bridged up it to reach a snow ledge.

By the time Pete had led the next pitch across snow-covered rocks he had lost all feeling in hands and feet. He took off his mitts and gloves to see that the tips of his fingers were blackened with frost nip. He asked Joe and me if we would move through into the lead. We now seemed close to the end of the extreme difficulties. A projecting buttress just in front was at last catching the sun and the angle was beginning to relent. I led across to the buttress, and then Joe went through to climb one more awkward pitch over a bottomless

Joe on the skyline followed by Al up the summit ridge.

rocky scoop, that thrust one out of balance and was particularly difficult with a rucksack. Beyond, though, it all began to open out, with the sun creeping over the crest of the broken ridge about thirty metres above and hurling jagged beams through the swirling spindrift. It was now possible to follow runnels of snow through the shattered rocks, scrambling up the broken ground towards the crest and the sun.

I pulled out over the top and found myself in a different world. I was on a broad platform that would have taken several tents, bathed in sunlight and out of the wind. Above, the ridge broadened, a winding snow trail between the rocks leading summitwards. I brought Joe up and the other two followed. We had taken five hours to climb about 152 metres. It was now two o'clock in the afternoon.

Pete, still concerned about his feet and hands, took his boots off to massage some life into his toes. I loaned him one of my down socks to give his frost-nipped hand greater protection than he could get from his frozen mitts. And then we set off again, but now we could move together, the only curb on our progress the weakness of lungs in the thin air. It was a slow steady plod upwards, picking our way past huge boulders that barred the crest of the ridge. In one place we even had to take off our rucksacks to wriggle through a narrow gap beneath a rock.

I was undoubtedly going slowly but was still determined to take my share out in front, aiming at twenty steps at a time and then a rest. As we slowly gained height, the ridge seemed to stretch in front of us for ever in a series of false crests. Glancing back the summit of Kongur Tiube still seemed slightly higher than ourselves. The light of the afternoon was beginning to soften as the sun dropped down towards the western horizon and still we plodded on. And yet we knew we were going to make it. Nothing could stop us now. It was just a matter of putting one foot in front of the other.

I was savouring the moment of success and knew an emotion of anticipation which actually brought tears to my eyes. I had the feeling of immense affection for the three others sharing this experience, who had given me such great moral and, at times, physical support.

The summit came as a surprise. Joe was out in front, pulled over a notch in the ridge, and poked his head back to shout down to me: 'I think you'll like what you see up here.'

I did. The ridge curved round in a gentle sickle of snow to what was obviously the summit just fifteen metres or so above us and thirty or so distant. Across the open easy-angled slope of the summit, at the other side of a broad col, was the other summit of Kongur, a distant rounded hump of snow. It definitely seemed lower than the one just in front of us. We sat and waited for the others, and then started for the summit. Joe, who was determined to film our success, unroped and went up first with the cine camera, stopping just short of the top to film Al, Pete, and me, trailing an empty rope, move up towards the summit. Joe wrote:

I had this clamp which I stuck on the ice axe, and I filmed the other three coming up and then filmed them going past me and standing on the summit itself. And then I thought it a bit daft if there are only three people seen on the summit, because my mum's going to think I'm dead or something, so I then rushed into the picture and knelt there myself so that I was in the summit film too.

The emotion of anticipation had somehow vanished in the practicalities of reaching the top. Pete had nursed the string of silk summit flags, the ensigns of China, the United Kingdom and the expedition flag containing the Jardine logo, all the way from Base Camp. He had never taken a flag to a summit before but the way he had cared for these seemed to show a liking for the symbolism that they contained, fluttering from his ice axe on that bleak snowy mound. It was bitterly cold with a fierce wind blasting clouds of spindrift over the summit. The sky above and around was a deep dark blue, clear of haze or cloud, but below was the cottonwool of cumulus clouds stretching out to the far horizon, hiding distant mountain peaks.

It was getting late, past eight o'clock in the evening and we still had no shelter for the night. We left the summit after about ten minutes, dropped back to the shoulder and then started looking for a suitable drift for our cave. Al found one just below and started digging. It took us three hours to carve out a shelter big enough for the four of us to squeeze into. Pete, worried about his frost-nipped hand, stayed outside, kicking away the snow with his booted foot as we shovelled it out of the entrance.

It was very nearly dark when at last the cave seemed ready. Joe and I had dug a broad but quite short shelter while Al had made a much narrower but longer slot. As Pete crawled into the hole, he exploded into recrimination, that Joe and I had been thoughtlessly selfish in just digging ourselves a luxurious abode with no thought of helping Al who had been working on his own. It was a short blazing row, engendered by fatigue and strain. That day Pete had done all the leading on the upper part of the ridge since Al had been struggling with a severe throat infection that sent him into paroxysms of coughing.

But the row died in apologies and we were able to snuggle into sleeping bags, light the stoves and at last have a victory brew of tea. There was not much else, for we had run out of main meals and just had some soup thickened with mashed potato powder, spiced with chillies. We were too tired to feel much elation, were still bruised by the argument, which had been a release as much as anything of the tensions built up by our days trapped in the snow cave and the isolation of our present position. It was two o'clock in the morning before we finally settled down in our cave just fifteen metres below the summit of Kongur.

RIGHT] *Joe takes off his rucksack to edge through a rock gap.*

OVERLEAF ABOVE LEFT] *Pete and Al lead up the summit ridge.*
BELOW LEFT] *On the upper part of the summit pyramid we could all move together.*

RIGHT] *Pete and Al on the upper part of the summit pyramid with the Karakol Lakes just visible in the middle distance.*

FOLLOWING SPREAD] *Al, Pete, Chris and Joe – the traditional summit picture.*

SECOND FOLLOWING SPREAD] *Al starts to dig a snow cave below the summit.*

17
The hair's breadth

13TH–18TH JULY 1981

I was woken by the light of the sun streaming into the entrance of the snow cave. I made a brew and then, while the others were creeping into full consciousness, I dressed and crawled out of the hole. During the night the wind had dropped to a steady breeze. It was still bitterly cold, but it was a perfect day with only a light scattering of clouds around the distant horizon. I walked back up to the summit – it was only a few metres, but now, with the entrance to the snow hole hidden by a curve in the ridge, I could have been on my own on what felt like the roof of Asia. There was a sense of space and distance I have never before experienced. In most mountain areas, even on the highest summit, the horizon is limited by surrounding peaks, but here, in the heart of Central Asia, Kongur was so isolated that the neighbouring peaks were dwarfed and the horizon formed an arc as perfect as if I had been far out at sea. The surface of the desert was concealed in a light brown dust haze, out of which the distant peaks, like foam-capped waves, rose on all sides. To the north-west, beyond the haze beneath which Kashgar must be hidden, was the distant range of the Tian-shan and to the west, mingled in cloud, were the Soviet Pamirs. Even the mighty bulk of Kongur Tiube and Mustagh Ata were subdued, while to the south, glimpsed through serried cumulus cloud, were the peaks of the Hindu Kush and in the far distance just a hint of K2, barely discernible on the far horizon.

The view to the north-east was barred by the mound of Kongur's other summit. The previous night it had definitely looked lower, but that morning it appeared to have grown, a trick no doubt of the light, for the sun was now to the east. But could it be higher than the summit on which I was standing? There was obviously not much difference. By the time I got back to the snow hole, the others were beginning to emerge. We sat on the shoulder, poised between the notch which led to our route off the mountain, and the unwelcome second summit, which almost seemed to gain in height as we gazed upon it.

Reason told us to escape while we could. The weather was perfect, but for how long? We were a long way from safety. The fact that we could see neither our Advance Base nor our Base Camp, both of which were shielded by the bulk of Junction Peak, increased our sense of isolation. Yet Pete expressed the problem all too well: 'We'll kick ourselves for the rest of our lives if we don't make sure we've been to the top, and the only way to know is to go there.'

We eventually decided to dump our sacks on the shoulder and walk over. Pete and Joe were going to team up once again to allow Al and me to go at our own pace. Having made the decision, it was easy going at first down and across the summit slope towards the col

ABOVE LEFT] *Al and Chris coming back across the central summit, with Mustagh Ata in the cloud left.*
BELOW LEFT] *Looking back across the central summit to the main summit.*

Al and Chris crossing the wind slab slope of the main summit.

between the summits. Easy, but dangerous, for the slope had the crusty quality of windslab. Could the whole lot slide in a gigantic sheet? We kept a wide distance between the two parties and tried to tiptoe down. It was a strange sensation for the way was quite gentle with scree exposed on the other side of the col as we scrambled up by broken rocks. It was like walking along the ridge of Helvellyn on a clear winter's day. But the thinness of the air and the spaciousness of the view to either side belied the illusion. We came to the top of the slope. This was the central summit. From the viewpoint Michael Ward and I had had the previous year on the other side of the Gez gorge, it had seemed little more than a knob of rock on the summit plateau, but now, upon its crest, it assumed the stature of twin rocky summits linked by a sharp ridge of crumbling rock. We shuffled over it awkwardly and then down a steep snow field on the other side to the next col. The dome of the north-east summit was now before us. It was an easy walk, curving gently uphill. By the time Al and I got there, Joe and Pete were already sprawled on the snow, munching boiled sweets.

It was an agreeable anticlimax for looking back, the fin-like summit we had reached the previous night, stood proud and high projecting above the lip of the flat plateau on which we were sitting. It was undoubtedly the highest point on Kongur, though probably by not more than thirty metres or so. We turned round and started back, Al and I out in front this time. We always seemed to be ascending in order to get down on this climb. We had to plod back over the central summit and then across that dangerous slope to reach the main summit.

It was four-thirty in the afternoon when we were ready to leave once again, but there was no suggestion of spending another night in the summit snow hole. We all desperately wanted to get back to the food cache and the relative safety of the snow cave at the foot of Junction Peak.

Just before we set off, Joe reminded me of one more commitment that we had. Michael Ward had been given a message for peace with the request that it should be planted on the summit of Kongur. I buried the little card in the snow, the only token of our presence that we left behind.

Dropping down the ridge, we lost height quickly and steadily for we were no longer fighting gravity. But then we came to the shoulder above the difficult step. This was going to be awkward to reverse. We discussed the best route and finally decided to follow the crest and abseil down the steepest section. Pete was out in front, picking his way down the ridge, via a small gully and then to a rocky pinnacle poised on the brink of the sheer drop of the final step. He commented:

I go to the big block on the crest, lower myself around on its north side and find a large spike overhanging the west. It seems stable and I tie two slings together, to go round it. We must hurry and someone must go first and there's no reason why it shouldn't be me. I tie off the rope that Al and I have been using and hurl it down.

Pete about to abseil down the difficult step.

By this time Joe and I had caught up and sat crouched on a ledge above watching Pete prepare the abseil. He threaded the rope through a karabiner brake from his waist belt and then ran it under his thigh to give more friction. He started down the narrow crest of the ridge; it was awkward for he could swing to either side of it and constantly had to adjust his balance to counter the pull of the rope. He paused on the brink of the drop, decided to commit himself to the western slope and began a careful pendulum over a steep snow slope. The rope caught on a rock protruding from the snow. It shifted, rolled and was tumbling down towards Pete. It was the size of a football. Joe and I shouted out at the same instant:

'Watch out! Rock!'

But it hit him as we shouted. He shot down out of sight. It was an agonising few moments. Had he gone off the end of the rope? Was he dead, or unconscious with severe head injuries? And then a voice came from below, distant, slightly aggrieved: 'I've been hit on the head by a rock.'

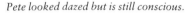

Pete looked dazed but is still conscious.

'We know, are you all right?'

'I think so.'

Al was the first to go down and then Joe. By the time I got there, Pete was sitting against a rock, looking dazed but conscious. It had been a narrow escape, for the rock had knocked him out for an instant – enough time for him to slide out of control down the rope. He had not tied a knot in the end of the rope and so he might very easily have gone off the end, in which case he would have fallen a few thousand metres to the glacier far below. He was probably saved by his hand which was guiding the rope, being drawn into the karabiners acting as a break. This jammed the rope running through them and the pain might well have brought him back to consciousness as his feet hit the snow at the bottom of the sheer section down which he had plunged unconscious and out of control.

Joe had checked Pete's injuries before I got down. The rock had hit him a glancing blow on the side of the head, by his left ear. There was a lot of blood, but the skull seemed intact. Had the rock been just an inch or so more central on his head the injuries might well have been more serious. Pete had been within a hair's breadth of death, for had he been unconscious or even semi-conscious I doubt whether we could have got him back along the knife-edged ridge and then back over Junction Peak. The margin between happy success and disaster is always so terribly fine in the high mountains.

By the time we had rigged another abseil, Pete, though still slightly giddy, was able to move unaided and we all slid down another thirty-six metres to below the steepest section of the step. We now had a traverse round its base back down to the col. It was awkward climbing on steep ground, with crumbling rock underfoot and poor belays, but soon we were back again just above the snow coffins we had left thirty-six hours before. The sun was balanced over Konger Tiube, bathing the rocks in the rich yellow light of sunset. We were determined however to get all the way back to the snow cave. Pete had now recovered and was once again out in the lead. Joe and I followed the other pair as we slowly picked our way over the crumbling gendarme, and then beneath the steep rocky pinnacle which was a golden brown in the last rays of the sun.

It was dark before we reached the end of the ridge, but as the sun vanished below the western horizon an almost full moon took over, bathing the mountains and desert in a cold, ethereal light. Far below on the glacier, bare ice glimmered, like the lights of a city seen from a high-flying aircraft. It was so light on the crest of the ridge that we could pick our way without the help of our head torches, but the fatigue was beginning to tell. I took just a few paces at a time before resting. Joe ambled along, patiently behind me. Down to the col and then the last climb. It was only eighteen metres or so, but seemed interminable, my body screaming its exhaustion.

The gaping hole of the snow cave at last; crawl in, lay out the foam mats, creep into sleeping bags, lie down and relax. I was too tired even to wait for the snow to melt for a brew and dropped into a deep sleep.

Next morning we had the one section of ascent and then from the top of Junction Peak it was downhill all the way. But it took us most of the day, particularly the slog through the deep snow of the traverse from the col back to the crest of the South-West Rib. Down below we had noticed two tiny dots. Were they a reception party or just rocks in the snow? We weren't sure. Then as we came over the brow of the South-West Rib we saw they were indeed members of the team.

Ploughing through deep snow on the shoulder of Junction Peak, but now it is downhill all the way.

Michael Ward and Jim Curran had spent eight days at Advance Camp. They had not seen any trace of us, but taking the storm into account, Michael had worked out that our food would run out by this day. If we did not return, then something must have gone seriously wrong. They had climbed up the South-West Rib to just above 6,000 metres. It was a really gorgeous day. Jim had been taking numerous cine shots and they had been examining Junction Peak constantly. At about 2.00 p.m. Jim did one more pan and they were about to go down when Michael suddenly saw us about half way down the ridge. They sat through the afternoon as we slowly came down towards them.

As we neared them Michael climbed up towards us. We stopped and told him our good news. There were handshakes, understatement that hid the warmth of our welcome and our own response, and then the final walk in the late afternoon sun back down to the camp in the Koksel Basin. We threw off our climbing harnesses and clothes, lay in the warm tents and were served endless brews of tea by Michael and Jim. It was good to relax at last; it didn't matter that Michael upset the panful of cannelloni over the tent. Have another swig of whisky, another coffee, and gaze back at the high outer wall of snow and sérac that once again shielded our summit.

Next morning the last walk uphill to go down, roped up in our pairs for the final time. We had a feeling of close unity and satisfaction as we sat on the col at the head of the Corridor and gazed back into the Basin against the shallow angled rays of the sun. Then it was down into the Corridor; no more rope between us, no more danger of hidden crevasses. There were so many firsts; the first trickling stream down the bare ice of the glacier, the first patch of moss, the first grass, the first primula. We were striding down the moraine ridge, the tents of Base Camp toy-like in size scattered over the grassy moraine that seemed startlingly green; it was so bright after our days of white snows, blue skies and black rocks. Someone had seen us in Base Camp; there was a shout and they all came rushing out.

They had grabbed the flags that flew outside the base tent and used the kitchen pots and pans as drums and symbols. We dropped down towards them and met in the little valley between moraine and hillside just above the meadow. We were all shouting with joy, experiencing a relaxed delirious happiness that it was all over. Liu Dayi, his careworn face transformed by a happy smile, embraced me, muttering: 'Ah Bonington, Bonington,' as a parent would do to a wayward child back from some adventure. To me the most important feature of this wonderful welcome was that when they saw us, they had no knowledge of whether we had climbed the mountain or not; they were just so relieved to see that we were alive and were welcoming us back as friends returned from danger.

It summed up the entire spirit of the expedition. It was formed of several disparate groups of people – the four climbers, the scientists, Jim Curran the film maker, David Wilson our interpreter, and our Chinese support team, who had got us to the foot of the mountain and looked after us so well when we were in Base Camp. The aims of these groups could so easily have begun to conflict. That they didn't was partially due to the personalities involved and partially to the way that Michael Ward had interwoven the research and climbing programme. As a result there was never a feeling of 'them and us' amongst the team, everyone being happy to muck in with whatever work had needed doing. This was epitomised by the effort that Jim Milledge and David Wilson made on our behalf in carrying our food half way up the South-West Rib on the final push for the summit. It was certainly one of the happiest expeditions that I have been on.

Down at the base tent we took off rucksacks and gear for the last time, downed bottles of Xinjiang beer and told the stories of our adventures during the last eight days. Then, in the mid-afternoon a yak ambled into Base Camp carrying not only our mail but a crate of champagne sent by our sponsors. The timing could not have been better, as we drank their health and ours in pint plastic mugs in the afternoon sun. The following night we had an expedition feast when the entire team, Chinese and British, sat down to demolish course after delicious course cooked by Wang, who barely found time to sit down himself. Toast followed toast, in champagne, beer, whisky, and a lethal Xinjiang whisky that Mr. Shi Zhanchun had presented to us when he had bade us farewell in Urumchi at the start of the expedition. Charlie was the chief toastmaster, drinking to everyone, from our bank managers back home (and possibly, though I don't clearly remember, the Inland Revenue), to eternal friendship between the Mount Everest Foundation and the Chinese Mountaineering Association.

It was a happy, mellow evening, the climax to a successful expedition when everyone came home, and yet it could so very easily have been very different. Perhaps for this very reason our celebration had an unconsciously frantic level.

Just how close is the margin between success and failure was to be cruelly brought home to us a fortnight later. As we pursued our own boistrous celebration the Japanese had just started their climb on the precipitous northern side. They had some very strong climbers and they also wanted to make the ascent in alpine-style. Three of them set out for the summit bid and were seen by a local herdsman, tiny dots against the snow, through a break in the cloud. They were close to the summit but then the clouds rolled in and they were not seen again. It will probably never be known how they met their deaths, or whether they reached the summit. It could well have been we who had vanished high on the slopes of Kongur.

We left Base Camp the next day, a column of smoke marking a bonfire of burning rubbish. Once the ashes and empty tins had been buried, a few discoloured patches on the grass where our tents had been those last weeks were the only signs left of our occupation. The marmots had the meadow to themselves once more as we turned our back on Kongur. Kongur was elusive again, hidden, inscrutable within a cap of cloud, and yet as we wandered down over the rolling moraine, my memories were held, as they still are, by those intense days above 7,000 metres. There were moments of total despair, when I felt I could no longer push myself any farther. It was the encouragement of the other three that had helped me break through momentary weakness. But there were many more moments of pure elation; the satisfaction of leading the rock gendarme, even though it led nowhere; the huge empty beauty of desert, snow and cloud mountains; of friendships grown stronger through the greater knowledge we had of each other's strengths and weaknesses in a world that was at the same time so enormous in terms of space and yet so small in terms of people.

It is this intensity of experience that draws us back to the mountains again and again, to set us planning the next trip, and the one after that, before the last one has barely begun. Nine months later, in my Lakeland cottage, I long once more for those wide open spaces and vistas of unclimbed, unexplored peaks stretching in every direction to the farthest horizon.

RIGHT] *Al traversing back beneath the rock gendarme in the sunset.*

OVERLEAF ABOVE LEFT] *Al and Michael on the col at the head of the Corridor.*
BELOW LEFT] *A warm welcome to the successful team from the Chinese Base Camp staff.*

Appendices

I

Members of the expedition and diary of events

THE BASE CAMP TEAM] *l to r, Edward Williams, David Wilson, Michael Ward, Charlie Clarke, Jim Milledge and Jim Curran.*

THE CLIMBING TEAM] *l to r, Chris Bonington, Al Rouse, Pete Boardman and Joe Tasker.*

THE TREKKING PARTY] *l to r, Jim Boswell, Adrian Gordon, Tom Harley, David Newbigging, Carolyn Newbigging, Martin Henderson and David Mathew.*

THE CHINESE PERSONNEL] *l to r, Zhang Xueshan (interpreter), Chen Jianjun (high-altitude assistant), Liu Dayi (liaison officer), Wang Yuhu (cook), Song Ziyi (high-altitude assistant).*

MICHAEL WARD, M.D., F.R.C.S.,
Expedition Leader

Born: 26.3.25;
married with one child, living in London.
Consultant surgeon and lecturer in clinical
surgery at the University of London.
Education: Marlborough College,
Peterhouse (Ironmongers Exhibition),
Cambridge; London Hospital.

One of Britain's leading mountaineering scientists.
He was a member of the 1951 Everest Reconnaissance and medical officer to the successful 1953
Everest expedition. From September 1960 to July
1961, at the Silver Hut (5,800 m) in the Everest
region, he carried out research into the long-term
effects of high altitude on man, made the first ascent
of Ama Dablam (6,856 m) one of the steepest and
most beautiful peaks in the Everest region, and led
the attempt on Makalu (8,470 m). He led expeditions in 1964 and 1965 carrying out geographical
exploration and medical research in North Bhutan.
Since 1976 he has been engaged on research into the
effect of continuous exercise on fluid balance and its
possible relationship to the cerebral and pulmonary
oedema of altitude with Edward Williams and
James Milledge.

He has been a Hunterian Professor at the Royal
College of Surgeons of England and Dickson Asia
lecturer at the Royal Geographical Society. Chair-
man of the Mount Everest Foundation, 1978–80.
Founder's Medal of the Royal Geographical
Society, 1982.

CHRISTIAN BONINGTON, C.B.E.,
Climbing Leader

Born 6.8.34; married with two children,
living in the Lake District.
Author, photographer and lecturer.
Education: University College School,
London; Royal Military Academy, Sandhurst.

One of Britain's leading mountaineers, who has
made many new routes in Great Britain and the
European Alps, including the first ascents of the Old
Man of Hoy in the Orkneys of Scotland (1966), the
Central Pillar of Freney on Mont Blanc (1961), first
British ascent of the North Wall of the Eiger (1962).
In the Himalayas he has made the first ascents of
Annapurna II (7,937 m) in 1960, Nuptse
(7,879 m), the third peak of Everest in 1961, Bram-
mah (6,416 m) in Kashmir in 1973, Changabang
(6,864 m) in the Garhwal Himalaya in 1974 and
the Ogre (7,285 m) in the Karakoram in 1977. He
was leader of the successful Annapurna South Face
expedition in 1970, and the Everest South-West
Face expedition in 1975.

Founder's Medal of the Royal Geographical Society, 1974. M.A. (hon.), University of Salford; D.Sc.
(hon.), University of Sheffield.

PETER BOARDMAN

Born 25.12.50;
married, living in Switzerland.
Author and mountain guide.
Education: Stockport Grammar School,
Nottingham University,
where he read English Literature.

A mountaineer with a long list of difficult Alpine climbs to his credit, including five British first ascents in the European Alps. He has climbed extensively in the Hindu Kush, where he made alpine-style ascents of the North Faces of Kohi Khaaik and Kohi Mondi, and in the Polish High Tatras, East Africa, Caucasus, New Guinea and Alaska. In the Himalaya he reached the summit of Everest (8,848 m) on the successful 1975 Everest South-West Face expedition. In 1976 with Joe Tasker, in an outstanding lightweight two-man assault, he made the first ascent of the West Wall of Changabang (6,864 m); was also a member of the 1978 and 1980 British K2 (8,612 m) expeditions. In 1979 he made the first ascent (and without oxygen) of the North Ridge of Kangchenjunga (8,586 m), the third highest mountain in the world, and the South Summit of Gauri Sankar (7,010 m).

He is now director of the International School of Mountaineering in Leysin, Switzerland. He has written many articles on mountaineering and his book *The Shining Mountain* won him the John Llewelyn Rhys Memorial prize in 1979.

Member of seven Himalayan expeditions including four to Kishtwar as leader between 1965 and 1974, and made the first ascent of Swagorohini (6,111 m) in 1974. Member of Kanjiroba Himal expedition in 1969 and medical officer to the Everest South-West Face expedition in 1975.

He has been engaged in research on the effects of lack of oxygen on the eye at high altitude. He is joint editor with Michael Ward and Edward Williams of *Mountain Medicine and Physiology* and honorary medical officer to the British Mountaineering Council.

JIM CURRAN

Born 1.1.43;
single, living in Bristol.
Senior Lecturer in Media Studies,
Bristol Polytechnic.

For twenty years he has been an active climber in Britain, the European Alps and more recently the Karakoram as a climbing cameraman. His expeditions include the successful ascent of Trango Tower in 1976 and he was leader of the British Barnaj II expedition in 1978.

He has produced four films on climbing and mountaineering: *A Great Effort*, an historical documentary based on the writings and poems of Menlove Edwards, a renowned pre-war rock climber, which was a prizewinner at the 1977 Trento Film Festival; *Barnaj*, a documentary of the overland drive to India, and of climbing and exploration in Kashmir; *Trango*, featuring the first ascent of a famous granite spire in the Karakoram; and, most recently, *The Bat*, a film reconstruction of the first ascent of an extreme rock face on Ben Nevis, which has already won two awards at mountaineering film festivals.

CHARLES CLARKE, M.R.C.P.

Born 12.2.44;
married with two children,
living in London.
Consultant neurologist
at St. Bartholomew's Hospital, London,
and Essex Area Health Authority.
Education: Rugby School,
Gonville and Caius College, Cambridge,
and Guy's Hospital.

JAMES MILLEDGE, M.D., F.R.C.P.E.

Born 23.8.31;
married with two children,
living in Hertfordshire.
Consultant physician,
specialising in chest medicine,
and a scientific staff member of the
Medical Research Council,
Northwick Park Hospital, Harrow.
Education: Rydal School, Colwyn Bay and
University of Birmingham.

He was a member, with Michael Ward, of the Silver Hut expedition in the Everest region in 1960/61. He spent the winter at 5,800 m carrying out research on the long-term effects of high altitude on man; made the first ascent of Puma Dablam (6,400 m) and took part in the attempt on Makalu (8,470 m). Between 1962 and 1972 was on the staff of Christian Medical College, Vellore, South India. In 1964, in a Himalayan scientific expedition, he studied the differences between Sherpas and lowlanders at altitude. More recent research has included studies on the effect of hill-walking on water and salt balance, and in 1980 he led a scientific team to the Gornergrat, Switzerland (3,130 m) to study the effect of altitude and exercise on the hormones concerned with water and salt balance.

In the last few years he has ski toured in the Alps, traversing the Oberland in 1976 and the Haute Route in 1978 and made a ski ascent of Mont Blanc in 1980.

He is an outstanding mountaineer, who has pioneered and soloed many extremely difficult routes in summer and winter in Great Britain and the European Alps. He has also made twelve first ascents in the Andes of South America, including the South Face of Yerupaja. In the autumn of 1978 he was a member of a four-man party which climbed the Southern aspect of Jannu (7,710 m) in the Eastern Himalaya and in the autumn of 1979 made the first ascent of the North Face of Nuptse, both ascents using bold alpine-style tactics.

He is a director of Mountain Experience Climbing School.

JOE TASKER

Born 12.5.48;
single, living in Derbyshire.
Shop owner.
Education: Ushaw College, Durham
and Manchester University,
where he read Sociology.

ALAN ROUSE

Born 19.12.51;
single, living in Sheffield.
Mountain guide.
Education: Birkenhead School,
Emmanuel College, Cambridge,
where he read Mathematics.
He also played chess for Cheshire.

He has made many remarkable ascents in the European Alps and in the Himalaya, where he has pioneered routes of extreme technical difficulty. He made the first British ascents of the North Face of the Dent Blanche in 1973 and in 1974 of the East Face of the Grandes Jorasses. In 1975 he made the first British winter ascent of the North Wall of the Eiger. In the Himalaya he was a member of a two-man team to climb Dunagiri (7,060 m) in 1975, and in another remarkable two-man expedition in 1976 he made the first ascent of the West Wall of Changabang (6,864 m) with Peter Boardman; also a member of the British K2 (8,612 m) expeditions in 1978 and 1980, and in 1979 made the first ascent (and without oxygen) of the North Ridge of Kangchenjunga (8,586 m).

He is a director of Magic Mountain Climbing Shop.

EDWARD WILLIAMS, M.D., PH.D.

Born 7.10.23; married with three sons, living near Guildford.
Director of the Institute of Nuclear Medicine at the Middlesex Hospital Medical School and Professor of Nuclear Medicine in the University of London.
Education: King's College London and the Middlesex Hospital Medical School.

For twenty-five years he has been actively interested in physiological changes resulting from exposure to oxygen lack. He was leader of a series of scientific expeditions including the high-altitude physiological expeditions to the Vallot Observatory, Mont Blanc, in 1960 and the Plateau Rosa expedition in 1967; he has also been a member of many other such expeditions. He has contributed extensively to the physiological and medical literature in this field and been responsible for original discoveries made in the Himalaya relating to the role of the endocrine system in man's response to oxygen lack.

He has climbed extensively in the European Alps and has made first ascents in the Karakoram.

DAVID WILSON, PH.D.

Born 14.2.35; married with two sons, living in London.
Education: Glenalmond, Keble College (Abbott Scholar), Oxford.
Since his school days in Scotland, he has been deeply interested in mountaineering and general exploration. At Oxford he was secretary of the University Exploration Society and a member of a university expedition to Somaliland.

After National Service in the Black Watch and on leaving university, he entered the British Foreign Office in 1958 and has served in a variety of posts including the British Embassy in Peking. He also studied Chinese for two years in Hong Kong.

He left the diplomatic service in 1968 to become editor of the *China Quarterly* at the Contemporary China Institute of the School of Oriental and African Studies, London.

In 1974 he rejoined the diplomatic service and after working for three years in the Cabinet Office, went to Hong Kong as Political Adviser, 1977–81. At present he is head of the Southern Europe Department at the Foreign and Commonwealth Office.

Members of Trekking Party

DAVID NEWBIGGING
CAROLYN NEWBIGGING
MARTIN HENDERSON
DAVID MATHEW
JAMES BOSWELL
TOM HARLEY
ADRIAN GORDON

Chinese Personnel

LIU DAYI *Liaison Officer*
ZANG XUESHAN *Interpreter*
JIN YINGJIE *Manager*
SONG ZIYI *High-altitude assistant*
CHEN JIANJUN *High-altitude assistant*
WANG YUHU *Cook*
ZHANG BAOHUA *Cook*

Chairman of Mount Everest Foundation

MICHAEL WARD 1978–80
SIR DOUGLAS BUSK, K.C.M.G 1980–2

Committee of Management

SIR DOUGLAS BUSK, K.C.M.G., *Chairman*
CHRIS BONINGTON, C.B.E.
GEORGE GREENFIELD
THE RT. HON. THE LORD HUNT, K.G., C.B.E., D.S.O.
MICHAEL WARD
PHILIPPA STEAD *Matheson & Co.*
CHARLES CLARKE *Secretary*
DENNIS GRAY *BMC*
MARTIN HENDERSON *Matheson & Co.*

Co-ordinating Office/Sponsors

London
MARTIN HENDERSON
PHILIPPA STEAD

Peking
DAVID MATHEW

Hong Kong
T. T. HARLEY
P. A. FARNELL-WATSON

Diary of events

1972	Michael Ward makes first approach to China.
1978	China Sub-Committee of Mount Everest Foundation formed.
Autumn *1979*	Chairman Hua Guofeng visits U.K. Sir Douglas Busk and Michael Ward meet him and Chinese Foreign Minister, Huang Hua.
1980	
19th Feb.	Michael Ward and Chris Bonington fly to Peking.
26th Feb.	Protocol for Mount Kongur signed by Mr. Shi Zhanchun and Ward.
29th Feb.	Ward and Bonington meet David Newbigging, Chairman of Jardine, Matheson & Co., Ltd., who agrees in principle to sponsorship.
5th March	Al Rouse invited to join reconnaissance.
25th May–1st June	Michael Ward flies to Peking to attend symposium on scientific investigations carried out on Qinghai-Xizang plateau
28th May	Bonington and Rouse leave for Hong Kong.
4th June	Ward, Bonington and Rouse with liaison officer, Liu Dayi, fly to Urumchi. Ward lectures at Xinjiang Medical College, Urumchi.
7th June	Team fly to Kashgar.
10th June	Team reach Karakol Lakes.
12th June	Team reach Base Camp.
18th June	Bonington and Rouse make first ascent of Sarakyaguqi (6,200 m).
19th June	Rouse injures ankle.

29th June	Bonington and Ward reach the Koksel Col, 5,700 m.
4th July	Party moves by bus to Gez Karaul.
6th July	Bonington and Ward climb wall of gorge to north of Gez.
7th July	Team set out up Kurghan Jilgha and camp at Serai.
9th July	Bonington, Rouse and Ward climb Arakler Ridge.
11th July	Bonington and Ward climb Karatash (5,440 m).
20th July	Team return to Kashgar.
1st Aug.	Team return to England.
3rd Sept.	First meeting of complete team. Research programme involving expedition members starts in U.K. at Northwick Park Hospital (Milledge), St. Bartholomew's Hospital (Clarke), and Middlesex Hospital Medical School (Williams).

1981

13th May	Team leave Heathrow for Peking.
15th May	Ward and Milledge fly to Shanghai to lecture at Institute of Physiology.
16th May	Rest of team and trekking party fly to Urumchi.
17th May	Clarke and Williams lecture at Xinjiang Medical College, Urumchi.
19th May	Team fly to Kashgar. Williams and Clarke start research programme.
22nd May	Team drive by bus to Karakol Lakes.
23rd May	Rouse, Tasker, Wilson, Gordon, Harley, Mathew and Carolyn Newbigging drive to Tashkurghan.
24th May	Tashkurghan party return to Karakol Lakes camp.
25th May	Ward and Milledge reach Karakol Lakes. Bonington, Boardman, Clarke, David Newbigging, Jim Boswell and Henderson set out on trek.
26th May	Trekking team climb Point 4,870 to east of Mustagh Ata. Rouse and Tasker walk up moraine to recce site for Base Camp and return.
27th May	Trekking party return to Karakol Lakes. Rouse and Tasker leave Karakol Lakes to camp just short of eventual Base Camp site.
28th May	Bonington, Boardman, David Newbigging, Boswell, Henderson, and Gordon walk up to establish Base Camp. Ward, Clarke, Milledge, Williams, Wilson, Carolyn Newbigging, Harley and Mathew, with Chinese staff, yaks and camels, stop half way.
29th May	Everyone reaches Base Camp.
31st May	Trekkers' Peak (Point 5,490 m) climbed by Bonington, Boardman, Tasker, Henderson, David Newbigging, Gordon, Curran and Milledge.
1st June	Carolyn Newbigging, Harley, and Mathew leave for Karakol Lakes. Second camel and yak caravan complete gear to Base Camp. Research programme starts at Base Camp.
3rd June	David Newbigging, Boswell, Henderson and Gordon leave for Karakol Lakes. Bonington and Tasker filmed by Curran and Wilson, recce route up Corridor into Koksel Basin. Boardman and Clarke climb Rognon Peak.
5th June	Boardman, Rouse, Tasker with Curran and Wilson move up to Advance Base in Koksel Basin. Clarke and Wilson climb Toothed Peak.
6th June	Boardman, Rouse, Tasker, Curran and Wilson reach Koksel Col and then Boardman and Tasker climb South Ridge to 6,200 m before returning to Koksel Basin.
7th June	Koksel party returns to Base.
9th June	Boardman, Rouse and Tasker set out to attempt southern 6,710 m peak. Camped at 6,000 m. Clarke, Milledge, Wilson, Williams, set out to attempt Sarala Peak.
10th June	Boardman, Rouse, Tasker return because of bad weather but other party sit it out in their camp.

11th June	Clarke, Milledge, Wilson, Williams return to Base.
13th June	Bonington, Boardman, Rouse, Tasker with Curran and Wilson move to Advance Base.
14th June	Climbing team move to Koksel Col. Milledge and Wilson climb Sarala Peak.
15th June	Climbing team establish camp other side of Pimple at 5,990 m.
16th June	Climbing team reach shoulder at 6,400 m on South Ridge and return to Pimple col camp.
17th June	Climbing team return to Advance Base. Milledge and Wilson climb to 6,040 m.
18th June	Climbing team climb South-West Rib to 6,270 m, camp and then snow hole.
19th June	Climbing team return to Base.
21st June	Curran, Wilson, Clarke and Williams move up to Advance Base.
22nd June	Curran and Wilson move up to Koksel Col and establish camp. Clarke and Williams return to Base.
23rd June	Climbing team move up to Advance Base.
24th June	Climbing team move up to camp on shelf at South Ridge at 6,200 m. Ward and Milledge move up to Advance Base. Curran and Wilson move up to top of Pimple.
25th June	Climbing team climb South Ridge and camp on top at approx. 7,320 m. Milledge and Ward to Pimple and return.
26th June	Climbing team traverse Junction Peak ridge, camping on crest. Curran and Wilson drop back to Advance Base.
27th June	Climbing team dig snow cave at col between Junction Peak and summit pyramid at approx. 7,160 m.
28th June	Climbing team reach end of knife-edged ridge to foot of summit pyramid and then return.
29th June	Climbing team return to Advance Base.
30th June	Climbing team, Ward and Curran return to Base.
3rd July	Ward and Williams move up to Advance Base.
4th July	Climbing team, Wilson and Milledge move up to Advance Base. Ward and Williams go up to Koksel Col and return.
5th July	Climbing team move up to snow cave on South-West Rib at 6,200 m. Wilson and Milledge carry food up to 6,000 m and return to Advance Base.
6th July	Climbing team reach snow cave on Junction Peak at 7,160 m.
7th July	Climbing team rest in snow cave. Ward and Curran to Advance Base and remain there until 15th.
8th July	Climbing team move to foot of summit pyramid and dig snow 'coffins'.
9th July	Bad weather. Stay in coffins.
10th July	Bad weather. Stay in coffins.
11th July	Bad weather. Stay in coffins.
12th July	Kongur summit reached. Camp in snow cave just below top.
13th July	North-East summit reached and return to snow cave below Junction Peak.
14th July	Return to Advance Base. Met by Ward and Curran on South-West Rib.
15th July	Climbing team, Ward and Curran return to Base Camp.
16th July	Williams, Clarke and two high-altitude assistants to Advance Base to collect tents.
18th July	Return to Karakol Lakes.
19th July	Return to Kashgar.
22nd July	Return to Peking.

II

The history of the exploration of the
Mustagh Ata–Kongur Massif

by Michael Ward and Peter Boardman

The Mustagh Ata–Kongur massif lies at the axis of many ranges – they belong as much to the eastern Pamirs as to the western Kun-lun, and are linked by mountainous country northwards to the Tian-shan and southwards to the Karakoram and the Himalaya. It stands a huge and obvious wall separating the Takla-makan desert from the Pamir plateau.

It is no longer fashionable to talk of Euro-peans 'discovering' areas that have been in-habited for thousands of years, and the Mus-tagh Ata and Kongur massif lies beside old well trodden routes that were used by human-ity before the beginning of recorded history as channels of trade, spiritual and material, be-tween the early civilisations of India, China and the west. The massif dominates the hori-zons of all who look eastwards across the Pamirs, and all who look south from the oases of the Taklamakan desert – it was known long before it was described.

The first Arab geographers regarded all the mountains of Europe and Asia as linked together – they described the land masses of the world as a desirable woman with a long girdle of mountains encircling her ample mid-riff from the Pyrenees to the Himalaya. Later they called the region of the Pamirs Bam-i-dunya – 'Roof of the World'. Herodotus told of unicorns and gold-digging ants in this re-gion. The long line of skinny mountains de-picted by Ptolemy in the second century AD continued to be reproduced on maps as late as the eighteenth century.

Chinese control of the area has fluctuated ever since the first occupying army was sent there from the east in 138 BC. One of the most dramatic campaigns was in 747 AD when a Chinese expeditionary force travelled from Kashgar across the Pamirs and ousted the Tibetans who had overrun the area at the time.

From the fourth to the seventh centuries Buddhist monks passed by the massif from China to India in search of their religious heritage. Two such pilgrims who wrote down what they saw were Fa Xian (AD 399) and Xuan Zang (AD 624). Both crossed the Chichiklik pass, south-east of the massif on their way from the Taklamakan desert to the frontier zone of Tashkurghan.

In the second half of the thirteenth century Marco Polo traversed from west to east across the Pamirs in 'forty good days'. His account skates over the actual route followed, but conveys the barrenness, the cold and his im-pressions of the local inhabitants – 'idolators and utter savages, living entirely by the chase and dressed in the skins of beasts. They are thoroughly bad.'

In 1603 the Portuguese Jesuit missionary, Benedict de Goes, travelled through the region on his way from India to China. For over two hundred years after this, there is no record of a European passing by again. In the 1820s it is likely that the wild American adventurer, Alexander Gardiner, travelled this way. Then the true 'exploration' began, with the start of the triangular 'Great Game'.

From the 1820s to 1980, the exploration of the Pamirs and the Kun-lun, and the Kongur and Mustagh Ata massif bridged between them, has been politically sponsored. Where-as elsewhere in the world, traders, mission-aries, geographers and other scientists have initiated the exploration, where the three empires of Russia, China and the British in India met, the dictates of power have been paramount.

During the nineteenth century, the Great Game explorers had, in varying proportions, three political objectives: to map and plot the watershed and, in particular, identify the main source of the Oxus, to help settle the frontier; to reconnoitre all passes with a view to their invasion threat/potential; to assess and develop trade and alliances with the local people.

The detail of these fascinating intrigues can be traced in the select bibliography. However, despite the sinister power politics, most of the European visitors relished the thrill of exploration as John Keay remarks in his book, *The Gilgit Game*: 'some of the privileged agents and soldiers, who did get there look suspiciously like freelance explorers doing political work simply for the travel opportunities it afforded.'

First Briton on the Roof of the World was Lieutenant John Wood, in February 1838, but his Pamir travels were too far to the southwest for him to note the Kongur-Mustagh Ata massif and it was not until 1868 that Hayward, as he skirted the Taklamakan desert towards Kashgar, noted and plotted a 'large peak' to the south. During the 1860s the Russians began an intensive exploration of the Pamirs, whilst in 1869 and 1870 two native agents working for the British also passed through. All appear to have failed to mention the massif specifically. Then, in 1873, the British exploration of the region suddenly became less haphazard. The 350-strong British mission to Kashgar under Forsyth was one of the biggest ever sent from India and was the grandest ever seen in Xinjiang. It had an almost unlimited field of enquiry. Considerable geographical work was carried out by members of this mission during which an enormous mountain was spotted south of Kashgar; Trotter, one of the surveyors, calculated its height to be 25,000 feet (7,620 metres). Then Trotter, his companion Gordon, and two others, journeyed south over the Chichiklik pass to Tashkurghan.

There were still some gaps to be filled in, and in 1885 one of the greatest explorers of the nineteenth century, Ney Elias, was sent by the British authorities on a one-man mission to do this. Elias covered a lot of 'new' ground. From the Taklamakan desert he crossed the snow-covered Karatash pass and traversed between what we now know to be Kongur and Mustagh Ata and he became the first European to reach the Karakol Lakes. His map, compiled from the surveys of Hayward and Trotter, omitted Mustagh Ata, but he realised that this was probably the mountain sighted by the Russian explorer Kostenko in 1883 and he set about calculating the heights of the mountains now before him. Trotter had called the 7,620-metre peak Mount Tagharma – this name Elias now transferred to

Mustagh Ata, and eager to impose British names in the area he renamed Trotter's peak Mount Dufferin after the current Viceroy of India. However, it is evident from the sketches that Elias made at the time that his Mount Dufferin is Kongur Tiube (Kongur I), and he failed to notice the highest peak of the range, Mount Kongur (Kongur II).

The names that Elias allocated only lasted on maps for ten years, for when the Anglo–Russian Pamirs Commission finally met in 1895 the British agreed to adopt the local names of Kongur and Mustagh Ata. However, despite conflicting opinions from the Russians and the Swedish explorer, Sven Hedin, Elias' estimate that Mustagh Ata was lower than Kongur Tiube was eventually vindicated.

In 1890 Francis Younghusband accompanied by George Macartney went on a successful mission to establish an official British presence in Kashgar. In doing so he followed in Elias' footsteps to the shores of the Karakol Lakes, from where he described Kongur Tiube and Mustagh Ata as 'huge masses looking over the Roof of the World, with Russia, India and China round their bases'.

In 1894 Sven Hedin lived for nearly a year in the region of the Karakol Lakes and during the period he took time off from serious exploration to make the first mountaineering attempts in the region. Hedin had little previous mountaineering experience, no rope or knowledge of acclimatisation, and usually insisted on staying on the back of a yak. However, he made four persistent attempts on Mustagh Ata. For his first two he chose the northerly of the two western ridges that reaches up to the lower, northern, summit of Mustagh Ata. He estimated his high point as 6,300 metres (20,670 ft). Then he tried the ridge of the main peak but reached only 5,640 metres (18,500 ft). He made his final attempt again on the northern ridge on 16th August, and camped at his previous high point, only to be turned back by strong winds the next day. Hedin returned to the recording of astronomical observations and thermometer readings at lower levels, and on 4th October he almost drowned in the Karakol Lakes when a leather boat he had made and was taking soundings from drifted out of control and nearly sank. Although he must have known that it was already on the Russian maps, Hedin later claimed to have bestowed the name of Mustagh Ata. He did not measure its height, but adapted Trotter's measurement of Kongur Tiube and gave it 7,800 metres. By describing the 'unchallenged pre-eminence' of Mustagh Ata he became yet another in a long succession of people to fail to notice the elusive summit of Kongur.

In 1899 the north side of Kongur was surveyed from a six-mile base line near Kashgar by Derby – but he only obtained a height of 23,250 feet (approximately 7,090 m).

From the south and west, the summit of Kongur is not at all obvious, because it is hidden by the mountain which in 1981 we called Junction Peak. In July 1900 Sir Aurel Stein, the well-known archaeologist and Central Asian explorer took some excellent photographs from the Karakol Lakes which showed considerable detail of the Kongur group, and he became the first person to mention and evaluate the two peaks of Kongur Tiube and Kongur. Like Hedin, Stein also attempted Mustagh Ata by its northerly western ridge and also used yaks to considerable heights. He turned back at 20,000 feet (approximately 6,100 m), his two Hunza guides having reached 21,500 feet (approximately 6,550 m) the previous day and finding their way barred by a notch. Four years later the great Russian geologist Bogdanowitsch also made an unsuccessful attempt.

The positions of the peaks in the massif were not clearly assessed until the 1920s by C. P. (later Sir Clarmont) Skrine who was the British Consul General at Kashgar for two years. Skrine linked together previous impressions from the north and south of the massif from the advantage of viewpoints gained during his exploration of the Shiwakte and Tigarman groups of peaks to the east. Skrine approached these groups, which are a jumble of lower 20–21,000 feet (6,000–6,400 m) peaks from the Karatash river. He took photographs of the top hundred and thirty metres visible of the East Face of Kongur, and also photographed the mountain from the south-east. Having made plane table readings from the north and east and calculations in conjunction with Stein's readings from the south, Skrine travelled to the south himself. He journeyed to India from Kashgar via the Gez river gorge between Kongur Tiube and the next mountain to the north-west, Chakragil, and passed by the Karakol Lakes. The photographs and plane table readings he took on this last journey slotted in most of the final pieces of the jigsaw. The position and height of Kongur Tiube (Skrine's Kongur I) was fixed, and the evidence for another and higher adjacent peak, Kongur (Skrine's Kongur II), was conclusive.

During the political upheavals of the 'thirties and 'forties few Europeans passed by the massif. Nevertheless, the mountains were slowly becoming more accessible. In 1935 Sir Eric Teichman became one of the first people to make the Peking to Kashgar journey in a motor vehicle, from where he travelled to India on horseback. He photographed Kongur Tiube and Kongur from the Karakol Lakes.

In 1947 the famous British mountaineering partnership, Bill Tilman and Eric Shipton, joined up once again. Shipton was then Consul General in Kashgar, and Tilman travelled to Tashkurghan to meet him for a fast characteristically lightweight attempt on Mustagh Ata. They very nearly reached the summit, but Shipton was insufficiently acclimatised and suffered frostbite in his feet. 'Bill and I agreed,' said Shipton, 'that we had never been so cold before while actually climbing.' Later, Tilman estimated that they had been some seventy metres below the 24,758 feet (7,546 m) summit. It had been a serious effort and contrasted in style with the two expeditions to the mountain in the 1950s.

During the 1950s, relations between China and the Soviet Union thawed for a few years, enabling Soviet mountaineers to come and climb in the massif as members of joint expeditions. It was not until 1956 that mountaineering was formally introduced as a sport into China, and only men and women in their teens and twenties were instructed in it. In Communist countries a mountaineering achievement is usually judged in terms of its 'collective' success – a large party working together to reach the summit together. In these terms the Soviet–Chinese expedition to Mustagh Ata in July 1956 was an unqualified success, for never in the history of mountaineering have so many people made the first ascent of such a high mountain at the same time, and all of them returned safely. After previously training and acclimatising in Mount Elbruz in the Caucasus, a large expedition, led by E. A. Beletskij, with deputy leaders, K. K. Kuzmin and Shi Zhanchun, approached the mountain in four-wheel drive vehicles up to Base Camp, and by pack animals on the lower slopes. After studying aerial photographs they chose the same route as Shipton and Tilman had tried – the southern of the two westerly ridges. Over twenty-one days the team established a line of camps and on 31st July, thirty-one climbers (nineteen Russian and twelve Chinese) reached the summit. Their names were E. A. Beletskij, K. K. Kuzmin, V. S. Rachimov, E. I. Ivanov, A. S. Gozhev, A. E. Kovyrkov, P. K. Skorobogatov, V. I. Potapov, A. V. Sebastianov, I. D. Bogatjev, V. A. Kovaljev, I. A. Shumichin, B. L. Rukodelnikov, Jo. I. Tjernovlivin, G. N. Senatjev, B. D. Dmitrijev, R. G. Potaptjuk, I. G. Grek, A. I. Sidorenko, Shi Zhanchun, Xu Jing, Shi Xiu, Hu Benming, Chen Rongchang, Liu Lianman, Guo Decun, Liu Dayi, Peng Zhongmu, Weng Qingzhang, Peng Shuli, Chen Deyu.

This expedition had another higher goal – the summit of Kongur. There was not much time left, since they were due to leave the area on 20th August. Kiril Kuzmin led a reconnaissance to investigate a way round Junction Peak to Kongur, and it is possible that they reached the Koksel Col. But whichever way they tried to reach it 'the main peak of Kongur was still way beyond and remained as unapproachable as ever'. It was obvious that the mountain would require an independent expedition, and that there might be more feasible routes lying to the north, or the east up the Chemi glacier. Kuzmin's reconnaissance returned, and they decided to attempt the south side of Kongur Tiube instead – it was nearer, and at least they could see it properly.

Led by Kuzmin, the climb was accomplished in an impressive single push of five days. The climbing team – six Soviets and two Chinese – set off on 12th August, supported by pack animals and nine other climbers. They crossed the Konsiver river, yaks carrying all the loads and the climbers up to 5,000 metres. On the third day, three of the support team returned, and on the fifth day the remaining six dropped back, leaving the eight

climbers to continue to the summit on 16th August. They were K. K. Kuzmin, V. I. Potapov, B. L. Rukodelnikov, E. I. Ivanov, W. P. Sibirjakov, P. S. Rachimov, Peng Zhongmu and Chen Rongchang. The experienced Soviet climbers said that the climb was 'technically complicated'.

Since 1956, the massif's summit heights have been quoted consistently as Mustagh Ata – 7,546 metres, Kongur Tiube – 7,595 metres, and Kongur 7,719 metres.

For the next twenty-four years, no climbers from outside China were allowed into these mountains. The period of co-operation between China and the U.S.S.R. did not last the 1950s, and the Soviet Union resumed stating vaguely in the 1960s that Kongur is situated in 'the Eastern Pamirs, China/U.S.S.R.'. At the time of writing in 1982, the border in the Kongur region remains in dispute, with China maintaining that the present line is no more than a temporary demarcation.

Nevertheless, despite the absence of outside stimulus, mountaineering here did not stop entirely. In 1959, Mustagh Ata received its second ascent – this time by an 'all-Chinese' mixture of Han, Tibetan, Kirghiz and Tadjik. Thirty-three of the fifty members reached the summit, including eight women. Then, in 1961 an expedition including ten women attempted Kongur Tiube. After establishing Base Camp on 16th May they were on the climb for a month, progressing during clearings in the generally bad weather. The ice cliffs had altered formation and the route was different to that of 1956. One climber died in an avalanche. On 17th June, two Tibetan women, Phundob and Sheirab were among the summiters.

In 1980 the region opened up officially – British and Japanese groups reconnoitred Kongur and on 21st July three Americans (including the woman skier, Jan Reynolds) skied Mustagh Ata. The three-man British reconnaissance led by Michael Ward, investigated all sides of the mountain except the east, where bad weather prevented them from linking up from the Kurghan valley with Elias' 1885 route across Karatash pass and Skrine's 1921 explorations of the Shiwakte and Tigarman groups.

Before leading the British Mount Kongur expedition to success in 1981, Ward asked the

Chinese authorities in Peking about the mountain, and they said that it had never been attempted, no photographs were available, and that it was a mysterious and enigmatic peak – the closer one got to it, the less one saw. Also in 1981, as well as the first ascent of Kongur by the British expedition described in this book, a fourteen-man Japanese expedition led by Takashi Kawakami made the third ascent of the South Face of Kongur Tiube – Yoichiro Yamaguchi and Shigeyuki Koga reaching the summit.

Meanwhile in June 1981 three Japanese skied Mustagh Ata before joining the expedition to the north side of Kongur. On 7th August two members, including the leader Sakahara and Kimihara Matsui, of a four-man Japanese expedition, made the first ascent of the lower (approximately 7,500 m) northern summit of Mustagh Ata. On 16th September a joint American–Canadian group of Lloyd Gallagher, Pat Murrow and Stephen Bezruchka skied another new route on Mustagh Ata, using the next glacial system south to the two previously attempted and climbed.

The 1981 Japanese attempts on the northern side of Kongur ended in tragedy. Under the general leadership of Ryuichi Kotani, a double attempt with Base Camps in separate valleys was made – a large siege of the East Ridge from the Kurghan valley under the climbing leadership of Naoki Takada and a three-man alpine-style attempt on the North

Ridge. Progress on the East Ridge was slow, because it was unexpectedly difficult and the high-altitude assistants were insufficiently acclimatised. Meanwhile, on 16th July Yoji Teranishi, Mitsunori Shigi and Shin'e Matsumi set out from Base Camp at 3,700 metres up the North Ridge carrying nine days' food. They were last seen on 23rd July at 6,500 metres and then the weather deteriorated. A local Kirghiz told a Chinese interpreter that he saw an orange tent on a ridge between the north-east and main peaks through fast moving clouds on 28th and 29th July. When the weather cleared on 3rd August no trace of the climbers could be seen, and the party on the East Ridge were too far away to search for them. It is possible that, having reached the top, they were killed in an avalanche during their descent. The expedition was abandoned soon after.

As for future exploration of this complex area, it seems likely that the region will continue to be politically sensitive. Nevertheless as long as access continues to be allowed, there are countless possibilities. The climbed tops of Kongur Tiube, Junction Peak, Kongur and Kongur NE are only four high points in a multiple-summited ridge above 7,000 metres and there are many walls and ridges to attempt. And in 1982, thirty-five years after he said it, Shipton's statement still holds true: 'the East Face of Kongur has not yet been seen by western eyes.' It seems unlikely that it holds the key to an easy way to the top.

III

Medical science

by Michael Ward, Edward Williams, James Milledge, Charles Clarke

Prolonged Exercise, Oedema and Altitude

At the present time in the Himalaya alone about 200,000 people trek to high altitude each year, and their number is growing. As a result mountain sickness has ceased to be a rather esoteric illness of interest to only a few travellers and is now quite a common experience since it affects to some extent about half of those who go to altitude.

Though usually a benign condition lasting about forty-eight hours, it has a number of potentially lethal complications, the most important of which are cerebral and lung oedema. Another manifestation is retinal haemorrhage, which, if it affects the macula, causes blindness. Finally there is chronic mountain sickness, or Monge's disease, which affects those who live permanently at altitude, and who become intolerant. This was first described in South America. Recently Chinese scientists have reported cases from Tibet, though so far none have been seen in the high-altitude populations of the Himalaya.

Although oxygen lack is the main cause of mountain sickness it has become obvious that there are other contributory factors, and these seem especially important in cases of cerebral and pulmonary oedema which particularly affects the fit, the young and the strong energetic trekker or mountaineer.

An examination of a number of the case records of those with these complications seemed to indicate that the severe and lethal cases occurred after a period of continuous severe exercise lasting several hours. It has been known in some neuro-surgical patients that oxygen lack causes oedema of the brain and some cases of mountain sickness are known to have papilloedema (swelling of the disc around the optic nerve due to cerebral oedema). In fact there is a growing feeling that though oxygen lack is the cause of mountain sickness, it may produce the clinical features by causing alterations in fluid balance. We wondered therefore whether continuous exercise by itself could either cause oedema or aggravate oedema already present as a result of the oxygen lack of high altitude.

Although a good deal of research work has been done on the effects of exercise of short duration, and even up to several hours, such as occurs in a marathon or cross-country skiing, very little has been done on the prolonged exercise of many hours duration over several days that hill walkers take. Even less has been done on the effects of this type of exercise on fluid balance and its hormonal control under these conditions.

In 1976 Edward Williams and Michael Ward did four consecutive days hill walking in North Wales to see if this kind of exercise had any effect on urine output. They found that on the last day of exercise and during the following three rest days that they passed unusually large amounts of urine. It looked as though, despite the loss of fluid due to sweat and excessive breathing during exercise, some mechanism had been brought into play which caused water to be retained during exercise. When exercise stopped this mechanism was switched off, and the retained fluid was unloaded from the body.

In the last few years studies have been carried out by us in the United Kingdom and European Alps which have revealed some of the mechanisms involved in the formation of what is now called 'Exercise Oedema'. The expedition to Kongur allowed us to extend this work both during the ascent in eight hours from Kashgar (1,200 m) to the Karakol Lakes (3,500 m) and throughout the six weeks spent at 4,570 metres and above.

Prolonged exercise at sea level

The amount of exercise taken during a day's trekking in the Himalaya, or a normal Alpine climbing day results in between 60–100 per cent more energy expenditure than that used whilst living a semi-sedentary life. This means using about 4,500 calories per day as opposed to 2,500 calories per day. This exercise represents a six to eight hour day, covering ten to fifteen miles, with an ascent and descent of between 900 and 1,200 metres each day.

The effect of this amount of daily exercise over a period of days, which is what an energetic hill walker would be perfectly capable of doing in the British Isles, produces both a retention of fluid and a shift of fluid from inside to outside the cells. The fluid accumulates partly in the blood vessels and partly in between the cells. The effect of gravity will cause a swelling of the feet and ankles into which the tip of the finger can be impressed – so-called 'pitting' oedema. Even if obvious pitting oedema is not present, measurements of the volume of the leg below the knee show an increase at the end of the exercise period. Also oedema of the face has been noted.

Body water is controlled by the antidiuretic hormone from the pituitary gland. But in our study we found that levels of this hormone did not change with exercise.

Another way of controlling water is through sodium. If sodium is retained, so is water. The control of sodium movement in the body is through a series of hormonal mechanisms.

We found that on exercising, the activity of renin (a kidney hormone) increased and this in turn led through a series of intermediate hormones to an increase in aldosterone, a hormone in the adrenal gland (see below). This in turn led to retention of sodium and therefore water, causing oedema. On successive days of exercise sodium accumulated, but by the fourth and fifth day, this reached a maximum

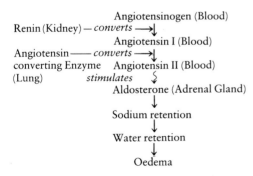

Angiotensinogen (Blood)

Renin (Kidney) — *converts* ⟶↓

Angiotensin I (Blood)

Angiotensin —— *converts* ⟶↓
converting Enzyme   Angiotensin II (Blood)
(Lung)   *stimulates* ↕

Aldosterone (Adrenal Gland)
↓
Sodium retention
↓
Water retention
↓
Oedema

level. When we stopped taking exercise all the retained sodium was excreted in the urine together with extra water.

We also found that the 'fitter' the individual was, the less renin and aldosterone he secreted and the less sodium and water were retained. In one 'unfit' subject the retained fluid became visible as oedema.

In addition to the increase in water in between the cells (oedema) we found that there was an increase in the amount of plasma or fluid part of the blood during exercise.

The increase in fluid between the cells and in the plasma comes partly from an increase in total body water, the result of less water being excreted than taken in, and partly also by fluid inside the cells coming out into the extracellular space.

These mechanisms occur in certain other conditions such as pregnancy and in chronic heart and lung disease, where a definite shift of fluid from intra to extra cellular fluid occurs, causing oedema.

Effect of altitude alone on renin–aldosterone production

This has been investigated by Edward Williams and his colleagues in the Karakoram in 1956. They showed that the Na/K ratio of the saliva had changed in such a way as to suggest that aldosterone secretion was diminished rather than increased. Aldosterone studies were later carried out by them after a rapid ascent without exercise to 3,500 metres in the European Alps. This confirmed that ascent to altitude *without exercise diminished* aldosterone secretion.

Effect of prolonged exercise at altitude on renin–aldosterone production

The effect of prolonged severe exercise at altitude might at first sight be expected to produce a large increase in aldosterone secretion, sodium and fluid retention associated with gross oedema, since oxygen lack is, like exercise, a stimulus to the kidney to secrete renin.

Controlled experiments in 1980 at the Gornergrat 3,130 metres above Zermatt in Switzerland were carried out by a team led by Jim Milledge, when an ascent to that altitude from 1,000 metres was made in a few hours. Exercise started immediately and continued for five days.

As expected, the secretion of renin was greatly increased and much above the level obtained on exercise alone at sea level. Aldosterone secretion rose also but not in the same proportion. At sea level the relationship between renin and aldosterone during exercise was proportional. At altitude this relationship had been uncoupled. Although the sensitivity of aldosterone to renin was still present, it was much less marked. As a result, the amount of sodium retained was less than anticipated, and the fluid changes on exercise at altitude were of the same order as those observed at sea level.

The explanation may lie in the secretion of angiotensin converting enzyme (ACE). It is known that in dogs who are suffering from chronic oxygen lack ACE is secreted less than in dogs who have a normal oxygen uptake.

A simple laboratory experiment confirmed that a similar fall in ACE secretion happened in man during hypoxia. Estimations of ACE at the Gornergrat and on Kongur have shown that altitude had the same effect. In both the members of the trekking party and expedition members in China there were few if any symptoms of mountain sickness. It could be speculated therefore that a decrease in ACE secretion might protect the individual from massive oedema when he exercises on first going to altitude, and it is possible that in those with lung and brain oedema, ACE activity does not fall, but we could not test this hypothesis as no cases of severe mountain sickness occurred on the expedition.

Mountain sickness may result in cerebral oedema and, as already indicated, the dividing line between the two conditions can be hazy. Also both cerebral and pulmonary oedema may occur together and the hypoxia resulting from pulmonary oedema will make the cerebral oedema worse, so this combination is particularly lethal.

Papilloedema is evidence of cerebral oedema and in the early stages it may be present without obvious clinical features. Retinal haemorrhage also occurs in 40–50 per cent of newcomers ascending to 4,000 metres and above. Charles Clarke monitored each member of the expedition throughout our period on Kongur. No member of either the expedition or trekking party in China had any evidence of papilloedema or retinal haemorrhage during the period they ascended from Kashgar to the Karakol Lakes and then to Base Camp or above. This was because acclimatisation was adequate and no acute mountain sickness occurred.

Blood and Erythropoietin Studies

One of the best known effects of altitude is an increase in the red blood cells which was first noted by Viault in 1890 whilst working in the Andes of Peru and Bolivia. This is due to a hormone erythropoietin which stimulates the primitive red cells in the bone marrow to produce mature cells that enter the blood.

Previous methods for estimating erythropoietin used animals and only large changes in the blood could be found. Very recently a radioimmunoassay technique, developed by Dr. Mary Cotes of the Clinical Research Centre, Northwick Park Hospital, which uses test tubes, made this estimation much more sensitive. In China the sudden ascent to altitude with a prolonged stay followed by a sudden descent provided a good clean and clear cut situation in which erythropoietin production was switched on and off.

Preliminary results show that a few hours after arrival at altitude (the Karakol Lakes, 3,500 m) from Kashgar (1,200 m) the level of erythropoietin in the blood was raised. That is, the stimulus to red blood cell production had started.

Ascent to Base Camp caused a further rise, whilst during the next six weeks at and above Base Camp the levels in the blood slowly declined but remained above the value obtained at sea level.

On descending to Kashgar at the end of the expedition, erythropoietin production fell to below sea level values.

We checked the mass of red cells by measuring the relative volume of these cells in a given volume of blood (the Packed Cell Volume). This increase lagged behind the level of erythropoietin, taking days rather than hours. The PCV rose slowly, reaching a plateau after about a month during the period we were at Base Camp and above.

On descent to sea level about six weeks are required before the PCV returns to normal.

In one subject who showed no increase in the PCV (as occasionally occurs in high-altitude natives) yet who climbed Kongur, the level of erythropoietin production was similar to the others. There was no evidence of blood loss and it may be that the target cells in the bone marrow, normally stimulated by erythropoietin, were not responding normally.

The high number of red blood cells seems to predispose to thrombosis and a number of cases of lung and brain thrombosis, some of them fatal, have been reported in young mountaineers at altitude.

One of the reasons for the gangrene occurring in frostbite is due to the increased concentration of red cells in the small vessels of the skin. Obviously high altitude increases this concentration and for this reason it could be that frostbite at high altitude is commoner at a given temperature than at sea level. This increase may also have implications in the cause of pulmonary oedema as thrombi have been found in the small vessels of the lung in people dying of this condition.

Exercise and Oxygen Transport

On previous scientific expeditions to high altitude in Nepal it has been shown that Sherpas who are born and bred there differ from lowlanders in that the way they transport oxygen from the air to the tissues is more efficient. This has been confirmed in South American high-altitude dwellers, but not so far by Chinese scientists studying Tibetans.

In particular they breathe less at a given rate of work or exercise and their heart rate continues to rise up to 180–200 beats per minute, whereas lowlanders at altitude seem to have a limitation of heart rate around 150 beats per minute. Also if Sherpas are given a low oxygen mixture to breathe they do not overbreathe, whereas lowlanders when given a similar mixture do so.

One of the things that we wished to find out was whether experienced climbers who had been many times to, and do well at altitude, have developed an oxygen transport system as efficient as that of the high-altitude native.

In order to do this we started eight months before the expedition left the U.K., carrying out exercise tests at Northwick Park Hospital using a treadmill.

In the field we used a twelve-inch step on and off, which we stepped in time to a metronome timed to go fast or slow according to the amount of work we wished to perform.

During the experiment we measured the amount of air breathed in and out, the amount of oxygen taken in, and the heart rate at increasing work rates up to the maximum. We also repeated the whole test whilst the subject breathed a low oxygen mixture when at sea level, in order to see the effect of acute oxygen lack. At high altitude when at Base Camp we breathed a high oxygen mixture. In this way the sensitivity of the carotid body and the respiratory centre in the brain, both of which are concerned with oxygen assessment, were tested by changing the oxygen content of the inspired air at sea level and at high altitude.

Both high-altitude dwellers and those with chronic bronchitis can get a hyperplasia, or enlargement of the carotid body, due possibly to constant stimulation of the cells. A tumour of the carotid body (chemodectoma) has been noted in high-altitude dwellers and this is a form of environmental cancer due to oxygen lack. Our results on Kongur showed that the climbers had a higher level of oxygen uptake when working at their maximal rate. In other respects they were remarkably similar to the scientists. The rate of breathing and heart rate on exercise were similar, as was the rate of increase of breathing at altitude.

At sea level and at altitude both groups showed a similar response of heart rate on exercise. At sea level both mountaineers and scientists could go up to 200 beats per minute. At altitude in both groups the heart rate increased but did not rise above 150 beats per minute however heavy the work, whereas Sherpas can go up to 200 beats per minute at altitude. Perhaps in lowlanders there is some mechanism that limits the rise in heart rate when exercising at altitude and this may be protective. This mechanism seems to act after a period at altitude, because on acute exposure to low oxygen the heart rate in lowlanders can go above 150 beats per minute.

One difference between the mountaineers and scientists on Kongur was that the mountaineers showed less change of breathing when exposed to low oxygen.

Also their reduction in maximum oxygen consumption at altitude was less than the scientists experienced. In this way they resembled, to a degree, the physiology of Sherpas.

Scientific Equipment

Hormone studies

A good deal of equipment was needed as well as an electricity supply. We took two mains voltage petrol driven generator sets. Similarly we took two of each sort of centrifuge needed. Each one of a pair of such essential scientific equipment was packed separately. The same yak or camel did not carry both.

We had to become familiar with maintenance and be able to carry out minor repairs. Petrol engines need oxygen in order to function. The engine is tuned so that oxygen from the air is mixed in exactly the correct proportion with vaporised petrol so it is obvious that at high altitude this delicate adjustment is upset. The manufacturers provided parts for a simple modification to be made as we went higher, but even so the engines needed a great deal of coaxing, especially as few such machines start easily at sub-zero temperatures.

Instead of the familiar hypodermic syringe and needle we used evacuated glass test tubes of standard laboratory size to which was fitted a bung which, in use, was pierced by a special double-ended needle. One end of the needle was placed in a superficial vein, and the other pierced the bung, the blood flowing freely into the vacuum in the test tube. These 'Vacutainers' were highly satisfactory.

One of the two sorts of centrifuge was designed to use accurately-made fine-bore tubes into which blood was placed. After spinning at a known speed for a timed period the blood in each tube was separated into a column of cells with on top a clearly separated column of clear plasma. These two columns were then measured in an instrument designed for the purpose, the length of the blood-cell column expressed as a percentage of the length of the total original blood column providing a measure of the quantity of oxygen-carrying cells in the blood. This percentage is called the haematocrit, or Packed Cell Volume.

The other centrifuge was provided with containers into which fitted the 'Vacutainers' used for obtaining the blood. It was a standard, but tiny and robust, piece of laboratory apparatus. We had to take one to pieces to

repair it twice, but otherwise had little trouble. The generators and centrifuges were usually used on the ground in the open air and they stood up to violent fluctuations of temperature, to driving snow and wind, and also performed well on the uneven surface.

Rapid freezing in the hospital laboratory is simple: one puts the small samples of blood serum without delay into a deep freeze. Our expedition solution to this problem is not well known. We took two 25-litre Dewar flasks (like large thermos flasks) and in Peking filled each with a mixture of solid carbon dioxide and liquid nitrogen. When liquid nitrogen and solid carbon dioxide are mixed together, the temperature is $-195.8°C$ and it remains at this temperature until all the liquid nitrogen has boiled off. The temperature then slowly rises to that at which carbon dioxide begins to sublimate, which is $-80°C$. The specimens therefore were stored at a temperature that varied between these two levels and arrived back in the laboratory at $-80°C$. Preliminary experiments had been carried out in England to confirm this and, under best conditions, the cooling material lasted for about 140 days. Under field conditions 90–100 days is probably a safe period to assume. These flasks were so essential, not only on the mountain but for transport of the serum specimens back to England, that we never let them out of our sight. Although weighing about 50 lb apiece we had them as hand luggage in aeroplanes, took them from place to place ourselves, had them in our hotel rooms, and finally back-packed them. These were the only baggage items not carried by camel or yak.

The properties of materials change at the temperature of liquid nitrogen. A piece of rubber, for example, if hit, will shatter, not bounce. Thus special low-temperature sample containers had to be used. They were of 2 ml each and made of a special plastic with flexible plastic screw cap. When tightly screwed they were additionally sealed with low temperature tape and the label, always written in pencil, was also covered with this tape. The method was highly successful, as no sample tubes were damaged, no labels obliterated, and no leakage of contents occurred. All arrived at the laboratories in London still deep frozen.

At the Karakol Lakes and at Base Camp we

Step tests at Base Camp.

carried out some of the scientific work in a tent, but much of it had to be done outside. At Base Camp we often could not start scientific studies until about 11.00 a.m. because the low temperatures prevented certain instruments from functioning and also made it impossible to carry out, by the chemical method employed, analysis of oxygen and carbon dioxide.

Exercise tests

The best way to measure the real work done by a subject who is exercising is to measure the amount of oxygen taken in each minute, then to relate breathing or heart rate to this value at a number of different increasing work rates. On Kongur the different work rates were achieved by increasing the rate of stepping up on to the twelve-inch step and by adding a load – a rucksack full of rocks – for the maximum work rate. The classical method for measuring oxygen consumption is to collect the expired air via one-way breathing valves and elephant tubing into a large bag known as a Douglas Bag. Professor Douglas, a physiologist from Oxford, was with J. S. Haldane on one of the best known altitude expeditions to Pike's Peak in America in 1911 and was still to be seen in the laboratories at Oxford in the 'sixties. The bags he developed were made of rubberised canvas but most Douglas Bags are now made of plastic. These become brittle below freezing point and if unfolded at this temperature are liable to crack. We took care to expose them to the sun and have them warm before using them. Expired air is collected in this way over a carefully measured time and then, after a sample has been taken into a greased syringe, it is emptied through a gas meter, the volume is corrected for temperature and so the volume of air breathed per minute is calculated. The sample has to be analysed for oxygen and carbon dioxide. Nowadays in the laboratory this is usually done very quickly by electronic analysers but on Kongur we used an old-fashioned but

Jim Milledge using the oxylog.

beautiful blown glass apparatus – the micro Schollander. This is very delicate and Jim Milledge, who was responsible for this work, carried the apparatus as hand luggage by air to Kashgar, and as part of his load up to Base Camp. The powdered reagents had been weighed into vials and at Base Camp were made up with deionised water.

This classical method was very tedious and it soon became apparent that we would have difficulty in getting through all the exercise tests we had planned, especially as we wished to do tests breathing both air and oxygen enriched air equivalent to sea level. So we also used another method of measuring oxygen consumption, using an apparatus called an Oxylog, recently developed at the Clinical Research Centre at Northwick Park Hospital. This is a small portable electronic device weighing about five pounds. Using one-way breathing valves the subject's expired air passes through the apparatus. A small representative sample is extracted and pumped over one of a pair of oxygen sensors. The other sensor samples air. The difference in the signals from these sensors is proportional to the oxygen taken in by the subject. On the input port of the breathing valve is a small electronic whirligig which rotates as the subject breathes in. The signal from this is proportional to the volume of air breathed. The apparatus multiplies these two signals after appropriate corrections and displays the result – oxygen consumption – on a digital display. It also shows the volume of gas breathed per minute, each value being updated every minute. To use it we simply noted the two values each minute,

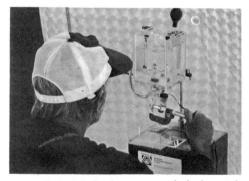

Jim with the Scholander apparatus he had carried carefully all the way from Northwick Park.

and after three to five minutes at each work rate we got steady readings. We checked the accuracy of this apparatus against the classical method and used the older method for maximum work rates where the very high volumes of breathing were too much for the Oxylog. Essentially the Oxylog is a portable laboratory.

Retinal photography

Changes in the retinal vessels were observed by serial angiography following the injection of fluorescein dye, using a motor-driven camera. This was carried out in a darkened tent by Charles Clarke.

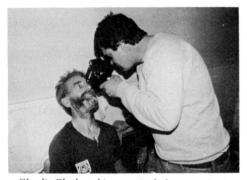

Charlie Clarke taking a retinal photograph of Edward Williams.

Acknowledgement

We should like to thank the following authorities for granting leave of absence: the City and East London Area Health Authority (Teaching) (Michael Ward); the Middlesex Hospital Medical School (Edward Williams); the Medical Research Council and the North West Thames Regional Health Authority (Jim Milledge); and the Governors of St. Bartholomew's Hospital (Charlie Clarke).

We should also like to acknowledge the work of staff at Northwick Park Hospital, Harrow, particularly Mrs. Helen Mozoro and Mrs. Anne Rhodes of the Lung Function Laboratory who helped with the pre-expedition experiments, and Nigel Luff and David Catley of the Division of Anaesthesia, Clinical Research Centre, who analysed the gas and blood samples.

MW, EW, JM, CC

References

PUGH, L. G. C. E.
'Blood Volume Changes in Outdoor Exercise of 8–10 Hours Duration', *Journal of Physiology* (London), 200 343–351 (1969)

WILLIAMS, E. S., WARD, M. P., MILLEDGE, J. S., WITHEY, W. R., OLDER, M. W. J., FORSLING, M. L.
'Effect of the Exercise of Seven Consecutive Days Hill Walking on Fluid Homeostasis', *Clinical Science*, 56 305–316 (1979)

WARD, M. P.
'Exercise Oedema and Altitude', *Proceeding of Symposium on Qinghai-Xizang (Tibet) Plateau*, Science Press, Peking, China Vol. 2. *Environment and Ecology of Qinghai-Xizang Plateau*, p. 1415–1421 (1981)

HEATH, D., WILLIAMS, D. R.
Man at High Altitude, (2nd Edition), Churchill Livingstone (1981)

WARD, M. P.
Mountain Medicine: A Clinical Study of Cold and High Altitude, Crosby Lockwood Staples (1975)

'Exercise Oedema' *Lancet*, 1 961–2 (1979)

MILLEDGE, J. S., CATLEY, D. M.
'Renin, Aldosterone, and Angiotensin Converting Enzyme During Exercise and Acute Hypoxia in Man', *Journal of Applied Physiology*, 52 320–323 (1982)

MILLEDGE, J. S., BRYSON, E. J. CATLEY, D. M., HESP, R., LUFF, N., MINTY, B, D., OLDER, M. W. J., PAYNE, N. N., WARD, M. P., WITHEY, W. R.
'Sodium Balance, Fluid Homeostasis, and the Renin–Aldosterone System During the Prolonged Exercise of Hill Walking', *Clinical Science*, 62 595–604 (1982)

WILLIAMS, E. S.
'Electrolyte Regulation During the Adaptation of Humans to Life at High Altitude', *Proceedings of the Royal Society* Series B. 165 266–280 (1966)

IV

Fauna and flora of the Konsiver valley

*by Charles Clarke, Martin Henderson
and Chris Grey-Wilson*

The terrain

Unlike the more familiar mountain areas of the Alps and the Himalaya, where pine-filled valleys lead to high grassy meadows, this region of Xinjiang is a stark and stony rolling desert land, poorly vegetated and entirely treeless.

The Konsiver river valley, whose floor near the Karakol Lakes is at 3,500 metres, lies between the little known Kongur massif and Mustagh Ata (7,546 m), a prominent peak well known to early travellers in the area. The valley is some twenty miles wide with pastures a mile either side of the Konsiver river, before it passes into steep gorges near the Karakol Lakes, providing good grazing for several thousand sheep and goats tended by Kirghiz tribesmen. Yak and camel are also kept but it is difficult to estimate their numbers. Certainly we had difficulty securing fifty yak to carry our equipment from the Karakol Lakes to Base Camp. The Kirghiz are skilled horsemen and breed horses in their settlements near the Lakes. Donkeys are also kept.

Either side of the pastures by the Konsiver river desert hills rise slowly towards the snow line, at 4,570 metres in early June, somewhat higher in July. The main Kongur–Kongur Tiube Ridge at about 7,000 metres forms a continuous barrier to the east and north, while across the valley to the south-east Mustagh Ata and its satellites form a more discrete massif. To the west of Mustagh Ata the Pamir–Karakoram Highway runs through to the town of Tashkurghan and onwards to Pakistan. Lower hills of 4,570 to 4,875 metres which form the Russian frontier lie to the west of the highway. These hillsides are barren, supporting very sparse grazing for occasional herds of yak and camel. The moraines of several glaciers from the Kongur massif (of which the Koksel Glacier is the longest, reaching within five miles of the river) divide the desert hills. Tucked between them are a series of grassy alluvial meadows each less than a square mile in area and often marshy.

Wildlife

Such barren land does not support a wide variety of animals. Marmots are abundant in and alongside the small grassy meadows between 3,900 and 4,575 metres. In the desert hills between 2,800 and 3,900 metres we also saw hares in large numbers.

Marco Polo sheep (*Ovis poli*) were once common in this region but have been hunted extensively by the Kirghiz. Though rare here they are said to be more common around Tashkurghan. We saw several pairs of *Ovis poli* horns – one spanning a metre and weighing twelve kilos – and on two occasions saw three fine sheep whilst trekking at 3,900 metres on the way to Sarala Peak. We were told that there were no ibex or other game prized for their horns.

The only small mammal we saw was the pika which lives among moraines at 4,570 metres.

Footprints of what we think was a fox were seen on several occasions in the snow at about 4,750 metres.

Wolves are said by the Kirghiz to be present and sometimes kill sheep and goats, although we never saw any. Snow leopards and bears are unknown in the region.

Notes were made of the birds in the area. At the Karakol Lakes were several pairs of Ruddy Shelduck (*Tadorna ferruginea*), some Yellow-headed Wagtail (*Motacilla citreola*) and Grey Heron (*Ardea cinerea*), one of which was found nesting on a small island. On one occasion we saw a solitary Common Redshank in the shallow waters of the lakes, and no doubt other migratory birds were also present. Our camp beside the lakes attracted Dark Kite (*Milvus migrans*) who waited close by in the hope of scavenging scraps of food. Hill Pigeon (*Columba rupestris*) were also seen. During the trek up the Konsiver river in late May, a Pied Wagtail (*Motacilla alba*) was sighted beside a mountain stream at 2,650 metres.

At Base Camp two pairs of the superb

Guldenstadt's Redstart (*Phoenicurus erythrogaster*) became quite tame and we saw them with their young in early July. Chukor Partridge (*Alectoris graeca*) were frequently heard and seen at Base Camp. Rock Bunting (*Emberiza cia*) and Jungle Crows (*Corvus macrorhynchos*) or possibly Raven (*Corvus corax*) were common throughout the area.

A Golden Eagle (*Aquila chrysaëtos*) flew over Base Camp on several occasions. Another bird of prey with a striking white body and leading edges, probably an adult Himalayan Griffon (*Gyps himalayensis*), was seen once on Kongur at 6,000 metres and again over Base Camp. Yellow-billed Chough (*Pyrrhocorax graculus*) were also seen on Kongur.

Flora

The striking contrast between the well-watered meadows, such as our Base Camp, and the dry desert hills supported a wide variety of flowers which bloomed during our stay from late May to mid-July. Some alpine species such as primulas, buttercups and edelweiss were familiar but most of the desert plants were unknown to us.

We collected and pressed over 150 plant specimens for the Royal Botanic Gardens, Kew, and are most grateful for their help in identifying all the specimens.

The flora of the extreme western part of Xinjiang province is scarcely known and any collection of specimens from the region is certainly of great interest to botanists.

It is clear from the collections made by the British Mount Kongur expedition that the flora of the region adjacent to and including the Mount Kongur massif, part of the Pamir plateau, has close affinities with that of the neighbouring parts of the U.S.S.R., north-east Afghanistan and north-west India; a region made up of the Pamir mountains, the Wakhan corridor (often referred to as the Little Pamir) the Taghdumbash Pamir and the Karakoram. The flora is not rich, indeed it is rather depauperate, as one might expect from such a high and remote area where the extremes of climate, the short summer and rather low precipitation preclude all but the hardiest plants. The plant communities are sparse, often composed of scattered individuals or small groups nestling on the ground, or sheltered by rocks and cliffs. There are no trees (except in the lower sheltered valleys) and any scrub is low and generally found adjacent to streams and rivers. Large expanses of pasture are rare, and again generally associated with streams and spring lines. Despite this, however, the region has a unique flora, a mixture of local endemics and widespread temperate montane species which occur from the European mountains east to China and Japan and including the drier parts of the Western Himalaya.

The collections number 179 dried specimens in total and these have been presented to the Royal Botanic Gardens, Kew. They were collected by various individual members but should be cited in future as 'British Mount Kongur Expedition 1981, no. 1, 2' . . .

The following list of species is arranged in alphabetical sequence for families and genera. Numbers refer to individual collections – in some instances the same species was collected more than once. Identifications were made by various members of the Kew Herbarium staff.

FACING PAGE 200, ABOVE LEFT AND RIGHT] *Sibbaldia tetrandra, Silene gonosperma.*

BELOW LEFT AND RIGHT] *Aster flaccidus, Chorispora macropoda.*

SPREAD, ABOVE LEFT TO RIGHT] *Pleurospermum linoleyanum, Androsace chamaejasme, Potentilla multifida, Primula nivalis.*

BELOW LEFT TO RIGHT] *Saussurea gnaphalodes, Iris loczyi, Rhodiola sp. Crasulaceae, Primula ceae.*

LEFT, ABOVE LEFT AND RIGHT] *Sibbaldia tetrandra, Saxifraga sanguinea.*

BELOW LEFT AND RIGHT] *Leiospora excapa, Oxytropis microphylla.*

BERBERIDACEAE
Berberis kaschgarica Rupr. 22.

BORAGINACEAE
Arnebia sp. 179
Lappula cf. *microcarpa* (Ledeb.) Gürke 5, 6

CARYOPHYLLACEAE
Silene gonosperma (Rupr.) Bocquet 59, 155

CHENOPODIACEAE
Chenopodium foliosum Ascherson 161

COMPOSITAE
Ajania tibetica (Hook.f. & Th.) Tzvel. 49, 78
Aster flaccidus Bunge 76, 89, 102, 144
Leontopodium nanum (Hook.f. & Th.) Hand.-
   Mazz. 75, 81, 111
Leontopodium ochroleucum Beauv. 154
Saussurea gnaphalodes (Royle) Sch. Bip. ex Klatt
133, 137
Taraxacum leucanthum (Ledeb.) Ledeb. 168, 176

CRASSULACEAE
Rhodiola amabilis (H. Ohba) H. Ohba 146
Rhodiola cf. *integrifolia* Rafin. 61, 121
Rhodiola rosea L. 108
Rhodiola cf. *rosea* L. 70, 71
Rhodiola wallichiana (Hook.) Fu 163

CRUCIFERAE
Arabis sp. – immature 14
Chorispora macropoda Trautv. 105, 106
Christoleia crassifolia Camb. 77
Dilophia salsa T. Thoms. 112 *pro parte*
Leiospora excapa (C.A.M.). Durrand (=*Parrya
   excapa* C.A.M.) 50, 125
Torularia sulphurea (Korsh.) O. Schulz 2, 20, 40,
52, 79, 80
Torularia sp. 7

CYPERACEAE
Carex rigida Good 4
Carex stenophylla Wahlenb. 94, 105
Carex cf. *stenophylla* Wahlenb. 151

EPHEDRACEAE
Ephedra sp. 118

GENTIANACEAE
Gentiana prostrata Hke. 135, 143, 150
Gentiana riparia Kar. et Kir. 174
Gentiana sp. 149
Swertia aff. *marginata* Schrenk 136, 156

GRAMINAE
Deyeuxia compacta (Munro ex Hook.f.) Hack. 60,
110, 152, 173
Elymus schrenkianus (Fisch. & Mey.) Tzvel. 153,
170
Poa spp. 84, 172

HIPPURIDACEAE
Hippuris vulgaris L. 43

IRIDACEAE
Iris loczyi Kanitz. 1, 25, 88, 116
Iris lactea Pallas 9, 10, 11

LABIATAE
Nepeta sp. 140
Scutellaria przewalskii Juz. 8

LEGUMINOSAE
Oxytropis microphylla DC. *vel aff.* 123, 141

Oxytropis cf. *stracheyana* Bunge *vel aff.* 37
Oxytropis spp. 54, 171, 179

LILIACEAE
Allium polyphyllum Kar. & Kir. 31, 117
Lloydia sp. 93

PAPAVERACEAE
Corydalis cf. *gebleri* Ledeb. 16
Corydalis stricta Steph. ex DC. 119, 132
Papaver pavoninum Schrenk 51

PLUMBAGINACEAE
Acantholimon diapensioides Boiss. 23, 34, 115

POLYGONACEAE
Polygonum sp. 167
Rheum kialense Fr. 42
Rheum sp. 29, 120

PRIMULACEAE
Androsace chamaejasme (Wulfen.) Host *vel aff.*
95, 107, 131
Androsace septentrionalis L. 18
Androsace sp. – sterile 55
Primula algida Adam. 3, 21, 26, 27, 46, 57, 63,
100
Primula nivalis Pall. 44, 58, 62, 164
Primula sibirica Jacq. 178

RANUNCULACEAE
Clematis pamirolaica Grey-Wilson *ined.* 82
Halerpestes sarmentosa (Adams) Kom. 91
Ranunculus acris L. 19
Ranunculus pulchellus C. A. Mey. 114, 157
Ranunculus sp. 96

ROSACEAE
Potentilla bifurca L. 165
Potentilla dryadanthoides Juz. 166
Potentilla fruticosa L. cf. var. *pumila* Hook. f. 128
Potentilla multifida L. 113, 158, 159, 160
Potentilla salesoviana Steph. (= *Comarum
   salesovianum* (Steph.) Asch. & Graebner) 56,
83, 86
Potentilla sericea L. 65, cf. 97
Potentilla sp. nov.?, 33, 35, 38
Sibbaldia tetrandra Bunge 48, 66, 72

SAXIFRAGACEAE
Saxifraga flagellaris Willd. 47
Saxifraga hirculus L. 147
Saxifraga sanguinea Franch. 67

SCROPHULARIACEAE
Pedicularis spp. 139, 175

TAMARICACEAE
Myricaria dahurica Ehrenb. 41

UMBELLIFERAE
Pleurospermum lindleyanum (Klotzsch) F.
Fedtsch. 145

VIOLACEAE
Viola thianschanica Maxim. 127

In addition, the following mosses (Bryophyta)
were collected:
Bryum sp. – sterile 87
Leptodictyum riparium (Hedw.) Warnst. 92
Tortula caninervis (Mitt.) Broth. 98

Chris Grey-Wilson
Royal Botanic Gardens, Kew

V

Health and medical equipment

by Charles Clarke

The choice of drugs and medical equipment on climbing expeditions is now well established; we used a scaled down version of the kit I took for Everest South-West Face in 1975 and I acknowledge freely the advice given by my predecessors. The only notable additions were vaccines against plague and rabies (which we carried with us) and the main exclusion was that we decided (unwisely) not to take any intravenous infusions. The result was a kit weighing about sixty kilos – or one yak load. Details of the equipment are listed at the end of the appendix.

Some medical observations on our journey to Base Camp

In pleasant contrast to many countries which we have visited during climbing expeditions to remote areas, the glimpses we had of China were uniformly healthy. We saw no obvious evidence of malnutrition, leprosy or other chronic disease. We visited and lectured at the Medical School at Urumchi, capital of Xinjiang, and learned something of the standard of practice there. It seemed impressively high: there was a cardiovascular surgical unit, a neurosurgical unit and radiotherapy centre. There is also a small general hospital in Kashgar and a long established Uighur hospital which specialises in traditional medicine, particularly in the herbal treatment of vitilligo. We learnt in conversation that hydatid disease (a parasite of sheep) was a common problem and that carcinoma of the oesophagus was more common in Kazaks than in other races in Xinjiang. (The Kazaks are nomads in Northern Xinjiang.)

Goitre, from our own observations, is apparently absent around Kashgar and on the Pamir plateau – in contrast to the seventy-five to eighty per cent incidence in some villages south of the Himalaya and Karakoram ranges, for example in parts of Nepal and Baltistan. We were unable to determine whether the condition had been eradicated by using iodised salt for over a generation or whether the lack of goitre reflected an inherent absence in this region. The older locals told us that they never remembered seeing goitres in their grandparents.

We were not called upon to give medical assistance to the small local population around the Karakol Lakes.

The expedition's health

Gastro-enteritis, the scourge of many expeditions, was almost entirely absent. We had one case and attributed this to the fact that our Chinese diet did not suit him. The credit for the general lack of trouble should go not to our own personal hygiene but to Mr. Wang our cook, who like all Chinese boil *all* water before drinking it. Chinese cuisine which demands that freshly cooked food be brought immediately to the table undoubtedly helped. We also had a conventional lavatory (a plastic seat on a wooden thunderbox mounted over a hole in the ground) which avoided accidental contamination of our water supply at Base Camp.

Despite the good health of the expedition in general, the beginning of our stay at Base was marred by a most unpleasant 'flu-like illness. Three of us were ill for over a week. Chris Bonington also fell ill and within twenty-four hours had a firmly established left lower lobe pneumonia – a potentially fatal disease before the advent of antibiotics. Luckily this responded well to treatment and within two weeks he had returned to his usual form; it thus seemed reasonable for him to take part in both the first and second assaults on Kongur.

Our other worry was Lui Dayi, our liaison officer who developed a small gastrointestinal haemorrhage at Base. This responded well to conservative management but made me feel that intravenous fluid replacement

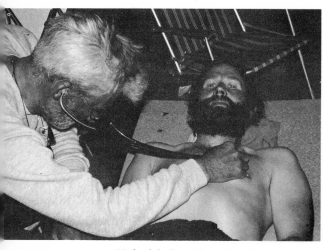

Michael declares Chris clear of infection.

might well have had a place in our equipment.

The only other problem came by way of our research projects. Edward Williams noticed that Joe Tasker had a surprisingly low haematocrit of thirty-five per cent in Kashgar; despite his being symptomless I attributed this to hookworm acquired on one of his many previous expeditions and treated him with Alcopar and iron tablets. The haematocrit climbed briskly into the normal range.

We had little in the way of acute mountain sickness and attributed this to our very gradual acclimatisation; we took around two weeks to climb from 3,500 to 5,500 metres.

Medical equipment

DIAGNOSTIC SET

Stethoscope, aneroid sphygmomanometer, auroscope, ophthalmoscope, thermometer, multistix, spatulas, notepad, pencil.

DOCTOR'S READY KIT

This travelled with us and then went to Advance Base.

1	Elastocrepe bandage
2	crepe bandages
4	safety pins
10	Tulle gras dressings
10	assorted Steristrip
10	antiseptic wipes
1	2" Micropore tape
1	1" Micropore tape
24	Panadol tabs
100	Codeine Phosphate tabs 30 mg
60	Lomotil tabs
5 ml	Chloramphenicol eye ointment
100	Fortral caps 50 mg
100	Valium tabs 5 mg
1	Iodex with Wintergreen
3	Lignocaine 1 per cent 5 ml
5	Largactil Inj. 50 mg
5	Omnopon Inj. 20 mg
30	Dalmane caps
2	Lasix Inj. 50 mg
8	Lasix tabs 40 mg
24	Amoxil caps 250 mg
16	Septrin tabs
24	Strepsils
100	Decadron tabs 2 mg
1	scissors 7"
1	Zinc and Castor Oil cream 110G
1	toothed forceps 6"
4	assorted sutures and needles
6	2 ml syringes and needles
1	Spencer Wells forceps

MAIN PHARMACY – BASE CAMP

100	Amoxil caps 250 mg
96	Septrin tabs
200	Maloprim tabs
5	Ketamine 10 mg/ml Inj. 20 ml
10	Xylocaine 1 per cent 5 ml
10	Amoxil Inj. 500 mg
10	Largactil Inj. 50 mg
30	Omnopon Inj. 20 mg
3	Decadron Inj. 100 mg
4	Tetanus toxoid Inj.
200	Lomotil tablets
200	Codeine phosphate tabs 30 mg
9 × 24	Strepsils (lozenges)
500	Soluble Aspirin tabs 300 mg
100	Valium tabs 5 mg

10	Valium Inj. 10 mg
100	Decadron tabs 2 mg
25	Ventolin tabs 4 mg
1	Ventolin inhaler
25	Anthisan tabs
25	Stemetil tabs 5 mg
4	Anusol ointment 25 G tubes
10	Tineafax powder 25 G
1000	water sterilising tablets
2	Lorexane (louse) powder 100 G
6	Calamine & Glycerin Cream 35 G
2	Betnovate ointment 100 G
25 G	Mercurochrome crystals
25 G	Crystal Violet crystals
25 G	Brilliant Green crystals
100	insect repellent wipes
100	antiseptic wipes
1	Zinc and Castor Oil Cream 110 G
18	Lenium shampoo 42 G
40	Eversun 7 suncream and lipsalves
50	Opilon tablets
50	Ronicol tablets
50	Largactil tabs 50 mg
20	Minims Benoxylate
200	Panadol tabs
50	Gelusil tabs
50	Lasix tabs 40 mg
5	Lasix Inj. 50 mg
100	Brufen tabs 400 mg
4	Xyloproct ointment 30 mg
36	Anusol supps
3	Chloramphenicol eye ointment
2	Betnesol eye drops
200	Orovite tabs
100	Ferrous sulphate tabs 300 mg
50	Fortral caps 50 mg
100	Diamox tabs
6	Merieux Inactivated rabies vaccine
2	Vials plague vaccine 20 ml
60	Benzyl Penicillin Inj. 600 mg
30	Chloramphenicol Inj. 1.2G
100	Chloramphenicol caps 250 mg
200	Dalmane 15 mg caps

DRESSINGS

100	Melolin 10 × 10 cm
100	Melolin 5 × 5 cm
5	Elastoplast bandages 7.5 cm
10	Elastocrepe bandages 7.5 cm
5	Coban self-adherent wraps
2	Elastoweb bandages 7.5 cm
2	cotton wool 100 G
2	absorbent lint 100 G
200	Elastoplast fabric plasters
50	'Anchor' dressings
10	'Op-Site' wound dressings
50	finger tip dressings
2	triangular bandages
100	assorted Steristrips

INSTRUMENTS

6	assorted scissors
2	artery forceps 6″
1	toothed forceps 5″
1	scalpel handle and 20 blades
1	dental upper and lower forceps
1	dental excavator
1	dental spatula
1	dental mirror
10	gutta percha fillings
1	neurosurgical burr hole kit
2	retractors
6	surgical gloves
10	Disposagloves
1	Ambu bag and airways
20	assorted syringes and needles
20	assorted sutures and needles
1	padded collar
2	urinary catheters and bags

Notes

1. We should have taken a wider range of hypnotics, though everyone found Valium and Dalmane acceptable.
2. More Gelusil or other antacids were needed; 'acid indigestion' is common at altitude.
3. I carried all 'DDA's in my personal luggage in a bag labelled First Aid Kit in which there was a detailed list. It seems quite impossible to complete the necessary formalities otherwise.

Acknowledgments

Almost all the medical equipment was supplied free of charge. We are most grateful to the many companies and individuals who gave assistance:

The Boots Company Ltd.; 3M (U.K.) Ltd.; Smith and Nephew Ltd.; Winthrop Laboratories Ltd.; Searle Pharmaceuticals; Parke, Davis, Ltd.; Roche Ltd.; Hoechst U.K. Ltd.; Bencard Ltd.; Astra Pharm. Ltd.; Glaxo Laboratories Ltd.; Merck Sharp & Dohme Ltd.; May & Baker Ltd.; The Pharmacy, St. Bartholomew's Hospital; Mr. David Caro, F.R.C.S., St. Bartholomew's Hospital; Allen & Hanburys Ltd.; The Wellcome Foundation Ltd.; Charles F. Thackray Ltd.; Wm. R. Warner Ltd.; ICI Ltd.; Servier Laboratories Ltd.; Cutter Laboratories Inc.; Seton Ltd.; Miss Elaine Edwards.

VI

Some comments on geology

by Edward Williams

Kongur, Kongur Tiube, and Mustagh Ata are the three highest peaks at the western end of the Kun-lun range which stretches across the centre of China from west to east. They are in a closely associated group in proximity to the Pamir plateau and are separated from the continuation of the Kun-lun to the east. The Kongur massif stands on an igneous rock base which tapers towards the east. On both the north and south of this belt of igneous rock are very old (perhaps 500 million years) but softer rocks. Technically, they are lower Paleozoic conglomerates and sandstones.

Chinese sources accept that the Kun-lun, including the high mountain group at its far western end, emerged as part of the same mountain upthrusting which formed the Tibetan plateau.

It must be understood that such geological examination of the area as was undertaken was carried out mostly during journeys made as part of the expedition and only minor specifically geological forays were possible. Thus only a tiny fraction of the area was examined in detail and in no sense must this appendix be read as a preliminary report on

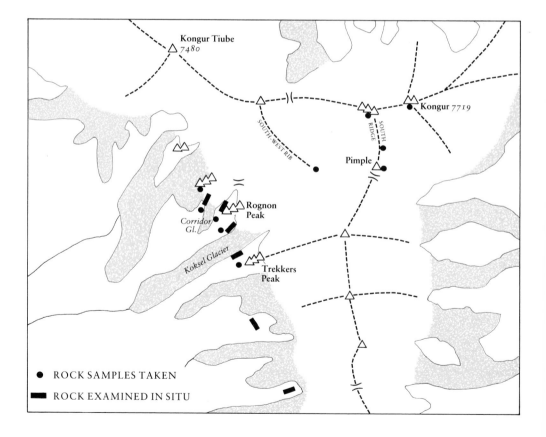

● ROCK SAMPLES TAKEN

▬ ROCK EXAMINED IN SITU

the geology of the whole Kongur Shan. Much more important: I am not a geologist.

Since the crust of the earth cooled and solidified about 4,000 million years ago many changes have taken place. For convenience this vast period of time has been divided into four periods, the fourth being the most recent and a far, far, shorter period than any of the other three. The fourth, or quarternary, period is in many areas mostly concerned with the effects of the ice ages, particularly the last.

Quarternary geology

Once we were through the Gez gorge and on the high land of the Karakol Lakes the exciting scenery was dominated by ice and the recent action of ice, although to the south the mountains were eroded into sharp ridges and peaks. This striking difference in the scenery as one looked away from the Kongur and Mustagh Ata massifs is accounted for by the softer rock to the south already mentioned. The unnamed ridge, rising to a little over 4,000 metres to the west of the Karakol Lakes was used as a vantage point to observe the topography of the Konsiver valley and of the slopes leading up to the Kongur Shan. Glacial deposits and erratics (rocks different from those of which the ridges are composed) are common on this ridge, approximately 500 metres above the valley floor.

If ice-carrying debris is moving, the general direction of such movement is shown on the ground after retreat of the ice by a tendency of surface features to be aligned according to ice flow directions. No such alignments could be seen from here. Apart from the alluvium of the Konsiver river and its tributaries and the gorges they have cut, the landscape is entirely formed of hummocky ground moraine.

Glaciers grind rock into very fine powder known as rock flour. The terrain is composed of this with scattered isolated wind-worn rocks, varying from vast pieces protruding ten metres above the surface to small boulders. These rocks are mostly schists (rocks transformed by pressure and heat) with very occasional coarse granite and gneiss. No pieces of quartz or quartzite larger than a few centimetres were seen nor did I find a single block of sedimentary rock.

The maximum depth of the river canyons examined was no more than about a hundred metres. The walls showed evidence of a minor degree of stratification but typically are of unsorted boulder clay. On the slopes to the west of the Koksel river drumlins are present with axes a few degrees south of an east-west orientation. These are long, narrow, whale-backed ridges often with a hard-rock steep face towards the direction of ancient ice flow, their long axis being along the direction of flow of the ice which formed them. I did not see any evidence of eskers, those sinuous ridges of debris marking the route of melt streams on the ancient ice, and there is no ancient terrace on the slope. Such a terrace could exist but has been overrun and buried by the vast modern moraines beneath which the landscape suddenly disappears on the higher slopes.

To the east of the Koksel river the ancient deposits are in lower relief with no drumlins seen and fewer rocks. All of the features are scoured by frequent high winds and the terrain, having a semi-desert vegetation, is subject to marked wind erosion.

Although few of the modern glaciers coalesce, their moraines from the Koksel north-westward form a continuous, immense, loose unvegetated rampart of about fifty metres above the ancient moraine surface. At its terminus the Koksel ice, as well as that of the unnamed glacier flowing from Kongur Tiube, still have a remnant piedmont form. A piedmont form of glacier is very rare outside polar and sub-polar regions. It occurs where a glacier extends beyond the end of the gorge it has cut and forms a flat lobe of ice beyond the mountain walls.

The common moraine had formed by the convergence at a higher level of the moraines of the individual modern glaciers. Between these are sequestered flat-bottomed, long, very narrow, triangular shaped valleys, terminated below by the abutting moraines and above by moraine-covered mountain slope. The Base Camp valley forms a good example. It is 150 metres wide at its upper end between the lateral moraine of the Koksel and that of the Corridor glacier. It is about one kilometre from here to where the two moraines at last abut. All of these tiny valleys into which I went are drained either through a narrow gorge or by a stream passing underground among the moraine boulders.

I examined the moraines of the Corridor glacier in detail and found evidence for at least three major advances of the glacier. One of these had transgressed older moraine, and spilled into one of the tiny valleys described. The Koksel had also at at least two points broken the present lateral moraine and at one of these points a tongue of ice had apparently protruded into the moraine-free valley.

The unnamed peak closing the head of the Base Camp valley was covered by the terminal moraine of its still existing 'permanent' ice. I examined the profile of this moraine to above 5,000 metres and recorded evidence of five forward oscillations of its ice. There could have been more because an advance of its ice beyond the termination of a previous advance would obliterate the morainic evidence of this. The lowest 'push ridge' ran across the slope of the mountain only 144 metres (at its highest point) above the valley floor and this advance presumably accounted for the loose moraine deposit reaching all the way to the flat meadow and covering totally the 'core' of the mountain.

I conclude from these observations that the last major glaciation produced a thick ice cap in this area. Towards the end of the era the present Konsiver valley became occupied by static ice carrying a complete cover of debris, the exception being the flow of the then much larger ice drainage from the range as evidenced by the drumlins in the appropriate orientation. In relatively modern times there has been much more pronounced advance and retreat of the ice than one would expect by analogy with the European Alps.

Structural geology

In view of the extensive ice and snow cover of the massif I decided to examine the moraines and the rock burden of the glaciers as well as examining, and taking samples from, bedrock. I did not attempt to analyse the frequency of occurrence of the varieties of rock composing the moraines, or being carried on the moving ice surface.

Bedrock samples were taken from the Toothed Peak, Rognon Peak, and Trekkers' Peak. In addition I examined rock from the two outliers south-east in the same chain of peaks. The summit party collected samples from various points on Kongur itself. The sampling points are shown on the sketch map; typically three or four pieces were obtained from each point.

The five samples collected from the rock exposure a few metres below the snow summit of Kongur are a quartz-rich schist, a garnet mica schist, a quartz-rich schist cut by a quartz vein, an augen schist, and a piece of quartz. The single sample from the point between the 7,000 metre peak and the Kongur summit ridge is also a hard augen schist. The samples from the Pimple are each of a soft clay-mineral schist while the single specimen from the ridge rising above (the South Ridge) is a harder deformed schist with beaded quartz inclusions. The specimens from near the bottom of the South-West Ridge are flakes of thin quartz veins and quartz-rich hard schist.

The specimens from each of the outlying sites and the rocks examined on the line of outlying peaks show a striking uniformity. They are a hard quartz-rich, contorted, metamorphic rock with pieces of quartz vein up to one or two centimetres thick. The rock exposed on the lower cliffs of these peaks gives the distant appearance of stratification, so numerous are the thin long lines of quartz veins.

The moraines of the Corridor glacier and the rock burden of the moving ice are largely a mixture of soft mica schist, garnet mica schist, and rock from the adjacent outliers. The terminal moraine of the Rognon Peak is similar, as are the lateral moraines of the Koksel glacier. It is striking that the moving Koksel ice carries very little overburden and in this the predominant rocks are pieces of milky quartz.

It appears, therefore, that the ridges and summits of the main massif are likely to be of quartz veined hard schists while the re-entrants and even the great scoop of the ice-filled Koksel Basin could be of the friable clay mineral schists so common in the moraines. Somewhere in the centre of the source of the Koksel glacier is a quartz-rich formation. The line of outlying peaks are of a single form of metamorphic rock containing vast numbers of thin quartz veins. Before being divided by the outflowing ice into separate peaks this deposit probably formed one ridge. I found no exposure of sedimentary rock and no evidence in the moraines for their existence under the ice cover of the massif.

VII

Equipment and Food

Equipment
by Joe Tasker

Developments in equipment in the last few years have been one of the factors enabling small teams, such as ours was on Kongur, to operate as a mobile, self-contained unit on the highest mountains in the world. The improvements in clothing allow mountaineers to survive and even make progress in storms and weather conditions which, only a few years ago, would have halted the largest of expeditions. New designs and purpose-made climbing tools have facilitated progress in situations where every minute saved is valuable.

The purpose of this appendix is to single out and discuss those items of equipment which are newly developed and have not been well covered already in other expedition books.

The combination of plastic shell boots with quick release crampons, Gore-tex-covered down or synthetic insulations, and pile-lined Gore-tex mitts, makes the climber almost invulnerable to the worst of blizzards. Gore-tex covered down sleeping bags extend the time a down bag is usable, before the damp of melting snow draws the down into sodden lumps with little value as insulation. Lightweight but resilient dome tents are now available which are spacious and yet can withstand ferocious winds.

On Kongur we were able to move up and down the mountain as a group of four, carrying with us everything we needed in the way of food, clothing and equipment. Although we were part of a larger group, as a climbing team we were able to operate on the mountain without the supportive framework of pre-established camps that a large expedition often entails, and this was thanks to our modern, lightweight equipment.

We each exercised an individual choice regarding particular items of clothing, but the basic kit was the same for all. This consisted of a layer of thermal underwear, a layer of fibre-pile clothing (either a one-piece suit, or a two-piece jacket and salopette combination), a cashmere polo-necked sweater, and an outer layer of either a pair of Gore-tex-covered Thinsulate salopettes and jacket or a one-piece, Gore-tex-covered, down suit.

This clothing was designed with zips in the trunk and thigh area which went from the middle of the chest, underneath the crutch to the small of the back, so that we could relieve ourselves without having to undress completely or expose major parts of our anatomy to the cold winds and snow.

The most important garments were those forming the outer layer. The one-piece down suit is a long standing, well proven item of expedition clothing. The thick layer of down which covers the body and limbs is as effective as a mobile sleeping bag. Adding a Gore-tex cover to the down suit dramatically improved the use of the garment in that the main insulation layer was now encased in a waterproof, yet breathable outer skin. The down was protected from damp caused by contact with the snow, but the perspiration produced by exercise could escape through the fine, vapour-permeable membrane of the Gore-tex.

Gore-tex is a fabric with holes so fine that droplets of water cannot pass through it, but the infinitely smaller molecules of vapour can. This material has been one of the most revolutionary developments in mountaineering clothing for many years. It is not the absolute answer, but it is the best available at present. The limitations on its use tend to be in a very humid atmosphere, or thick mist, when effectively there is a vapour on the inside and the outside of the garment; in rain so heavy that it covers the garment completely, effectively sealing the holes through which the vapour should escape; and in very cold conditions, as the outer layer on insulated clothing, when the body's vapour is cooled before it reaches the surface layer of Gore-tex and no longer has sufficient pressure to be forced through the holes. The vapour then freezes and can be identified as a layer of ice crystals a short way inside the insulating layer, beneath the surface cover.

On Kongur we were trying a new synthetic insulating material, called Thinsulate, which was developed as a less bulky form of insulation than down or more traditional synthetics. It consists of microscopically tiny filaments of material, bulked out by larger, stronger filaments, designed to arrest the movement of air molecules and thus, as with most insulated clothing, to use the air itself as the insulator, keeping the weight of the garment to a minimum.

In a warmth for weight comparison, natural down, with its millions of tiny tendrils to arrest the movement of air, still holds the advantage over all synthetics, but the Thinsulate did give effective insulation without the same voluminous bulk that we have come to expect in mountain clothing. It also has the advantage of other synthetics in drying more readily than down once wet. Gore-tex, as an outer layer, thus need not serve quite the same purpose in keeping the insulator in good condition as is required with down; but it is equally useful to the wearer of Thinsulate, as a waterproof shell which does not let condensation form inside.

In the event insulation was a personal choice, two of us choosing down suits and two the Thinsulate jacket and salopette combination.

Fibre-pile, which we used as an under layer and in mitts is one of the most useful of the synthetics, being very comfortable to wear and widespread in its use. It has many applications and probably as interesting a future as any synthetic insulator. The mitts were also covered in Gore-tex, and though the combination worked well, thicker pile may well have been more useful, as one person felt that his hands were not warm enough. This was partly due to the necessity of taking off the mitt on difficult passages, and getting the light inner glove, worn for extra warmth, wet and finding it thereafter impossible to dry. Once cold, it was very hard to warm one's hands up again. Protection for hands on a mountain is one remaining area where improvements still need to be made.

Down sleeping bags covered in Gore-tex benefit similarly from the combination of the insulator and the protective layer as the down suit earlier discussed and, whereas only a few years ago sleeping bags could sometimes have their insulating properties greatly reduced in a few days, now it is possible to continue using them in snow caves and damp tents for many days at a time, as we had to during both the attempts on Kongur, without too big a fall off in their capacity for conserving warmth.

It was in 1979 that plastic boots with alveolite inners were first used by British climbers on expeditions and since then they have rapidly come to be accepted as the best form of protection against frostbite. A rigid plastic or nylon shell made on a mould similar to a ski-boot mould, has inside it a separate inner boot which can be of several materials, but the best so far developed is alveolite. This seems to be nothing more than a light closed-cell foam, but its warmth-keeping properties are out of all proportion to its insubstantial appearance. Unlike leather, alveolite does not allow condensation to escape, and socks do become damp. But this is a minor inconvenience if the foot is warm all day, and at night the sock and boot can be dried in the warmth of the sleeping bag.

The boots are very much lighter than conventional leather boots, which is a great help in keeping the overall weight carried to a minimum. The rigid shell also prevents the foot being compressed by crampon straps if the traditional method of attaching crampons to the boots is used. This means that the circulation is not restricted and the likelihood of frostbite in the toes is further reduced. We wore the boots with Yeti gaiters which completely cover the uppers, gripping them with a rubber shard, which we found needed gluing in place over the toe to prevent it creeping up. The sole is exposed, which is useful on either rock or in very deep snow when the crampons are removed. On this occasion we all suffered from numb feet and the reason could have been that we did not use a foam overboot which would give all round protection from the cold.

Crampons too have been further improved and models are available which can be attached to the boot by a heel and toe fastening similar in concept to a ski binding. This method saves time and effort buckling up straps and unbuckling them at the end of the day when ice has frozen them in place. Having crampons attached in this manner, with only the heel and toe firmly held, gives a feeling of uncertainty after the reliable, well tried strapping method, but once the adjustments are correctly made, provided there is sufficient flange at the heel and toe of a boot, the crampons do hold securely, even when kicked into the hardest ice.

Tents of a design which have two hoops which cross in the middle and are slotted into opposite corners of the ground-sheet provide a shelter which is stable and roomy. An inner tent can be hung from the poles and the outer tent, or flysheet, drawn tight on them, giving further protection and a tautness which strengthens the structure. The high dome shape allows one to sit up inside rather than have to stay lying on one elbow for most of the time when cooking. This makes a long, enforced stay in the tent more bearable and can even increase the number that can comfortably be accommodated. The shape of the structure is very strong and the stitching in the material is more liable to give way than poles to break even under the fiercest of winds. However the noise of such winds on the fabric is what made it difficult to sleep in these tents. If the wind is a constant problem on a climb it may be that it is more useful to carry a light aluminium shovel rather than a tent and dig out a snow cave, forming a shelter which is proof against wind, snowstorm and possibly avalanche. The shovels had a scoop-like shape and were very robust; we gave them a heavy battering in digging into often ice-hard snow, but they withstood any punishment we could give them. The weight of a shovel was small enough for us to take one all the way up the mountain as our only means of making shelter, as we had to do, just below the summit, before our descent. The weight of the shovel more than justified itself in the effort it saved had we had to dig all the snow caves with ice axes alone.

We took with us on the climb very light marker wands made from sectionised alloy tent poles. These were much more handy and also lighter than bamboo wands. It is important to have a fair-sized flag on them to make them more visible in white-out conditions.

In spite of the variety of stoves available and the emergence of new models, the stove we used the most on the mountain was the well-established ordinary Camping Gaz stove. It is extremely simple to ignite, is clean and uncomplicated. There are still many problems in using pressurised paraffin or petrol stoves at altitude. There have been too many occasions when the more complex mechanisms have gone wrong to encourage us to risk such a vital commodity breaking down due to the effects of altitude and cold. The simple Gaz stove with especially filled cartridges of propane/butane fuel may only run for three hours on one cartridge but it rarely malfunctions. Only if the rubber seal is hardened so much by the cold that it does not seal properly, or a coating of ice on the cartridge prevents a close seal, do problems occur. But this can be avoided by warming cartridges beforehand against the body in a sleeping bag and carefully warming the rubber seal over a candle or lighter flame.

These are the main items of equipment which were instrumental in our success on the mountain and which have seen significant improvement over the last few years. Of course we did not climb Kongur using these things alone. There were all the other pieces of equipment and clothing, the ropes, ice axes, socks, rucksacks etc., which all contributed to the success, and which we could not have easily dispensed with. A list of suppliers follows with our grateful thanks to them all.

Aiwa Co. Ltd. for short-wave radio, mini cassette recorders; Avon Inflatables Ltd. for rubber dinghy; Berghaus for Yeti gaiters; Blacks of Greenock for tents; Bollé (U.K.) Ltd. for H.A. goggles and sunglasses; Bowater Sacks Division for tarpaulins; James Boylan & Son Ltd. for walking boots; Bridon Fibres & Plastics Ltd. for ropes; Camping Gaz (G.B.) Ltd. for cooking stoves and fuel; Clogwyn Climbing Gear Ltd. for karabiners and pitons; Crompton Parkinson Ltd. for long-life batteries; Dale Agency for wool balaclavas; Damart Thermawear Ltd. for thermal underwear and gloves; Dunlop, Japan for tent; Europasport for Ramer ski sticks and socks; Field & Trek Ltd. for MSR & Optimus stoves; Fleetfoot Ltd. for Trg. shoes for recce; W. L. Gore & Associates for Gore-tex material; Great Pacific Iron Works for ice pitons; Hampton Works Stampings Ltd. for marker wands; Helly-Hansen (U.K.) Ltd. for fibre pile garments & Lifa underwear; Honda for portable generator; Interalp for ice axes; Iser, Marker Bindings for ski bindings; Jardine Air Cargo (U.K.) Ltd. for air freight; Javlin International Ltd. for Neoprene overboots; Karrimor International Ltd. for rucksacks and kitbags; Kay-Metzeler for foam mattresses; Kodak Ltd. for film and polaroid camera; Koflach, Austria for H.A. boots; Life Support Engineering Ltd. for oxygen bottles; Lyon Ladders for Petzl head torches and ascenders; McNairn Cashmeres Ltd. for sweaters; Marks & Spencer Ltd. for sweaters; Mont Edison for material for Lifa underwear; Montfort-Fuller & Hambly Ltd. for long socks; Morlands Ltd. for sheepskin boots; Mountaincraft Agencies for snow shovels; Mountain Equipment for sleeping bags, jackets, salopettes; National Panasonic Ltd. for tape recorders; North Face for tents; Phoenix Mountaineering Ltd. for tents; Pindisports Ltd. for Koflach boots; Prestige Group Ltd. for pressure cookers; Racal-Mobical Ltd. for radio transmitter; Red Rose Products for film dispatch bags; Royal Geographical Society for altimeters on loan; Salewa for tents, crampons, karabiners; Second Skin Wetsuits for wetsuits; Seiko Watches for watches; Smith & Nephew Tapes Ltd. for adhesive tapes; Snowdon Mouldings for tents; Henry Sutcliffe Ltd. for packing boxes; Swiss Cutlery (London) Ltd. for Swiss Army knives; 3M United Kingdom Ltd. for Thinsulate material; Troll Safety Equipment Ltd. for climbing harnesses and tape; Ultimate Equipment Ltd. for tents; Vango (Scotland) Ltd. for base tents; Wang Electronics Ltd. for word processor; Norman Walsh for training shoes (maker); Waterside Designs for training shoes (supplier); WCB Containers Ltd. for lockable boxes; Worthington Packaging Co. Ltd. for polythene bags; Yale Security Products for padlocks.

Food
by Charles Clarke

Eating a mug of pemican soup at 27,200 feet, as Peter Lloyd and I did in 1938, is, I think, an unparalleled feat and shows what can be done by dogged greed. For greed consists of eating when you have no desire to eat which is more or less the case anywhere above 23,000 feet. Of two equal candidates on an Everest expedition in an Everest party, it might pay to take the greedier, overlooking his disgusting habits at low levels, for the sake of his capacity to eat at higher.

So wrote Bill Tilman in 1976, and little can be added to his advice about high-altitude rations. You never get it quite right. On Kongur we needed food that was varied, palatable and of high calorie value but which, above all, was light. Our rations, planned by Al Rouse and myself, were determined quite simply by the personal preferences of the team on previous expeditions and upon the availability of food in the far west of China: there was no pemican in either.

High-Altitude Rations

Detailed lists of rations are available in Michael Thompson's food appendix in *Everest the Hard Way*. To this there are few additions and in principle we aimed to eat items that can be purchased from the supermarket in Britain, North America or Hong Kong.

Many varieties of dehydrated meat and vegetables are available and in my experience all suffer from similar disadvantages. They taste vaguely the same after several days at high altitude and probably because of the inevitable quantity of preservatives, in particular monosodium glutomate, few rehydrate well when the boiling point of water falls below 80°C. Our personal preference was for Mountain House Rations, well packed in tough aluminium foil, clearly labelled and with calorie values indicated on the packet. The taste for even this brand palled after several days above Advance Base but was alleviated to a large extent by the addition of fresh spices. Fresh onions, garlic and chillies and curry powder revolutionised the menus and, being themselves light, added little to the pay-load of the summit team. These Mountain House meals, supplemented with mashed potato, thin Chinese noodles or vermicelli, provided the basis for evening meals. A second group of main meals gave a welcome variety: aluminium foil-packed, ready-to-eat stews and pasta meals, though weighing nearly 250 gms per man day, are now available from several fast food companies. Though relatively heavy, they are edible hot or cold, palatable and easy to digest. We found them excellent at lower altitudes. Crosse and Blackwell Ltd. make a range of pasta meals whilst Survival Aids Ltd. of Morland, Penrith, Cumbria, market a wide variety of different brands of stews, bourguignons, chicken and turkey dishes.

Popular additions to high-altitude menus were the varieties of tea we carried (mint in particular) and the wide variety of the brands of chocolate, sweets and biscuits. The correct labelling of food and attractive packages are as important on an expedition as on commercial television – lemonade powder looks much like dried potato as Joe and Chris discovered on the first assault.

Base Camp Rations in Western Xinjiang

Since the Kongur Base Camp was near a road head which is a day's ride from Kashgar, fresh food was plentiful. We drove, ferried and finally penned at Base Camp, a flock of twelve Xinjiang sheep which gave us fresh meat throughout the trip. The most popular dishes were, without doubt, shish kebabs. Half a dozen chickens began the expedition at Base Camp, too, and during our two months' stay were slaughtered for fresh meat.

From Kashgar we had four consignments of fresh food – eggs, vegetables, melon, apples, plums, apricots, Xinjiang beer, (an excellent lager) which supplemented the Chinese menus of our industrious cook, Mr. Wang. In general we ate very well at Base but Chinese food takes long to prepare being the ultimate in a labour intensive industry with a 5,000 year history.

Comparing notes with other expeditions to China, we fared very well – Kashgar is a rich city for food and our cook worked hard for us. Base Camp was organised entirely by our Chinese staff and, despite its high price (£8 per man-day in 1981), was a success, qualified only by the inevitable longing for western meals towards the end of the trip. Expeditions to Tibet can rely on *no* local food other than tsampa and even that is sometimes hard to come by.

We gave careful thought to the subject of alcohol and even the more abstemious members of the team enjoyed the whisky (generously provided by White Horse Distilleries in plastic bottles) and the Xinjiang beer, brewed in Urumchi. We had, I regret, little sustained appetite for the ubiquitous Chinese spirit, *mao-tai* which tastes vaguely like schnapps and leads to a monumental hangover. The scientific members of the team noted that, when ignited, more than fifty per cent of a glass full of *mao-tai* would burn off leaving a dull grey liquid with little to recommend it.

I conducted a careful survey of likes and dislikes at Base Camp at the end of the expedition, a useful manoeuvre for the future. More than half the team either 'hated or could well do without':

Raisins	Nut crunch	Banana cream
Almonds	Syrup	pudding
Brazil	Luncheon	Foil tinned
nuts	meat	kidneys
Hazelnuts	Beef loaf	Game pâté
Tinned	Noodles	Oyster pâté
crab		Dried yoghurt

The following foods outside basic rations won the approval of at least eight over eleven members of the team:

Fresh cheese (Truckle, Cheddars and Stilton)	
Fresh salamis	Fruit cake
Sweetened condensed	Tinned fruit
milk	

There were, of course, the inevitable suggestions that I should have provided:

Wine	Pancake mix
Beer-making kits	Flapjacks
Clotted cream	Oatmeal blocks
Jelly and custard	'Hard tack' lifeboat
Coffee bags	biscuits
	Processed cheese

And a hundred-weight of fudge!

We thank in particular White Horse Distilleries Ltd. for our whisky and Callard & Bowser Ltd. for a liberal supply of a wide variety of sweets.

VIII

Still Photography and Film

by Jim Curran

Still Photography

With the unique opportunity of taking un-limited photographs in an area of the world virtually unseen by Europeans since the 1930s, and then only scantily recorded, the expedition members were perhaps more moti-vated than usual to take still photographs. Certainly by comparison with Nepal, where every nook and cranny has long since yielded up its secrets to the Sunday supplements, this remote area of Central Asia was crying out for the invasion of zoom lenses, motor drives and polarising filters without which no self-respecting expedition these days would feel complete. Perhaps for this reason the level of photography was both comprehensive and of a consistently high standard, even allowing for the combined experience of several old hands.

Apart from Chris Bonington, who used his well-proven Olympus OM system, and the inevitable appearance of the ubiquitous Rollei 35, the team were generously supported by Canon Cameras Ltd., who supplied a range of Canon F1's, A1's and Canonettes, as well as a wide selection of lenses. All the cameras func-tioned well throughout the entire expedition, despite some initial concern expressed by Canon that the A1's, with their electronic sophistications, could malfunction in extreme cold. This problem proved virtually non-existent, probably because the climbers were all too aware of the necessity of keeping cameras warm, either close to the body, inside tents and even inside their sleeping bags. To prevent condensation, their exposure to sud-den changes of temperature was also well known enough not to present problems.

Despite its weight, the sturdily built F1 proved itself to be a superb and reliable camera and was used extensively as far as Advance Base and above. Its only minor fault was the tendency for the meter needle situated in the viewfinder to jam occasionally, either because of the cold or, more likely (as this was noticed on several occasions even as low as the Karakol Lakes), because of the fine dust that covers the Pamir plateau and, as far as I could see, most of China. Glacier dust can be a major problem and seems to be far worse in the arid western end of the Karakoram and Pamirs. The horrible grating, squeaking noise that emanates from any zoom lens that has been taken to these areas is evidence of its insidious penetration of every moving part of a camera which, with all the care in the world, can never be totally eliminated.

All the Canon lenses were excellent, giving crisp definition. In particular the very wide angle 17mm lens was much appreciated, giv-ing almost distortion-free images and avoid-ing the unsettling 'curvature of the earth' phe-nomena. It is a particularly useful lens for climbing shots, enabling close-up action to be framed in the context of vast surroundings.

Kodak 25 and 64 were by far the most popular film and at a guess would account for ninety per cent of all exposed film. Very few of us (and I must include myself) used much black and white, with the exception of Chris Bonington, who as usual headed the list by a long way in both volume and quality of films shot.

But, of course, despite equipment however sophisticated, it is still the person behind the camera, his skill and commitment that make all the difference between mere competence and brilliance. It says a lot for all four climbers high on Kongur that they brought back such a superb set of slides, particularly on an expedi-tion where the persistent foul weather was a continual drain on energy and will power. Unfortunately the only gap is in extensive coverage of the technically hard section at the base of the summit pyramid. This was simply due to the fact that for much of the time all four climbers were out of sight of each other on the steep and very complex terrain. But this is more than compensated for by the thousands of slides, from Peking, the Great Wall of China, through to Kashgar, the Karakol Lakes, the nomadic Kirghiz and the huge open spaces of the Pamir plateau that have enabled us to bring back some idea of the haunting and mysterious part of Central Asia that we were so privileged to experience at first hand.

Film

'Mountaineering is a difficult subject to film at the best of times. Anyone in their right mind would not choose to go to China and try and do it on his own.'
Chris Lister CHAMELEON FILMS

'Filming in the Himalayas must be dead easy with all those spectacular views.'
Anonymous young climber in a pub.

The above remarks, made just before I left on the Kongur expedition, were to stick in my mind for the following twelve weeks.

Despite my previous involvement with several mountaineering films, and four previous expeditions to the Himalaya, the elation of joining the Kongur expedition with the unique chance of filming in a remote area of China was rapidly tempered with a mounting trepidation. What was I letting myself in for? The one-man-band rôle that I had frequently got away with in the past, was probably the main reason for being invited. Yet this could so easily prove to be my undoing should I or the equipment fail on what was obviously going to be a major project, quite unlike my light-hearted forays to the Karakoram and vastly more costly and complex than, for instance, filming *The Bat and the Wicked* in a week on Ben Nevis.

I knew from experience that the film gear had to fulfil several apparently contradictory criteria. It had to be completely reliable, yet weigh as little as possible, be simple to use at altitude while giving high quality results, and be compact enough to be carried high by, at the most, two people. It was also inevitable that the climbers themselves would do most, if not all, the filming above 6,100 metres, apart from whatever telephoto shots I could obtain by going as high as possible.

At an early stage I decided that the only sync-sound would be in the news reports for ITN. These would be shot on Super 8 sound-on-film using specially modified cameras adapted by Canon Cameras for a previous Everest expedition. These reports would be sent regularly (we hoped) to London for transfer and editing on video. By doing this I hoped that little or no 16mm footage would have to be sent unaccompanied across China. In the seemingly likely event of any getting lost it would not be irreplaceable in the main documentary film to be shot entirely on 16mm Eastmancolour 7247 stock. Ironically the only 16mm film sent back *did* go astray in the Konsiver river capsize incident, together with all our letters and postcards. But it was good to learn after the expedition that all five reports that made it to London were shown on 'News at Ten' and at least one was subsequently shown on Chinese television.

The choice of three 16mm cameras I took were based on established reliability on many similar ventures. The Canon Scoopic 16 M.S. has time and again proved itself both easy to use and has given results comparable with much larger, heavier and more sophisticated cameras. It uses 100 ft daylight loading spools and each small battery is advertised as being able to run 16 rolls. They did just that even in cold conditions. The batteries were recharged on a Lucas solar panel – a small triumph for ecology over the scientists' noisy petrol-powered generators! The Scoopic was not winterised as I assumed from Chris, Al and Michael's description of the recce that the weather at Base Camp and as far as the Koksel Col would be much the same as the Karakoram where at altitudes under 6,100 metres it is often far too hot. In fact it was intensely cold for much of the expedition yet the Scoopic performed perfectly as far as the summit of the Pimple, where on a bitter day it ran 800 feet of film without so much as a hiccup.

It is also interesting to note that film, which gets brittle in extreme cold, never snapped, presumably due to the easy angles of the Scoopic's lacing system. Also using 100 ft rolls and regularly cleaning the gate between rolls eliminated any of the dreaded hairs in the gate that seem to occur only on brilliant or irreplaceable shots! While on the subject of damaged film it cannot be emphasised too strongly to any aspiring expedition film maker that a changing bag must be used at all times. The extremely bright sunlight even at quite moderate altitudes will cause severe edge fogging otherwise. The intense light at altitude also means that neutral density filters were necessary above Base Camp and with the Scoopic this is simplicity itself. Using a ND4 over the lens, linked to another over the automatic exposure meter, there is no need to compensate by changing aperture or ASA. Despite the widely ranging extremes encountered in the high mountain scenery the Scoopic gave perfect and consistent exposure from the dim interior of a Kirghiz yurt to the midday glare of the Koksel Basin.

My back-up camera was that old warhorse the clockwork Bolex A16 RXS. It was scarcely used except in conjunction with a 600mm Olympus lens and an Olympus/Bolex adaptor. The results, though sharp, were very flat and appreciably inferior to the Scoopic.

For high altitude the climbers relied on a clockwork driven Bell and Howell Autoload. This used 50 ft cartridges that are simply slotted into the camera which is little more than a tin box with a fixed lens. Joe Tasker took it to the summit and returned with 700 feet of perfectly exposed footage including a summit sequence that must be amongst the best film ever shot at such an altitude. The Autoload was winterised and had previously been used

successfully on the West Ridge of Everest in winter, a test that speaks for itself.

For wildtrack sound I relied on two cassette records; a Marantz Super Scope and a Sony TCS 300, plus a Nagra SN – the baby relative of the Nagra 4. This, though little bigger than a cigarette packet, gives superb quality sound. Its only drawback is that it uses tiny spools of 1/8 inch reel-to-reel tape which can be exasperating to thread in cold conditions and virtually impossible wearing gloves. In all about 15 hours of sound was recorded as well as 10,000 feet of film exposed.

For much of the film I relied heavily on the help of others. With the coercion, cooperation and possible corruption of David Wilson in particular but also Al Rouse, Michael Ward and Edward Williams (who will never forget carrying the big tripod up the Koksel Col), I was able to shoot all the footage I needed up to 6,410 metres. Beyond this Joe Tasker must take full credit. My thanks must also go to Nick Shipley, Leo Dickinson, Michael Morris, Martin Henderson and Pippa Stead for their very real help, advice and consideration, as well as the whole Kongur team. The film is, at the time of writing, nearing completion and Chris Lister and Allen Jewhurst of Chameleon Films have already shown their customary skill and expertise in making it a reality.

IX

Buzkashi

by Sir Douglas Busk

Among my other disqualifications for the chairmanship of the Mount Everest Foundation, is a considerable smattering of oriental languages. *Buzkashi* derives from two Persian words: *Buz* (goat) and *Kashidan* (to pull). The game was 'invented' by the Afghans, a somewhat violent race as in the past the British and now the Russians have discovered. It was originally played with a live goat. How long the animal survived is not known, but as the British discovered in the past and the Russians are discovering now, the Afghans are also a frugal race and doubtless ate the goat after the game, during which the meat had been tenderised.

At Tashkurghan the majority of players and spectators were probably Tajiks (Persian speaking) rather than Kirghiz (Turki speaking). Just over the nearby frontier to the west lies the Soviet Republic of Tajikistan and to the south-west the Wakhan region of Afghanistan, also Persian speaking.

Buzkashi cannot really be equated with polo, the etymology of which is the word for ball in the language of the Baltis, a Himalayan tribal group. Polo (with a ball) has long been played in Hunza. Many European expeditions have witnessed and described it over the years and some daring westerners have even taken part, so far without a fatality.

The danger of the game was increased by the use of a heavy local hardwood to make the balls. One of the most eminent mountain explorers of all time, Dr. T. G. Longstaff, served during the first war with the British officered Gilgit Scouts, a tribal levy raised to preserve the peace in this isolated and tumultuous portion of what was then the Empire of India. He relates in his book, *This my Voyage*, that he had to be invalided home as a result of a direct hit on the temple by a rising polo ball. The light bamboo root balls, now standard throughout the world, have since been introduced to the Karakoram.

The supreme example of a polo ground is to be seen today in the great *maidan* (square) in Isfahan, where the stone goal posts at each end, erected by Shah Abbas (1557–1628) are still standing. One of the buildings on the long side of the *maidan*, the Ali Qapi, was built as a grandstand for the Shah and his guests. Alas, the *maidan* has now been desecrated by flower

From the Karakoram and via Persia and India polo reached the west, but no occidental country to date has tried to introduce *Buzkashi*. We have gokarts, why not gopulls?

The buzkashi *at Tashkurghan.*

X

On Names

by David Wilson

Deciding on the correct rendering of foreign names is always a problem. In theory dealing with names in Chinese characters ought to be easy. There is an established modern system for romanising Chinese, pin-yin, which is now used in China and widely overseas. But the new form of romanisation produces some unfamiliar twists to names which are more familiar in older forms, either the Wade-Giles system or its modified variant as used by the Chinese postal service and appearing on many maps: thus, in pin-yin, Peking becomes Beijing, Mao Tse-tung becomes Mao Zedong and the province where the expedition took place changes from Sinkiang to Xinjiang. All this is easy enough for the China specialist to understand; but not for the ordinary reader.

An even harder problem is that the place names in the Kongur region are in minority languages. They do not transfer easily into the limited range of sounds available in Chinese characters. The Chinese characters for Kongur come out as Gong-ge-er and Kashgar changes into Kashi. Romanised Chinese maps, besides being too small scale to show many local names, add to the complexities by sometimes attempting to give an approximation of the local name rather than a straight rendering of the Chinese characters; Kashgar can appear as Kaxgar as well as Kashi. But for many local names in the Kongur region we had no access to a modern written version, in either Chinese characters or romanisation, since we had no large scale maps of the area. As for pre-war maps and the accounts of knowledgeable travellers, they provide a number of conflicting variants, or use forms of transliteration which might confuse the ordinary reader. Sir Clarmont Skrine, a considerable expert on the area who was briefly Consul General in Kashgar, wrote in the *Geographical Journal* in November 1925 about some of the places visited by the expedition. In that article he uses the form Qungur for Kongur and similarly uses a 'q' for names which are more commonly spelt with a 'k'. Doubtless he had good linguistic arguments on his side; but it would have been confusing to follow his example.

With this background, we decided that the spelling of names in the book should be based on a compromise between purism and pragmatism, with the emphasis on the latter. For nearly all Han Chinese personal and place names we have used the modern pin-yin spelling instead of the older forms; e.g. our liaison officer is referred to as Liu Dayi (not Liu Ta-yi) and the province in East China is romanised as Shandong and not Shantung as it would be on older maps. But we have retained older and better known forms of romanisation for a small number of names which we thought would be confusing in the new version, e.g. Peking, Mao Tse-tung or Urumchi.

For names originally in a minority language we have tried to find the most commonly used version and have not attempted to work through the distorting medium of Chinese characters: thus Kashgar, Kongur, Tashkurghan and Mustagh Ata. Where, as with some mountain names which only feature incidentally in the story, we have thought that it will be useful for readers to have the version as it appears on romanised Chinese maps as well as that normally used in British maps, we have put the Chinese pin-yin version first and the other version in brackets after the first use; thus Xixabangma (Shisha Pangma) or Mount Gongga (Minya Konka).

The method we have used may not be scientific; but we hope it will prove both readable and useful.

XI
Select Bibliography

ALPEN, DIE (Swiss Alpine Club Review) 1960, No. 2. (Mustagh Ata 1959)

AMERICAN ALPINE JOURNAL 1982, 'Muztagata 1981'

BERGKAMERAD DER April 1961 (Mustagh Ata 1959)

BLACK, C. E. D., *A Memoir of the India Surveys 1875–1890.* (Account by Ney Elias) London 1891

GILLETTE, NED, 'American Skiers in China's "Wild West"' (Mustagh Ata 1980), *American Alpine Journal*, 1981

HEDIN, SVEN, *Through Asia*, Vol. I. Methuen, 1898

HIGH MOUNTAIN PEAKS IN CHINA, 1981, supervised by Chinese Mountaineering Association, co-published by The People's Sports Publishing House of China, and The Tokyo Shimbun Publishing Bureau of Japan

HOPKIRK, PETER, *Foreign Devils on the Silk Road*, John Murray, 1980

IWA TO YUKI, No. 85, December 1981; accident to Japanese team on North Ridge of Kongur, 1981; Muztagata 1981; Kongur Tiube 1981

JACKSON, W. A. D., *The Russo–Chinese Borderlands*, D. Van Nostrand Company Inc., 1968

KEAY, JOHN, *When Men and Mountains Meet*, John Murray, 1977

KEAY, JOHN, *The Gilgit Game*, John Murray, 1979

LAMB, ALASTAIR, *The China–India Border*, Chatham House Essays, Oxford University Press, 1964

MILLER, J. INNES, *The Spice Trades of the Roman Empire*, Clarendon Press, Oxford, 1968

MIRSKY, JEANNETTE, *The Great Chinese Travellers*, University of Chicago Press, 1974

MORGAN, GERALD, 'Kungur and Mustagh Ata – A Case of Mistaken Identity', *The Journal of the Royal Central Asian Society*, Vol. 56. Part 1, February 1969

MORGAN, GERALD, *Ney Elias*, George Allen and Unwin, 1971

MYRDAL, JAN, KESSLE, GUN, *The Silk Road*, Gollancz, 1980

POLO, MARCO, *The Book of Ser Marco Polo*, translated and edited, with notes by Sir Henry Yute, 2 Vols, 3rd Edition, London, 1903

SEAVER, GEORGE, *Francis Younghusband*, John Murray, 1952

SHIPTON, ERIC, *Mountains of Tartary*, Hodder & Stoughton, 1951

SKRINE, C. P., 'The Alps of Qungur', *Geographical Journal*, Vol. 66, No. 5, November, 1925

SKRINE, C. P., *Chinese Central Asia*, Methuen, 1926

STEIN, AUREL, *On Ancient Central Asian Tracks*, Macmillan, 1933 also University of Chicago Press 1974

TEICHMAN, ERIC, *Journey to Turkistan*, Hodder & Stoughton, 1937

WARD, MICHAEL, 'The Kongur Massif in Southern Sinkiang', *Alpine Journal*, 1981

YANG KE-HSIEN, *The Ascent of The Mustagh Ata*, Foreign Languages Press Peking, 1959 (1956 ascent of Mustagh Ata & Kongur Tiube)

YOUNGHUSBAND, F., *The Heart of a Continent*, London, 1896

Picture Credits

Index